The British Horse Society

COMPLETE

HORSE &
PONY CARE

The British Horse Society

COMPLETE
HORSE &
PONY CARE

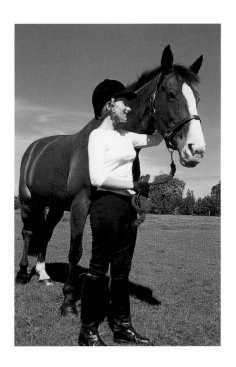

Collins

First published in 2005 by
Collins, an imprint of
HarperCollins*Publishers*
77–85 Fulham Palace Road
Hammersmith, London W6 8JB

The Collins website address is:
www.collins.co.uk

Collins is a registered trademark of HarperCollins Publishers Limited

10 09 08 07 06 05
6 5 4 3 2 1

The British Horse Society is a registered charity (no. 210504)
The British Horse Society website is **www.bhs.org.uk**

A catalogue record for this book is available from the British Library.

Created by: **SP Creative Design**
Editor: **Heather Thomas**
Designer: **Rolando Ugolini**
Technical advisor: **Margaret Linington-Payne**
British Horse Society consultants: **Jan Gigli, Helen Owens, Sheila Hardy**

Photography
All photography by Rolando Ugolini with the exception of the following:
Bob Langrish: pages 20, 201, 234, 235, 243, 256, 264, 265 and 274
Ifor Williams: pages 211, 212, 219
Margaret Linington-Payne: pages 32, 33, 116, 180, 196, 200, 278
Cover photograph: Rolando Ugolini

ISBN: 0 00 717467 5

Colour reproduction by Colourscan, Singapore
Printed and bound by LEGO, S. p. A., Italy

Acknowledgements
The publishers would like to thank the following for their help in compiling this book:
John-Paul Sheffield and Budgie and all their staff; Robert Shave; Dick Piggott and his Percherons;
Ann Rolinson and her Connemaras

Contents

Contributors

· ·

Catherine Austen

After graduating with an MA(Hons) in English from the University of St Andrews, Catherine won a place on the British Horseracing Board's Graduate Development Programme. After a year working at Ascot racecourse, she joined *Horse & Hound* where she is now Racing and Veterinary Editor. She is a Pony Club instructor and her ambition is to race-ride.

Karen Coumbe

Karen studied at Girton College, Cambridge, and qualified as a veterinary surgeon in 1984. She worked for five years in a mixed practice, and then moved to work solely with horses in 1989 after obtaining her certificate in equine practice. Since then she has become a partner at a Royal College of Veterinary Surgeons approved equine hospital in Mereworth, Kent. She is Veterinary Correspondent for *Horse & Hound*, has written equine books for the general public and edited the standard textbook for equine veterinary nurses. She is also an examiner for the new equine vet nurse qualification.

Judith Draper

Judith Draper is an equestrian writer and journalist who has been involved with horses all her life. She enjoyed several seasons working in flat and National Hunt racing before she turned to journalism. She spent thirteen years on the editorial staff of *Riding* magazine and from 1988-1991 was Equestrian Correspondent of The Daily Mail. She subsequently edited the British Horse Society's members' magazine British Horse for six years and has written a number of books. She is currently Equestrian Correspondent of the Mail on *Sunday*, Eventing Correspondent of *Horse International* magazine and a regular contributor to *Horse & Hound*. She is a member of the International Alliance of Equestrian Journalists and the British Equestrian Writers' Association.

Jeremy Michaels

Jeremy is a Fellow of the British Horse Society and currently Equine Director at Hartpury College in Gloucester. He also holds a masters degree in education, is a Chief Examiner, an associate inspector for Ofsted and the ALI, and a listed British Dressage judge. He teaches dressage and jumping at all levels, both in the UK and overseas, and competes regularly. An ex-Head of Training at the BHS, he is the presenter of numerous training videos and has written many articles for the equestrian press. He also undertakes expert witness work.

Seamour Rathore

Seamour Rathore is a journalist whose strong passion for horses led her to join *Horse & Hound* as Veterinary Editor and later as Dressage Editor. In 2004, she reported for *Horse & Hound* from both the dressage World Cup final in Düsseldorf and the Athens 2004 Olympics. Seamour has been a horse owner from the age of eleven, with a ten-year break away from the horse world in her twenties. She owns a skewbald Throughbred/Cob gelding.

Foreword

· ·

Owning a horse or pony is very rewarding and, of course, great fun, but it also brings responsibilities that will change your life. This authoritative book is a comprehensive guide to looking after your horse, providing you with all the information you need to keep him contented, fit and healthy.

As well as advising you on how to choose a horse, you will learn how to care for him on an everyday basis and build a good working relationship together which is beneficial for both of you. Communication works both ways and you need to understand and work for each other to get the best out of your partnership. It is essential to build a relationship of mutual trust and to learn to communicate effectively with each other.

The British Horse Society has considerable expertise in every aspect of practical horse care and is proud to be associated with this book. There is up-to-date information on every aspect of looking after your horse, from stable management and feeding to exercise and health care.

This essential guide is illustrated throughout with specially commissioned practical colour photographs, many in easy-to-follow, accessible step-by-step sequences, to show you in detail exactly how to look after your horse. These are accompanied by clear, precise information on what to do.

The British Horse Society is the only horse charity in the UK representing the wide range of issues affecting both horses and riders on a daily basis. It relies heavily on membership subscriptions and donations to fund its vital work, and by purchasing a copy of this book you are helping us to fulfil our mission.

Noel Edmonds
President, The British Horse Society

The British Horse Society

The British Horse Society was founded in 1947 when the separate equestrian bodies, The National Horse Association, and the Institute of the Horse and the Pony Club, decided to join forces and work together for the good of both horses and riders. Membership now stands at almost 60,000. In addition, there are 38,000 members of affiliated Riding Clubs.

As a registered charity, membership is vitally important to the BHS. Subscriptions provide the money that enables the charitable objectives of the Society to be met: promoting the welfare, care and use of horses and ponies, through the encouragement of good horsemanship and the improvement of horse care and breeding. The Society represents all equine interests.

Access and rights of way

New demands have been placed on the Society by changes in the last 50 years. The workload of the Access and Rights of Way department has grown in direct relation to modern farming methods and the expansion of urbanization. Intensive systems resulted in the ploughing up of ancient rights of way, and the rural rider is now faced with fewer safe places to ride. The BHS campaigns for greater provision of off-road riding and carriage driving by working with landowners and local authorities to reclass footpaths historically used by riders, to create new routes and to clear blocked bridleways. In May 2000, the BHS launched RIDE UK, a vision of a network of riding and driving routes throughout the country, with long-distance routes, such as the Pennine Bridleway, linking in to regional routes, such as Swans Way, which, in turn, will link in to local community routes. The aim is to provide suitable off-road riding for every horse owner, whether

they want an hour's hack from their yard or a month's long-distance ride. The BHS publishes a series of trail guides: ...on Horseback, giving details and maps of circular and linear rides in over 20 counties and regions using bridleways and quiet roads. Over 100 BHS Access Officers, co-ordinated by the Access and Rights of Way department, are in continuous consultation with County Councils and other organizations regarding provision for recreational riding.

Breeding and welfare

Perhaps the most important aspect of the Society's work is carried out under the Breeding and Welfare banner. However much the BHS does for the rider (and that includes non members) its prime duty is working for the well-being of the horse. The Society's aim is to prevent neglect and cruelty before it ever takes place. In other words, by educating and advising owners – particularly new owners – on correct management practices, potential problems can be nipped in the bud. Over 80 BHS County Welfare representatives, co-ordinated by the Welfare Department at Stoneleigh, support and advise horse owners throughout the country. As the ears and eyes of the Society, they are in an ideal position to identify horses that are suffering and advise their owners.

Active BHS participation on the National Equine Welfare Council, the Farm Livestock Advisory Council, the

Parliamentary Advisory Council for Transport Safety and the Joint National Horse Education and Training Ltd, to name but a few, ensures the future of the horse in the UK.

The British Horse Society is also responsible for administering affiliated Riding Clubs which promote fun and instruction whilst offering competition opportunities to riders across the country.

Safety

Safety is a major concern for everyone who rides and for the BHS. As a direct result of the Society's campaigning, the Highway Code introduced specific advice on horses on the roads. BHS Riding and Road Safety Tests are organized throughout the country, and a wealth of information is given on equipment and clothing, particularly hats. The BHS Safety Campaign aims to reduce the number of horse related traffic accidents by educating riders and motorists about the particular problems of riders as vulnerable road users. As part of the campaign, a leaflet and video, *Horse Sense for Motorists*, was produced in collaboration with the Department of Transport. The video won the Prince Michael Road Safety Award in December 1997. Road Safety representatives, co-ordinated by the Safety Department at Stoneleigh, train riders in roadcraft and examine candidates.

Training and education

The BHS has a large Training and Education department which handles over 12,000 enquiries each year. They administer a wide range of examinations ranging from Progressive Riding Tests for the recreational rider through to a full professional qualification structure. Qualified instructors work to ensure that horses are sympathetically trained and ridden. The Society believes that the public should be able to expect both a high standard of teaching and safety from riding instructors, and it has created a Register of Instructors to meet this need.

Since 1961 the BHS has run a scheme for the Approval of Riding Schools. Establishments that offer sound instruction in riding and horsemanship and whose premises, facilities and animals are properly looked after are given the BHS 'seal of approval'. There are about 950 BHS approved riding establishments in Britain and abroad. The system provides a useful guide for newcomers when selecting a venue, with details of each riding establishment published in *Where to Ride*. The British Horse Society also has an approved livery yard scheme up and running, to encourage livery yards to set high standards for their clients.

These vital aspects of work are co-ordinated and administered from the BHS headquarters with its permanent staff of 60. In April 1998, the BHS HQ moved to Stoneleigh Deer Park, Kenilworth, just a mile from the RASE Showground which had been their home for 21 years, ever since the move from Belgrave Square in London.

So how is it all done?

The Society is governed by a Board of Trustees who oversee the work which is funded largely by membership subscriptions. The national headquarters at Stoneleigh is supported by a network of regional and county committees – the hard working and enthusiastic volunteers without whom the Society simply could not operate. Representative volunteers offer expert advice at regional and county level in the fields of equine welfare, access and riding rights of way, and road safety, but committee members have the ability to represent the horse world on any subject. The committees are supported by Regional Development Officers who are full-time employees of the Society.

This is, of course, a very concentrated description of the BHS, its work and responsibilities. Anyone who would like to support the work of the BHS can contact the membership department. For full contact details, turn to the Useful Addresses section at the back of this book.

Chapter 1
Choosing a horse

• •

The decision to acquire a horse or pony is one of the biggest that you will ever make, and therefore it is very important to consider all the issues involved before you even think of buying one. Try to resist the temptation to 'fall in love' with a horse and then resolve that you must have it. Before you do anything else, you must decide what sort of horse is suitable for you. Look at and ride several horses and do as much checking as you possibly can before you part with your hard-earned money.

1.1 Buying a horse

The golden rule when buying a horse is that the onus is always on the purchaser to ensure that the horse is what they believe it to be and that it is suitable. This is known as *caveat emptor* — let the buyer beware. You should never take the seller's word for it when they say that the horse is sound, fit, healthy and suitable for you.

While many people in the horse world are honest and want to sell the right horse to the right owner, there are some unscrupulous people out there whose primary aim is to make money, regardless of the problems that may ensue. You should keep this at the front of your mind throughout all your deliberations and make the necessary checks that are outlined below before you purchase a horse.

Do your homework

Buying the right horse is exhilarating and rewarding. However, acquiring an unsuitable horse — one that may be difficult to handle (even with patient and devoted care) or with an on-going medical condition that means it spends long periods out of work — can be heartbreaking.

You should do everything you can to avoid this situation, which will not only be emotionally draining but could also create financial problems for both you and your family. So make sure you do your homework before you are tempted to buy any horse or pony if you want to enjoy trouble-free ownership.

At the very start of your journey to horse ownership, you should consider the following questions and try to answer them honestly:

Cost factors

The costs of owning a horse in the first year alone could exceed what you have paid for him. If you intend to keep your horse at part- or full-livery anywhere in the UK, for example, you could find yourself paying in the region of £3,000–5,000 a year in livery fees. And that does not even include the cost of the farrier, veterinary bills (including annual flu and tetanus jabs), dentistry bills, tack and equipment, including rugs, and show entry fees and travel, if you want to compete.

The other major financial outgoing that you really must include is the cost of regular lessons with a qualified riding teacher. A riding teacher will keep you and your horse on track and will be a confidante and valuable source of advice, particularly in the early months. Lessons do not come cheap, but regular ones will enhance your horse ownership immeasurably and mean that both you and your horse make positive progress.

Questions to ask yourself

- Can I afford to own a horse?
- Do I have time to own a horse?
- Will I keep the horse at livery or look after it myself at home?
- Is my riding sufficiently competent to manage alone?
- Is my knowledge of horse care adequate to ensure the horse's wellbeing?
- If I am buying my child a pony, are they committed to the project?

Making time

You may love the idea of owning your own horse but before you rush out and buy one, you should consider the following and think about your answers carefully and realistically:

- How many times a week can you ride? If it's only a couple of times, then perhaps you should consider the possibility of having a sharer (see page 17), or riding at one of the BHS approved riding schools.
- Can you undertake DIY livery yourself? Do you really have enough time to look after your horse on your own without any help?
- Can you take the time off work to attend visits from the farrier, vet and dentist? These professionals will rarely call at weekends or evenings.
- At what level of fitness will you need to keep your horse if you want to compete him at shows? Do you have the time to work him regularly and to keep him that fit?

RIGHT: *Choosing the right horse or pony is a very important decision and needs your careful consideration. The horse you buy will be your companion for many years to come and you will establish a working partnership.*

Riding proficiency

How many of the following activities have you done?

- Riding a horse bareback.
- Jumping a short course of fences of 0.7–0.75 m (2 ft 3 in–2 ft 6 in).
- Hacking out on a cold day.
- Walking, trotting and cantering with no stirrups.
- Getting on a horse that you have never ridden before without feeling worried or apprehensive.
- Riding a friend's horse while they were on holiday.
- Learning to cope with a spook, buck or disobedience on a horse.
- Riding forward in open countryside.

Someone who has done most of these things would be considered a *bona fide* novice rider. If several of these things fill you with fear, don't worry, but put off buying a horse until you have dealt with them. Confide any concerns you might have in your current riding teacher and work towards tackling them. If you are worried about riding an unknown quantity, how are you going to cope with trying out a prospective purchase?

Looking after a horse

If you are considering buying a horse, then your knowledge of horse care should be sufficient to ensure the horse is looked after properly.

- Do you know the basics of feeding?
- Can you bring in and turn out a sharp horse on a cold day?
- Can you muck out economically and swiftly?
- Can you tack up and untack?
- Do you know how to check whether tack and rugs fit?
- Could you confidently administer first aid to a sick or injured horse until the vet arrives?

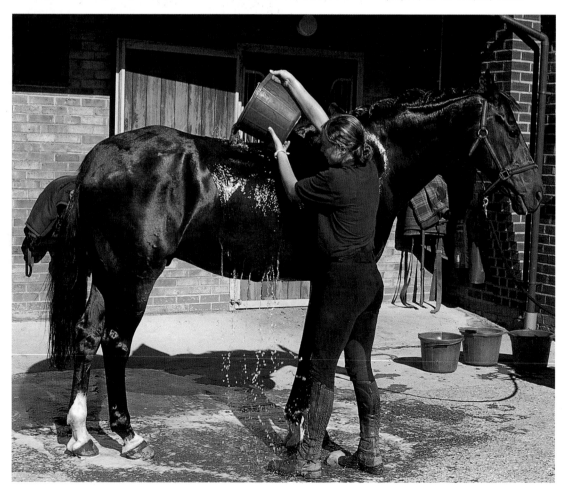

BELOW: *If you are thinking of buying a horse, you must ensure that you have adequate time to look after it properly on an everyday basis.*

RIGHT: *Get some experience of stable management by working for free at your local riding school.*

These questions are worth thinking about; perhaps before you take the plunge you could work regularly (for free) at a local riding school or livery yard. You will pick up many valuable skills, will probably be offered some free rides (which should complement regular, paid-for lessons) and improve your practical knowledge of horses.

All this would be good preparation for when you have sole charge of your own horse. It will also give you an invaluable insight into what horse ownership entails.

It is also worth considering the halfway house of sharing a horse for a year or so, prior to buying your own. The financial outlay and risks are less serious and it will help you decide if you really want to take the plunge. But remember to draw up a written agreement if you are going to share a horse, to avoid confusion and keep things straightforward.

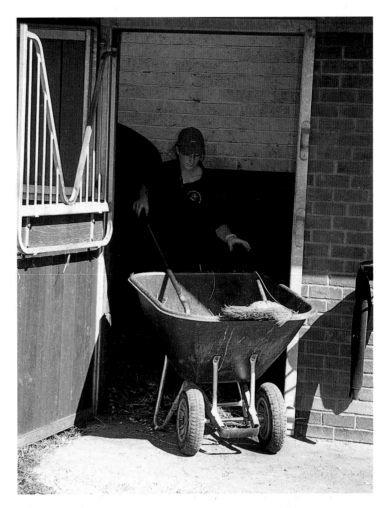

The next step

Once you have satisfied yourself that all the key commitment, know-how and financial concerns have been met, you should consider your particular circumstances further.

Will you be keeping the horse at home or at livery? If he is going to be kept at livery, how much will you have to do outside of the agreement? Some livery services do not include hard feed or tack cleaning, and there may be some days that they do not offer certain services. Your stabling and turn-out facilities may have an effect on what type of horse you buy.

Long-term considerations

Buying a horse is not an easy decision or a small step to take. On the contrary, you are committing yourself to a relationship which could last for many years and will eat up your time as well as your money. It is vital that you consider the long-term implications and the future of the horse. For instance, if you are buying a pony for a child, what will you do with him when the child has outgrown it? Would you sell him, loan him to a friend or keep him as a companion? If you are buying a horse for yourself, are you prepared to keep him into old age and retirement? And what will happen if the horse gets sick or your financial circumstances change? Horses are an expensive, ongoing financial commitment and the cost of keeping them should not be underestimated. It is not easy to sell or re-home an unwanted or outgrown horse or pony, and it can become a drawn-out process which may take many months. Therefore consider carefully whether you should buy a horse and whether you have the time and the money for such a responsibility.

1.2 Horses for novices

As a novice, your key concern should be to find a horse that is suitable for the type of riding you want to do and which has the type of character that you are looking for. Try not to get bogged down with the type of breed you would prefer; it is much more important that the horse is obedient, reactive to your forward aids, feels comfortable to you, and is uncomplicated to care for.

The horse's age

Age is a very important consideration when you are buying a horse. A novice rider is not the best teacher for a young or inexperienced horse, so you should opt for one that has 'been there and done that' and thus is in a position to teach you how it's done. You should probably rule out any horse that is younger than seven or eight, and certainly include those from eight up to fourteen or fifteen years.

Nowadays, thanks to improved veterinary care and correct feeding, horses routinely live into their mid-twenties, and so it can be more than worthwhile for a novice to consider the fifteen- to twenty-year age range. In this bracket, the likelihood of a veterinary problem is higher, but

that may be a risk worth taking for a sensible and experienced animal who has been well-loved by a good owner and which has an illness-free track record behind him.

A horse's age can be assessed approximately by examining the incisor teeth. However, don't attempt to do this yourself; ask an experienced person or, better still, your vet.

Size

Beware of buying a horse that is not the right size or does not have the suitable weight-carrying ability for you. Check this out with your riding teacher. The horse must not be too big for you — he will look imposing, but not with you dangling from his neck when he starts behaving badly because you are too small to 'keep him together'.

BELOW: *Horses come in all shapes and sizes. You have to consider which horse is the right choice for you.*

RIGHT: *All owners want a rewarding relationship with their horse which can last for many years.*

1.3 Which breed?

It is misleading to generalize about temperaments and to say which are characteristic of certain breeds. Many riders have happened upon incredibly lazy Throughbreds while Cobs can often be quite sharp. Here are a few pointers to help you.

General advice

■ All the native breeds, including Connemaras, Welsh ponies and Cobs, Irish Draughts and New Forest ponies, are always worth looking at, although some can be a little sharp.
■ Natives which are crossed with Thoroughbreds are the archetypal English riding horse or pony, and they are generally adaptable all-rounders, which are slightly lighter in build than a pure native but are able to winter out if necessary.
■ Pure Thoroughbreds are often used as hunters and they can make good hacks. However, a novice rider should avoid a horse that has been raced professionally, as there is often much undoing to be done before they are ready for a family role.
■ Warmbloods will often have lovely temperaments and they can be very rideable. These days, the top dressage and show jumping horses are predominantly Warmbloods, so they can reach high prices at the elite end of the market. But there are plenty of 'riding horses', which are bred every year for non-professionals.

BELOW: *Thoroughbreds can be very good all-rounders, but a novice rider should always avoid buying a former racehorse.*

Breed terms

Here are some useful descriptive breed terms to help you when you are considering which breed to buy.

BELOW: *Connemaras are renowned for their versatility and good natures. They are excellent for young riders.*

■ **Cob:** A sturdy, weight-carrying horse of no more than 15.3hh.

■ **Hack:** A lightweight horse of Thoroughbred type, usually ranging from 14.2–15.3hh.

■ **Half-bred:** A horse with one parent a Thoroughbred.

■ **Hotblood or Fullblood:** Applies to Eastern breeds, such as Arabs, and to Thoroughbreds.

■ **Thoroughbred:** A term to describe horses registered in the General Stud Book which trace their ancestry in the male line back to three Arab stallions.

■ **Warmblood:** Horses with a mixture of blood used for riding and driving.

1.4 Points of the horse

When people talk about horses and their conformation and anatomy, they will use a wide range of terms with which you must familiarize yourself.

Examining a standing horse

The rear end is the engine for movement. It is important that the hindlegs sit well under the body and do not trail behind when the horse is stood up on a hard, flat surface. Viewed from behind, the point of buttock should line up with the centre of the hock and create a straight line through the back of the cannon, fetlock and hoof. In the loin area it is desirable to have a good amount of muscle, making it easy for the horse to connect the momentum from the hind legs over his centre of gravity – giving a nice, balanced ride. The horse's ribs should be nicely rounded and just visible. The shoulder also plays an important role in the quality of the horse's movement. Ideally, it should slope 45–50 degrees from a horizontal line. This angle should be mirrored in the angle of the pasterns, too. An upright shoulder will normally result in short paces and make it difficult for the horse to lengthen his stride. The top line of the horse stretches from poll to tail and is a good indicator of how fit he is and whether he is an athletic mover. The line should be smooth and the withers should be a little higher than the croup. Another area where it is worth comparing horses is the way the head is set onto the neck. You should be able to fit two fingers into the groove behind the mandible.

Loins

Croup

Quarters

Point of hip

Point of buttock

Dock

Tail

Gaskin or 2nd thigh

Point of hock

Sheath

Stifle joint

Hock joint

Ergot

Pastern

Heel

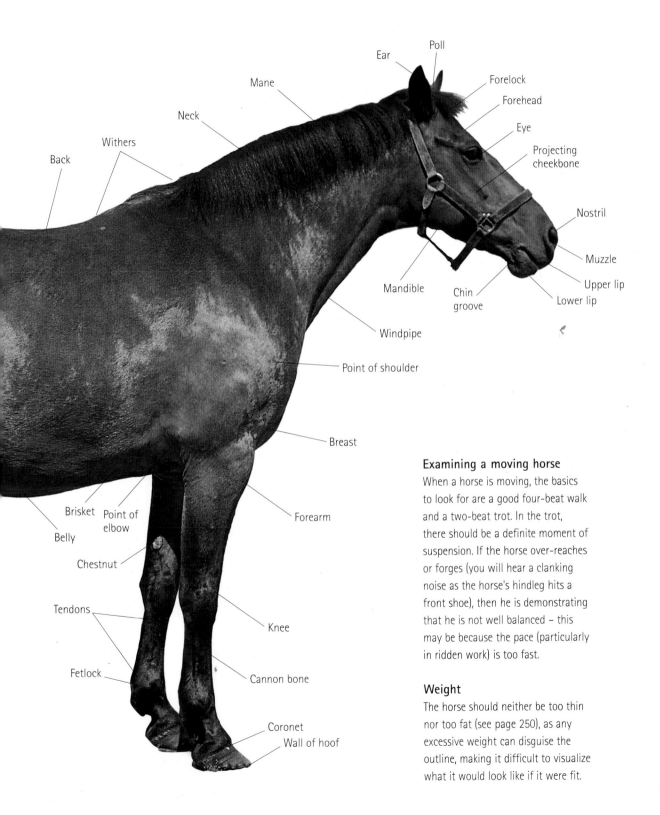

Poll

Ear

Forelock

Forehead

Mane

Eye

Neck

Projecting
cheekbone

Withers

Back

Nostril

Muzzle

Upper lip

Mandible

Chin
groove

Lower lip

Windpipe

Point of shoulder

Breast

Brisket

Point of
elbow

Forearm

Belly

Chestnut

Tendons

Knee

Fetlock

Cannon bone

Coronet

Wall of hoof

Examining a moving horse

When a horse is moving, the basics
to look for are a good four-beat walk
and a two-beat trot. In the trot,
there should be a definite moment of
suspension. If the horse over-reaches
or forges (you will hear a clanking
noise as the horse's hindleg hits a
front shoe), then he is demonstrating
that he is not well balanced – this
may be because the pace (particularly
in ridden work) is too fast.

Weight

The horse should neither be too thin
nor too fat (see page 250), as any
excessive weight can disguise the
outline, making it difficult to visualize
what it would look like if it were fit.

1.5 Conformation

Volumes have been written on this subject, but in order to accurately assess the strengths and weaknesses in any horse's conformation and movement, a trained eye which is borne of much experience is needed. This is one reason why it is imperative that you take an experienced person with you to viewings — they will be able to assess the horse more easily and see things more readily.

Conformation pitfalls

When you are viewing a horse and are trying to assess its confomation you need to pay particular attention to the aspects highlighted here.

Watching the movement

At a suitable point during a viewing, ask to see the horse walked and then trotted in hand. This way you can get to see the action, not just feel it.

Look for regularity in stride length and the absence of tripping. Watch out for dishing (the horse swinging its front legs to the side as well as to the front in forward movemement) and plaiting — the hind or front legs being put down in each other's path. View the horse from behind and watch if he pushes off with his hind legs to develop forward movement.

Hocks

The hock is a seat for common problems, often arthritic changes, so watch out for any signs of stiff hindleg action. Capped hocks (normally an enlargement on the point of the hock) are not necessarily a reason to rule out a horse unless you want to show him.

Fetlocks

The fetlock joint should appear flat rather than round. Look for lumps on the front or back, which may be a sign of age. On the inside, they indicate that the horse moves close and brushes. Non-bony lumps called wind galls are only unsightly and rarely cause problems.

Quarters

These should be nicely muscled and not higher than the wither. Watch the relationship between the point of the buttock and back of the cannon, which should be straight when the horse is standing square.

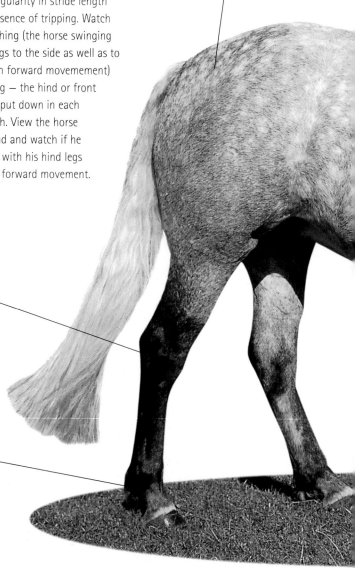

Neck

In old-fashioned horseman's tems, the 'neck should be well set-on and the shoulder sloping'. A horse with a low-set neck can be heavy in front to ride. A ewe-neck is to be avoided but is often the result of the horse being ridden in a hollow outline.

Back

The horse's back should not be too long; it can prove a weakness for weight carrying if it is, nor should it be dipped in the middle.

Head

This should be in proportion to the horse's size, lean and well set on to the neck so as not to affect respiration or ease of flexion, which can influence the control and balance of the horse.

Chest

This should be of medium width, not so narrow as to make brushing likely nor so wide as to roll in canter and limit the ability to gallop.

Forelegs

The tendons which run down the backs of legs should be heat-free and without swellings. The presence of either of these two things indicate possible tendon or ligament damage. This has the potential to be a severe problem that can mean many months of not working. Splints often form on the bones of young horses between the cannon and splint bones – just below the knee – but, once formed, rarely create a problem unless they are high enough to interfere with the joint.

Feet

Acquaint yourself with the different types of hoof conformation, ranging from boxy, upright feet to flat feet with low heels. At extremes, these types of conformation can cause tendon and/or bone problems. Historically, low heels have also been associated with a serious condition known as navicular, which is inflammation of the pedal bone – the last bone in the horse's leg, which is surrounded by the hoof.

1.6 Where to buy a horse

There are around a million horses in the UK today, and at any one time several thousand will be actively for sale. So, there is certainly no shortage of horses on the market, but where should you look in order to find the right one?

Before you start looking, you should have several criteria in mind: the horse's height, age, health, character and experience are the main ones. Of secondary importance, for the novice rider in particular, are breeding and competition record. A fit, healthy horse, which you can ride effectively and enjoy, is what you need.

Advertisements

For the first-time horse owner, the biggest selection of advertisements for horses for sale is available in the equestrian press. As well as national magazines, in most areas there is a local horse publication that you can probably pick up at your tack shop.

Being able to read between the lines of an advertisement is important. For example, a small 'P' at the bottom of the advert stands for private sale, while a small 'T' is trade, i.e. a dealer. For more information on commonly used terms and abbreviations, look at the table on the opposite page. Advertisers should always offer the following information on any horse or pony that is for sale:

- The age of the horse
- The height of the horse
- Breeding details
- Health information
- Additional details, such as 'good to shoe', 'box', 'traffic', 'clip', etc.

Word of mouth

Word of mouth can be a good way to find a horse, but you should exercise extreme caution. Do not rush into buying a horse that a friend of a friend thinks might be perfect for you. It won't do any harm to go and try it, but does it measure up to what you really want? At least, go and look at several other horses that are advertised through other media.

Teachers and trainers

Buying through your trainer can be a good way to buy a horse but beware of a few pitfalls. If you ride at a riding school and they have a horse that they believe is suitable, it can be all too easy to have a few lessons on the horse and become attached to it. However, buying a horse which has been in a riding school can bring problems. It may be extremely fit and eating a large amount

of hard feed – a lifestyle which you will have to change gradually. It may be 'institutionalized' and find life difficult outside of the school. Additionally, as a riding school horse it will be used to living with other horses and may not settle by itself.

If your teacher is freelance, then you must take the initiative and keep any possible buyer/seller relationship totally separate from the existing teacher/pupil one.

Auctions

Buying at auction is more suitable for very experienced horse people than novices. If you want to go down this route, then proceed with caution. Take an experienced horse owner with you. Examine the horse's vetting papers thoroughly and be clear about the different types of vet certificate.

You must try the horse before you buy; spend some time handling it and seeing how it reacts. Establish a rapport with the seller and provide as much honest information about yourself as you can. This gives them, in turn, an opportunity to be honest about the character, health and experience of the horse.

The real problem with buying at an auction if you are a novice is that

Commission

In those cases where you may be thinking of buying a horse or pony from someone you already know, such as your trainer or teacher, it is important to be clear from the start what the terms are. In particular, you need to know whether your go-between is working on a commission basis? While it is only fair that someone should be financially rewarded for bringing two suitable parties together, you should find out if this is the case. This is because some people may encourage you to buy an only half-suitable horse if they are likely to make money from the deal. So ask them outright whether they are on commission so that you all know where you stand.

there is not much time to deliberate, and therefore mistakes are more easily made. The horse is in one place at one time and may react differently elsewhere – for example, can you take the seller's word for it that the horse is safe in traffic if you don't get the opportunity to try riding him in these circumstances?

Dealers

Not all dealers are on the make, but as a novice horse owner, how are you to distinguish the sharks from the good eggs? It can be very difficult. One of the best ways is through word of mouth, but as a novice you might not know many people who would have heard about or dealt with a particular dealer.

Protecting yourself

There are various ways to protect yourself. Do you feel comfortable about the dealer's yard and the way in which they conduct themselves

BELOW: *Buying a riding school horse or pony for a child can seem a good option but there may be pitfalls.*

and treat the horses? Ask the dealer for contact details of previous clients and visit them and their horses. Ask for background on the horse you are interested in and phone up the previous owner to check it out.

Finally, consider a trial period (but use a contract) and don't hand over the horse's full price. Good dealers will behave with integrity and want to preserve their business and name. To some extent, you will only discover a bad dealer once you have been on the wrong end of the purchase of an unsuitable horse.

Local riding/pony club

Particularly in the case of ponies, you will discover that outgrown animals are often up for sale – this can be an excellent way for you to acquire a safe, reliable pony that knows the ropes. There will also be plenty of third parties who know the animal to ask for information.

Studs

Many studs will buy and sell horses, too. While they may be their own progeny, they may also do some

dealing as part of their establishment. Studs often sell youngsters that may be backed or ready for backing, but as a novice rider these are not the best sort of horses to start with. If they are selling older, established horses, then you should take the same precautions as with any dealer.

Explanation of terms

In advertisements, there are a lot of abbreviations (which saves the advertiser money). Here is an explanation of some of the terms that are most commonly used.

Dress: Dressage
SJ: Show jumping
XC: Cross country
ODE: One-day event
BD: British Dressage
BE: British Eventing
BSJA: British Show Jumping Association
TBX: Thoroughbred horse crossed with another breed, i.e. TBXID is a Thoroughbred X Irish Draught; a TBXConn is a Thoroughbred X Connemara
PC/RC: Pony Club/Riding Club
WHP: Working hunter pony
SHP: Show hunter pony
P (UK): Ponies (UK)
NPS: National Pony Society, a showing society
BSPS: British Show Pony Society, a showing society
Hann: Hanoverian
KWPN: Dutch Warmblood
SF: Selle Francais
FBW: Federation Baden-Wurttenberg
Old: Oldenburg
Hol: Holstein
Trak: Trakhener

1.7 Going to see a horse

Once you have some horses in mind, whether they are sourced from advertisements or word of mouth, speak to the sellers. Plan out how you are going to describe yourself, your riding ability and the sort of home you are offering the horse.

Discuss how best to describe your riding ability with your riding teacher. It is vital that you are as open and honest as possible, otherwise you could waste valuable time and money visiting an unsuitable horse, while a much better match for you is sold to someone else. If you are a first-time horse owner, have ridden for less than a year, or are nervous, you really should tell the seller in advance of a visit. They will then be able to help you to make a decision as to whether it is worth your visiting the horse.

You will often see the words 're-advertised due to timewasters' featured in advertisements; while this may not be the case, horse owners do get fed up with putting time aside for a prospective purchaser who has misrepresented themselves.

Of course, this can work in the opposite way, too, but it is just a part of buying. It is always worth riding a horse if you think that it might be suitable, but do not get on any horse that is displaying signs of dangerous behaviour. The person selling the horse should always ride the horse with you watching before you get on and also offer a brief description of what he is like to ride.

BELOW: *When you go to view a horse take a good look at him. Observe his behaviour as well as his conformation and watch him in action, too.*

Questions you should ask

When you are viewing a horse, ask the seller the following questions and, crucially, make a note of their answers. The most important one is: 'Why are you selling this horse?'

Basic questions

- How old is the horse?
- What breed is it?
- What types of work does it do?
- Has it had any competition success?
- How much experience does the person who owns or rides it currently have?
- How long has the current owner had the horse?
- Can they give a brief description of where the horse was before this home?
- Do they know anything about the horse's early years before they acquired it?

Veterinary questions

- Has the horse ever received veterinary treatment for lameness?
- What was the condition?
- What was the treatment and how long did it take to come right?
- Has the horse ever had colic?
- How serious was it and did the horse have colic surgery?
- Does the horse/pony have any history of laminitis?
- Has it had any other illness which has meant the vet has been called?
- Has the horse ever had an accident in the field, on the road, at a competition, in the stable or in the yard?
- What was the treatment and how long was the recovery period?
- Has the owner ever made a claim on the horse's insurance?
- If so, what are the details? Ask to check the policy; any exclusions will be noted on this year's policy.

Temperament questions

- Does the horse enjoy the company of people?
- Does the horse enjoy the company of other horses?
- Is the horse ever aggressive to people?
- Is the horse ever aggressive to other horses?
- How does the horse react to new people?
- Is it good in traffic?
- Do some types of traffic, i.e. motorbikes or tractors, scare the horse?
- Does the horse hack out alone and in company without problems?
- Is it confident around dogs, pigs, cows and children?
- Does it get strong when cantered on open ground?
- Does the horse enjoy shows or find them stressful?
- When stressed, how does the horse's behaviour change?
- Does the horse load easily? In a trailer? In a horsebox?
- Has the horse ever cribbed, wind-sucked or weaved? If so, how much and when?
- Is the horse happy to stand tied up?

Current rider questions

- What level is the current rider?
- Does the current rider compete the horse?
- In what disciplines and with what kind of success?
- Does the current rider carry a whip or wear spurs routinely?
- Who trains the horse and current rider?
- Can you speak to the trainer?

Stable management questions

- What current arrangements are made for the horse regarding turn out and stabling?
- What type of forage does it currently eat?
- What type of hard feed does it currently eat?
- Is it stabled in a barn or in outside boxes?
- Is the horse good to clip?
- Is the horse good to shoe?

1.8 The day of the visit

As the prospective owner, you must attend all viewings in person, preferably with an experienced horse person. Confirm that you are keeping the appointment made and make sure that you arrive on time, dressed suitably in riding gear.

Keep your eyes open. As you arrive, monitor the conditions on the yard, from the point of view of how the horses kept there are being stabled and also the behaviour of the other horses and any people on the yard.

Be businesslike, not over-friendly or excited. The person who is selling the horse should present the horse groomed but untacked. Spend some time in the stable with the horse, for a preliminary look over it, and then ask the owner your most important questions (see page 29).

Once you are satisfied that all is well, the owner should tack the horse up with you present and proceed to ride it for you. This will take some time, as all horses should be properly warmed up before being put through their paces. You must observe everything carefully. The horse should be shown to you doing all the things that you will wish to do with it, such as jumping a small round of fences. If everything seems satisfactory, you should ride next, not the experienced person you've brought along to advise, or the trainer.

Relax and take your time; ask the current owner as many questions as you like and remember 'safety first'. Again, if the horse is being bought because you want to jump with him, make sure you take him over at least one fence. If at any time you feel unsafe or out of your depth, bring the session to an end.

BELOW: *The owner should allow you to examine the horse closely before walking and trotting it up for you and then riding it.*

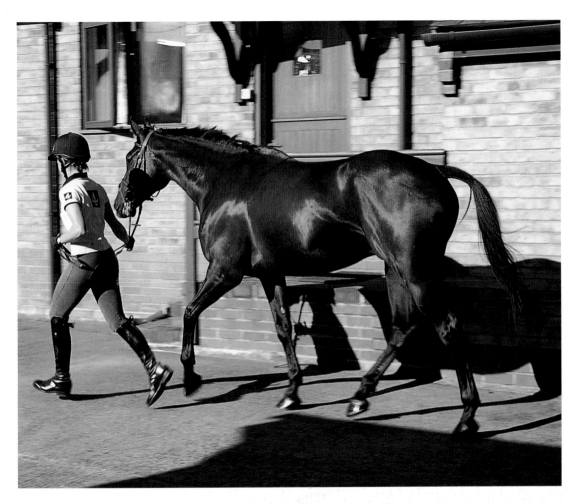

If everything seems in order, you could ask if your experienced friend or trainer could try the horse. But remember, the horse has already done a lot of work so it might be best to arrange a second visit. In addition, you may want to walk the horse round a field or down a nearby road or bridlepath, if he looks promising. But, again, don't expect this on a first visit.

A second visit for a good prospect can be arranged whereby you set the agenda — perhaps taking him for a short hack or onto the road, but get the owner's agreement beforehand. Never take a seller's word for it that a horse can do something, unless you have ridden the horse yourself in those particular circumstances.

Pitfalls at a viewing

Observation and questions are your best friends at a viewing. While the majority of vendors will be genuine, some are not. Look for possible signs that the horse was ridden before you came – sweat marks where tack has been, and unease when seeing the tack arrive for your trial.

Check the horse has adequate forage and water — it is one way to quieten a normally boisterous horse. At the other extreme, some people may even use sedatives to calm a

ABOVE: *Ask the vendor to trot the horse up for you and then watch the movements carefully from every angle: from the side, the front and from behind. Look out for signs of lameness or poor conformation.*

horse, so look out for inflammation of the soft tissue around the horse's eyes, a relaxed sheath in a gelding, and tripping. Don't ride a horse which you think may be doped; just make your excuses and leave.

If you intend to or have to hack on roads, then it is important that you try the horse in traffic. Do not just take the vendor's word for it.

Further checks

If the horse in question is being sold with a competition record or perhaps points from one of the competitive disciplines, then check this out with the appropriate sport organization.

To check the horse's registration with the breed societies, ask to see the papers and also take down the number, if the vendor has one.

A simple internet search will often bring up the contact details for the many breed associations and showing societies with whom you can make contact. They are always happy to help with advice and checking things out if you explain the situation in full.

You must go back and visit the horse more than once, increasing the level of detail and involvement each time. If the horse and the vendor are going to a show, then go along and watch them in action. You cannot have too much information about a prospective purchase. Don't rush into making a decision about the first horse you see; there is more than just one suitable horse out there for you and you owe it to yourself and your horse to look around.

Trial periods

Find out whether you can have the horse on a trial basis and draw up a contract outlining the terms on both

LEFT: *Try to ride the horse on several occasions before making a decision. If the owner will let you take it on a trial basis, this is the best option.*

BELOW: *When trying out the horse, put it through its paces and practise some trotting and cantering.*

sides, which may include a deposit changing hands. Most owners will not allow their horses to go out on trial and this is for good reason: in the wrong hands, a horse can be spoilt quickly and will then be returned as unwanted. The owner is then left without a proper sale and with a horse that needs to be rehabilitated, necessitating more money and time to be spent on the horse.

RIGHT: *If the owner will not allow you to take the horse on a trial basis, do make sure that you visit again and take him out for another ride to get the feel of him before deciding to buy.*

Viewing a horse summary

1 Before you contact the seller and arrange to go and see the horse, make a list of questions to ask over the phone to determine whether the horse is suitable and worth visiting. This will save you time and money.

2 Make a note of the seller's answers and consider them carefully before deciding whether to go ahead and arrange a visit. If you feel that the horse may be suitable, ring back and make the arrangements, explaining what you want to see and do, e.g. lungeing, jumping, hacking, etc.

3 Make sure that you arrange to take an experienced person with you, such as a BHS-qualified instructor.

4 Observe the horse being handled and check out its general health and body condition, especially the feet and legs. Look for lumps, bumps, abnormalities and telltale signs of old injuries.

5 Ask to see the horse ridden so that you can watch it being put through its paces and assess its movement and behaviour. Don't be afraid to ask the owner to lunge, jump, box or hack it down the road perhaps. This is not unreasonable and it will give you an opportunity to observe the horse and to decide whether it is safe.

6 If you and your adviser are happy that the horse is safe, then ask the vendor whether you can have a ride.

Ride the horse at a walk, trot and canter, and even try a little jump. Remember that he is unfamiliar and you need to get to know each other so do not be over-ambitious at this stage.

7 Do not make an instant decision now, however much you may like the horse. Ask any further questions that may be appropriate and then thank the owner, say that you will get in touch when you have made a decision, and go away and talk through the viewing with your adviser.

8 If you think of any questions that you forgot to ask or your adviser raises any issues, telephone the seller to resolve them and, if you are still interested, arrange another viewing.

9 Visit the horse again and ride it at least once to develop a feel for it. Again, if you are unsure, do not be rushed into making a decision but go away and think about it carefully.

10 If you decide that you want to buy the horse, then you are strongly advised to arrange for your vet to carry out a pre-purchase veterinary examination in order to reduce the chances of buying a horse with health problems.

11 If you decide not to purchase the horse, it is polite to let the owners know as soon as possible, so that they do not turn away any prospective buyers.

1.9 Five-stage vetting

Once you have settled on a horse and can tick all the boxes, then you are ready to make a purchase. Always get a five-stage vetting for a horse or pony first. There are several reasons why.

■ A five-stage vetting will make it easier to get good value insurance for the horse (saving you money in the long term).

■ Although you have done all your checks and asked pertinent questions regarding the health of the horse, the vet is in a much better position to judge its health.

■ The vet is a key person from whom you can garner further information concerning the horse's temperament and its suitability for you.

■ If you tell the vet what sort of rider you are and what you intend to use the horse for, he or she can bear that in mind during the vetting and advise you of any important issues.

■ The vet will be in a good position to observe the horse's behaviour and may provide insightful information that you have not picked up on. Ensure that your veterinary practice sends its horse specialist.

■ The vet will be happy to discuss the horse in an open manner with you, and you should take full advantage of this service and his or her advice.

BELOW: *The vet will want to observe the movement of the horse as he is walked, trotted up and turned.*

Practical steps

The five-stage vetting should, ideally, be carried out by a good vet who is known to you. Do not, under any circumstances, use the vendor's vet. If you don't know an equine vet in the area where your horse lives, use the internet site www.findavet.org.uk. This is affiliated to the Royal College of Veterinary Surgeons and allows you to do a search by area for a vet.

When you call to book the vetting, the veterinary clinic will need to know the exact details and address for the yard where the horse is. They will also need details of the horse (so the wrong one is not vetted) and the facilities (hard trot-up areas, surfaced arenas and lunge areas).

You also need to consider whether you would like a blood test to be taken at the vetting and whether you need any X-rays. The point of doing a blood test is for reference if a problem arises with the horse and there is a suspicion

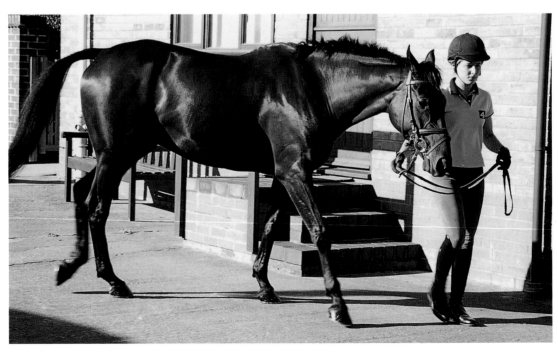

The stages of the vetting

Stage 1

A preliminary examination is made of the whole horse. This monitors the heart at rest, eyesight, mouth and teeth. Examination of the teeth will give the vet an approximate idea of the age of the horse as well as any problems that may make acceptance of the bit or eating difficult. The horse will be examined all over by hand (palpated), and the vet will check the horse's back and foot conformation and balance.

Stage 2

The vet will then trot up the horse on a hard surface for around 20–30 m. The horse will be backed up and turned sharply both ways, after which flexion tests will be performed and the horse trotted again. The flexion tests may highlight problems in movement brought about by arthritic conditions and other things, such as neurological diseases like shivers.

Stage 3

The horse is saddled up and the vet will monitor its reaction prior to a period of strenuous work. The aim is to monitor heart and lung health. The amount of exercise will vary according to the fitness and age of the horse. In ridden exercise, the horse's gait and response to the rider can be checked. The heart will be monitored again once the exercise is over and the tack removed.

Stage 4

While the horse recovers in the stable, the vet will monitor its health during recovery from strenuous exercise. The vet may also look over the horse again and palpate parts of its body.

Stage 5

The horse's feet will be inspected and then the horse will be trotted again. This is to discover if it has any post-exercise stiffness.

---

that its owner may have administered painkillers or even some dope for the vetting. The blood test is usually stored, rather than tested immediately, unless and until a problem arises.

X-rays are not necessary for a novice horse, which will participate in riding club and low-level affiliated classes. They can raise more questions than they answer and could well lead to further, expensive investigations, without offering any answers.

Buyer's report

The vet will produce a document that details all the veterinary findings, i.e. any signs of disease or injury, and will also offer a judgment on the suitability of the horse for the job intended and the rider. The vet will often give you a verbal run-through of this immediately, which can obviously help you decide your next move without delay.

Insurance

If the horse passes the vetting and you plan to buy it, get suitable insurance cover before you part with any money. This guards against injury, especially during transit to your yard. There are good and bad insurance companies; use one that your friends or riding teacher recommend. Cheap is not always best, so look for a company that settles claims swiftly and with minimum fuss.

RIGHT: *Loss of use branding indicates that a horse has had an insurance claim. Although an insurance company will not reinsure it, it may still be a suitable purchase for light work. Always investigate the reasons for this.*

1.10 Legal aspects

Your legal position will vary, depending on whether you have purchased a horse or pony from a private individual or from a business, i.e. a dealer or at an auction.

Private individual

Here the adage 'let the buyer beware' stands. You have no rights other than the description of the horse as it appears in the advertisement. It can, however, be useful to ask the vendor to send a document outlining the main aspects of the horse, i.e. the age, breeding, experience, height, lack of vices, behaviour when clipped, loaded, on roads, with the farrier, etc.

Dealer

When you buy a horse from a dealer, there is a piece of law known as the Sale of Goods Act 1979 (intended for miscellaneous second-hand goods) which protects the buyer in certain ways. The three main points of this are that the horse:

■ Must be fit and healthy as it is described.
■ Must be suitable for the purpose sold, i.e. for a novice rider who is a first-time horse owner.
■ Must be as described by the vendor; this covers the basics, such as height, colour, breeding, etc.

Nevertheless, it is still up to you, the purchaser, to check particular details, including health, behaviour, e.g. when loading, as well as the horse's history – has it ever been used in a riding school, for example?

Auctions

Auctions will have their own terms and conditions which are set out in their catalogues. Horses that are sold with a warranty will have a specified date by which they must be returned, i.e. seven days. However, if you buy a horse unwarranted, then you have no recourse if the horse is not suitable.

Horse passports

On February 28 2005, it became law for all horses to be sold with a passport, so make sure your purchase has one. You then need to contact the passport issuing office, which could be the BHS or a breed society – it will be clear on the passport — and notify them of your name, address and the horse's identification number. This needs to be done within 30 days of the change of ownership.

RIGHT: *Never rush into buying a horse. Once you have brought it home, it is difficult to send it back again.*

The cost of horse ownership

Apart from the initial cost of purchase, keeping a horse will involve a continual financial commitment. Unless the horse comes with its own tack, you will have to invest in a properly fitting saddle, bridle, girths, a head collar and lead rope, grooming equipment, first–aid kit, stable and turn-out rugs, yard and feeding equipment. All tack and rugs should be correctly fitted by a qualified, reputable person, whether it's new or second-hand. You, of course, will also need sensible, comfortable clothing, protective headgear, boots and gloves. Safety gear is essential and this cost should never be skimped on. Don't be tempted to save money by buying a second–hand hat which could have been damaged previously. Then there is the cost of keeping your horse, whether it's on your own land, in a rented field or paddock, in a stable or at livery. You will need to provide the horse with bedding, feed and forage, and will have to pay for regular visits from the farrier. These are just the basic costs of horse ownership. Additional considerations are the cost of dental, veterinary and routine health care, including worming and vaccinations, as well as treating ill health or injury. Because it is difficult to budget for these demands, you can take out insurance from a reputable equine insurance broker to cover you for veterinary fees. If you are a BHS member, you automatically receive public liability cover. Finally, if you are a novice or even a more experienced rider, you will still benefit from instruction. Regular lessons will help you to become a better and a safer rider. And if you plan to compete with your horse, there will be additional equipment, tack and clothing, as well as the entry fees to shows and competitions, not to mention a horsebox or trailer for transporting your horse.

1.11 Settling in your horse

The golden rule when settling in your new horse is to make things as similar to his old home as possible and introduce your own changes gradually. Within your capabilities, initially, you should keep the horse to the same stabling and turn-out arrangement as he had before you bought him. Try to obtain a few days' supply of his old forage and hard feed and introduce any dietary changes gradually.

Resist the temptation to shower the new arrival with carrots, apples, new rugs, gawping strangers, etc. However, do ride him for a short time, once he has had a few hours to settle in, or, at the latest, on the following day, if he is fit and used to regular exercise.

Do not leave it for too long before setting up your next appointment

LEFT: *It is important to establish a good relationship with your horse. He will soon look forward to your visits to feed, water or exercise him.*

with the farrier as the horse will be new on the list and you will need to give the farrier time to book him in to his diary.

Set up any other appointments that you may feel you need, such as a fitting with a master saddler for a new saddle or getting the horse's current saddle checked out.

Problem-busting

If there is a problem with your new horse, then talk to the previous owner about it. Be calm and tactful

and see if they can offer a sensible solution or might have experienced the same problem in the past. Always aim to solve problems amicably, but if you think there is a serious mismatch or the horse has been misrepresented in some way, you should do everything you can to get the owner to take the horse back – you may lose money but it will still make sense in the long run.

If you have bought the horse from someone in the trade, such as a horse dealer, then you should set out the problem in writing, tell them what you would like done and give them a date by which to reply. You can take a problem with a dealer to the local trading standards officer.

And finally...

It takes time to build a good working relationship and your horse will have to learn to trust you in order for you both to forge a mutually rewarding and long-lasting partnership – don't expect it to happen overnight.

The first few weeks

During this initial stage of coming to live with you, the horse will be adjusting and settling in to his new home environment. You can spend this time enjoying his company as you get to know him and he gets to know you. Make a point of spending time with your horse, looking after and feeding him yourself, and exercising him every day if possible.

You should also check out with the previous owner when the horse was last wormed and ideally ask your vet to perform a faecal egg count in order to make sure that your newcomer does not have a high worm burden and is not going to infect the pasture on which he will graze.

As well as checking for parasites, it is a good idea to arrange for a visit from the farrier to ensure that

he does not have to wait any longer than four to six weeks from his last shoeing. Your vet can inspect the horse's teeth for any signs of abnormal wear and any other dental problems. If you already own other horses or ponies, you should introduce him to them gradually in order to avoid any bullying and to allow changes in the established pecking order. Putting him in an adjoining field initially is a good option if this is possible.

It is also a good idea to take some riding lessons with your new horse and use this as an opportunity to improve your riding skills. There is always room for improvement, however experienced a rider you are, and the potential for learning for both you and your horse is endless. These early weeks can provide the foundations for a happy, healthy horse and a good future relationship between you.

Chapter 2
Housing your horse

• •

One of the best ways to keep our horses and ponies healthy and happy is to turn them out daily in a well-managed field. However, even when they can live out most of the time, there will be occasions when they need suitable housing – shelter from bad weather, for instance, or if a vet advises minimizing their movement to help recovery from injury or illness. Some people believe routine stabling is undesirable and all horses and ponies should be turned out day and night, but this is often impractical. Even when it is possible and appropriate, adequate shelter must be provided. A good regime for most horses and owners is to turn out either during the day and stable animals at night or vice versa, varying the turn-out periods according to the weather and grazing conditions. This allows the best of both worlds.

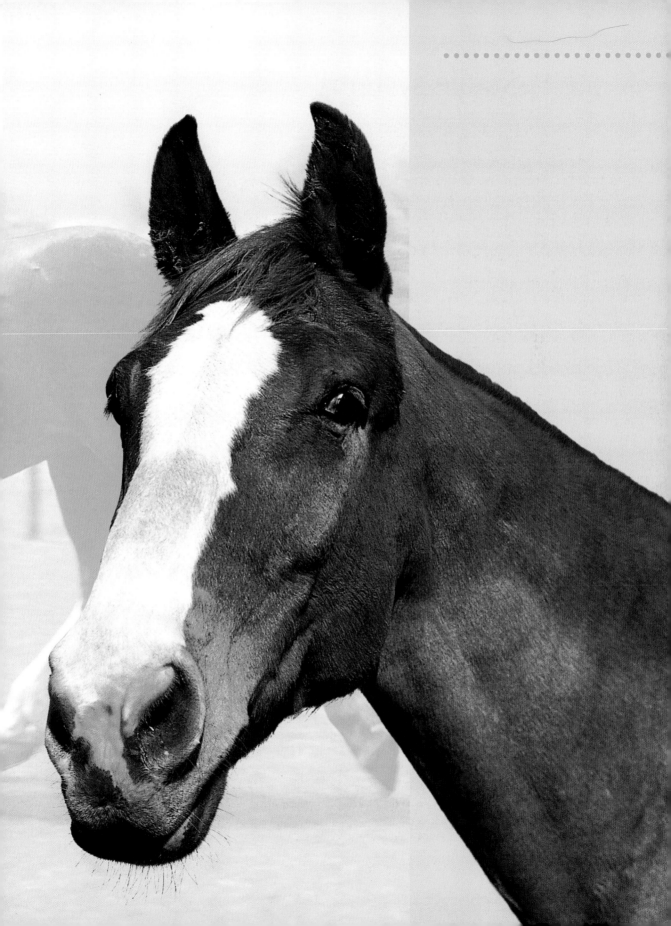

2.1 Stable systems

Most people keep their horses and ponies at livery, where facilities are rented and, depending on whether you opt for a DIY, assisted- or full-livery system, help may be provided. When assessing livery yards, stabling must be looked at as part of the overall package, but the same guidelines apply when you are building accommodation.

If you are able to keep your horse at home and can either put up new stables or convert existing buildings, you can create an ideal environment. However, even so, you may want to start off at livery so you have the support of a knowledgeable yard owner, perhaps one whose yard has been given approval under the British Horse Society's scheme.

Before taking the plunge and going it alone at home, you should examine your lifestyle and the time that you have available for looking after a horse. You will also need to consider whether your facilities are suitable – do you have a stable and a paddock and a properly fenced field for turning out and grazing?

Do you have a friend or family member who can help out? Every horse owner needs a back-up system for times when they are busy or go away on holiday. Before you buy a horse, try to answer honestly the following questions.

- If this is your first experience of owning a horse, then do you have someone knowledgeable to whom you can turn for advice?
- Do you have access to a safe area to school in? Even if you are not interested in competing, you and your horse will benefit from schooling sessions and lessons to keep you both interested and up to scratch. This includes riders who concentrate on hacking, as an obedient, responsive horse is a much greater pleasure to hack and is safer.

Planning permission

If you decide to go ahead and create a stable at home for your horse, it is vital to look at whether or not you need planning permission. This may apply whether you are building stables from scratch or adapting existing buildings, so you need to get advice from your local planning authority and, if necessary, from a solicitor with specialist equestrian knowledge.

Most planning authorities are reluctant to give their permission for permanent brick-built stabling for private use. This is because there have been cases where buildings supposedly constructed as stables quickly turned into accommodation for humans rather than horses. As a result, it is generally easier to get permission for timber stables.

Although stables manufacturers rarely become involved with individual applications, most will help by supplying drawings and illustrations of proposed structures. It is also a good idea to talk to any neighbours who might be affected by you keeping horses at home and allay their possible fears about noise, smell and inconvenience. This means thinking the project through down to the fine detail of where you are going to site your muck heap and how you will arrange for disposal of manure.

Down to basics

The foundations on which your stabling is built are just as important as the building itself. At one time, chalk was a popular flooring, but today concrete is standard because it is easier to keep clean.

If you are buying stables from a manufacturer, you will be sent a plan for the base and it is very important that it is prepared to these exact specifications. Laying concrete is a specialist job, and to aid drainage – to drains set outside rather than inside the box – the floor must be laid with a slight fall, or slope, to the rear of the box so that any urine runs out to external drains rather than pooling on the floor.

For most people, the best option will be to employ a specialist building contractor to do this job rather than attempt it themselves or to use someone with no experience of laying a stable floor.

RIGHT: *Most horses enjoy company and social interaction, whether it is looking out over the stable door or grazing together in a paddock.*

2.2 Stable specifications

There are two main stabling systems: external looseboxes and internal stabling which is constructed within an existing or purpose-built building. The indoor system is often called the American barn system, as it was first popular in the US.

Each system has its pros and cons. External stables are cheaper to build, but unless careful thought goes into their design, horses can seem isolated from their neighbours. Internal stables are more pleasant for those looking after the horses because they are under cover, but they are harder to ventilate and can lead to bullying between horses. In most cases, they are only feasible if you want to provide housing for at least four horses.

Size and cost

Individual stables, whether they are internal or external, should always be as large as possible. The minimum recommendations are usually 3.04 m (10 ft) square for a pony up to about 14.2 hands; 3.65 m (12 ft) square for a horse up to about 16 hands; and 4.26 m (14 ft) square for horses of 16.2 hands and over. It is important to recognize that these are the minimum recommendations and that all horses and ponies will appreciate having as much space as possible. Larger stables are also more economical in terms of bedding, as although you need to put down more to start with, they are usually easier to keep clean because droppings are less likely to be kicked around.

Although we all have to work to a budget, it is more economical in the long run to look ahead and build for future as well as present needs. For example, most manufacturers charge relatively less per unit for putting up, say, three stables and a hay store than for building just two stables. You will also find that you can never have too much storage space.

Linings and doors

In the same way, you should go for the best specifications that you can afford. Linings, which are also known as kickboards, for obvious reasons, to full height are more expensive than ones that go halfway up the wall, but they improve insulation as well as

LEFT: *Doors should be the correct height to enable the horse to look out over the top and observe what is going on outside in the yard.*

46

minimizing any damage to the stable framework from flying hooves.

Door openings should be at least 1.22 m (4 ft) wide to avoid the risk of a horse banging its hips as it goes in and out, and internal headroom should be a minimum of 3.65 m (12 ft) and preferably 3.8 m (12 ft 6 in). In theory, this could be reduced for a small pony but, in practice, the greater the headroom, the greater the volume of air, which helps with ventilation.

Conventional hinged doors should always open outwards so that if a horse got cast (stuck while trying to roll) against the door it would be possible to open it.

They must also have a sliding bolt at the top and a kickover latch at the bottom for security – some horses are accomplished escape artists. A galvanized metal anti-chew strip fitted to the top edge of the bottom door should help to prevent any damage from chewing by the horse.

Good ventilation

This is essential in order to keep your horse's respiratory system healthy, which is why it is important to keep the top half of your stable door open even in bad weather. If you are worried that your horse will get cold, add an extra or a different rug. Avoid draughts

ABOVE: *Outside looseboxes made of wood may need to be treated with a wood preservative to protect them and keep them in good order.*

which can give a horse a chill. Air vents should be at different heights to maximize the airflow. The general recommendation for outdoor stabling is that inlets should be just above horse height and outlets should be in the roof ridge, giving maximum air circulation. The air is warmed by the horse, then rises and goes out through the roof. For internal stabling, get some specialist advice relating to the design and layout of your building.

The roof

In both cases, whether you opt for external looseboxes or for internal stabling, the roof itself should be pitched rather than flat, again to provide the maximum volume of air inside the stable. There are several materials in popular use for outdoor stables and the choice usually comes down to your budget, but corrugated cement sheets or Onduline sheeting, which is a specially treated wood fibre, are both popular. Inserting a translucent perspex roof panel will let in more light.

An overhang on the roof over the door and front wall area of outside looseboxes is well worth having, as it gives extra shelter in bad weather for both the horse and the groom. In the case of prefabricated stabling, the overhang is usually an extension of the roof, but with brick or block stabling, it can be a continuation of the roof or even a separate material. Guttering is usually standard along the front of the stable and, again, it is often worth investing in some extra guttering at the back.

Drainage systems

Your stable will need some sort of drainage system, and you may need to get professional advice on which

ABOVE: *Stable roofs should be pitched rather than flat with an overhang to keep both you and the horse dry in wet weather conditions.*

is the best one to use. Looseboxes and barns should have a shallow slope of one in sixty towards the front or the back of the box.

Any liquid can be directed through a small opening in the centre of the wall at floor level into an open drain running along the outside of the stable wall. You can install removable traps to collect any straw and solids which might otherwise block the drains.

ABOVE: *Air vents can be set high up in the outside back walls of looseboxes to assist air circulation*

Floors

The stable floor should be constructed in such a way that it will provide comfort for the horse and not put strain on its legs. The optimum floor space for a horse should be 11–14 sq m (118–150 sq ft). The most commonly used material for floors is concrete. Easy to put down, it must be laid at a minimum depth of 15 cm (6 in) over a well-drained base of hard core and shingle. You must also install a damp course. The mix used must be extra hard to withstand the horse's weight and urine, and the surface should be roughened to make it nonslip.

Alternative materials include: chalk and clay, which are cheap but require more maintenance and are rarely used these days; composition flooring which is good but extremely expensive; porous floors which need a well-drained base and can be smelly; and rubber matting placed over the top of concrete, which saves time mucking out. Rubber matting should be used with some form of absorbent bedding, such as shavings or hemp, to absorb urine and help keep the horse's rugs as clean as possible. The benefits of matting are that it gives a warmer floor when the horse lies down, avoids the risk of capped hocks and elbows, and may allow you to use less bedding than on a concrete floor.

ABOVE: *An overhang extension of the roof over the stable door and front wall area will help to protect the horse and groom from bad weather and shade them from the sun.*

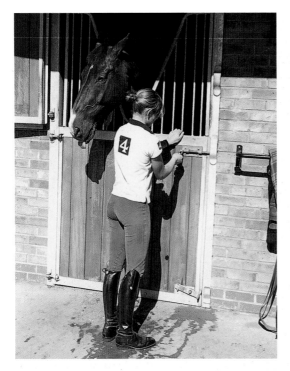

Electricity

Any electrical systems and wiring in a stable should be installed by a qualified electrician – even a low voltage can kill a horse. You will need a trip switch system with cabling running through unchewable metal pipes, and any switches positioned outside the box out of the horse's reach. You can install fluorescent lights or bulb fixtures high in the roof of the box, or bulkhead light fittings at a more accessible height for replacing and cleaning the light bulbs. All bulbs should have transparent covers.

Maintenance

The stable buildings, equipment and fittings will need regular maintenance to keep them in good condition and prevent deterioration. Woodwork will need to be treated with preservatives to ensure that it stays weatherproof and looks smart, as will any wooden doors and windows. Alternatively, you may choose to paint them but do not use toxic lead-based paints. Metal doors and windows made of rust-proof, galvanized iron or steel will not need any attention but their hinges might.

ABOVE: *Ensure that stable doors are closed and bolted. Many horses are accomplished escape artists.*

Other stable buildings

In addition to the looseboxes, it is a good idea if you have room to have a specially constructed feed shed which is built of brick or concrete blocks to discourage rats and other vermin.

You will also need a tack room which can be securely locked. Tack is a security risk and attractive to burglars; check with your insurance company before installing one. If you have the space and the budget, put in a sink with hot and cold water to make cleaning tack easier. You will need lighting but heating is not essential as there is must be no direct heat to leather saddles and bridles.

RIGHT: *A watering system is useful for providing fresh, clean water for filling water troughs and buckets.*

Optional fittings

Grids and grilles may be fixed to the top door of looseboxes. Made of steel rods or heavy mesh, they are available in several patterns as permanent or removable fixtures. V–shaped grids are sometimes used to prevent the action of weaving and may be unavoidable in some cases, but do not prevent the cause. They enable the horse to put his head and neck over the door, but the opening must be large enough for him to draw back without hitting his head.

2.3 Fixtures and fittings

Not everyone has the luxury of electricity in their stables, but it does make a huge difference, especially in the winter. Putting in an electricity supply is a specialist job for a qualified electrician, and it is important to make sure that everything to do with it is horse-, water- and vermin-proof.

Feeding

There are several different ways of delivering your horse's food. Feeding from ground level is the most natural way but it is not always practical because food and forage get mixed up in bedding. Haynets should always be set at eyelevel; if positioned too high, your horse will be stretching his neck at an unnatural angle to feed, and there will also be a risk that some of the hay seeds will fall into his eyes.

Hard feed is best provided in a feed bowl on the stable floor; this can be removed when the horse has finished eating. Some people use feed bowls that clip over the door, but this is an unnatural position for the horse. Permanent mangers in boxes should be avoided as they are a potential hazard.

Watering

Water must always be available for horses. Automatic water suppliers do have obvious benefits but you cannot monitor how much your horse is actually drinking. Buckets of water that are placed on the floor have the potential to be kicked over but are easily cleaned. Special bucket holders fixed to the wall can be used in cases where a horse is prone to knocking over his water bucket. Alternatively, an old tyre can often make a firm base for a water bucket to help prevent this happening.

BELOW: *You can use a clip-on feed container, which hooks over the lower stable door, but some people feel that these force the horse into an unnatural position when feeding.*

Occasionally you will come across a horse that likes to soak its own hay by dunking each mouthful in its water. In this case, it is usually best to supply a bucket of water near the hay as well as a supply of drinking water.

Bedding

There are many types of bedding available, ranging from traditional wheat straw to dried wood fibre and even elephant grass. One of the most important considerations is whether or not the bedding you choose will help to minimize the dust and spores in your horse's stable environment; in some cases, this may mean that wheat straw is unsuitable. Other factors that will influence your choice will include ease of handling and disposal, cost, availability and storage considerations.

It is important that, whatever type of bedding you finally decide on, it encourages your horse to lie down and rest in comfort without any risk of injuring himself. It should also keep him warm and minimize draughts. It should create a nonslip surface on the floor of the loosebox or stall, so that the horse cannot slip when he is moving around the stable. This will also help to reduce any jar to his legs when he is moving around or standing still on the hard floor.

Be aware also that some bedding materials, e.g. paper, can become particularly heavy to handle when they are wet, and they do not rot down easily. Other types may vary in quality; for instance, the wood shavings from one manufacturer may be significantly more dusty than those from another, even though both sorts could be marketed as dust-extracted bedding. Note you

ABOVE: *Wood shavings can make a warm, comfortable bed for a horse or pony. Many are dust extracted.*

should never use materials sourced directly from the building trade and which have not gone through a screening process; they may contain nails and other potential hazards.

Straw

This is widely used as a bedding material and has many advantages: the manure can be easily disposed of; it looks inviting and clean; and it is relatively cheap to purchase in years of good harvests. However, if it is eaten by the horse, it may cause allergies and coughing.

Wheat straw is preferable to barley or oat straw, but it is not always readily available. It must always be of

good quality, and the horse must be discouraged from eating it as this can make him overweight and affect his level of fitness. Spraying some non-toxic disinfectant on the bedding can help prevent this. Another problem with using straw as a bedding material is that it does create dust and it can act as a host to fungal spores. When these are inhaled, they can lead to allergic coughing.

Equipment

Only basic equipment should be fitted inside your horse's stable. This will usually comprise the following items:
■ A ring for tying up your horse when necessary
■ A water trough or bucket
■ A haynet and tie ring (optional)

RIGHT: *Shavings make a comfortable spore-free bed for a horse, but the manure can be difficult to dispose of.*

The old-fashioned system of deep litter bedding, where the bottom layer is left undisturbed for several weeks and fresh bedding put on top, is not recommended as vets say the build-up of ammonia from compacted urine and droppings is a severe threat to a horse's respiratory system. It is even more of a hazard when the stable has poor drainage. Deep litter bedding also generates heat and this, together with ammonia, predisposes the horse's feet to fungal infections.

Shavings and sawdust

Generally, compressed baled shavings are preferable to sawdust as they are less dusty. However, both will provide your horse with spore-free bedding. The other advantage is that the horse will not eat them, unlike straw. When packed in polythene bags, baled shavings are easy to store and they are relatively free of dust.

Damping down bedding

This practice is not recommended, so any bedding that is sufficiently dusty to need damping down is unsuitable for your horse. Damp bedding will provide an unsatisfactory environment which encourages the growth of mould spores.

Shredded paper

Shredded paper or cardboard, which can be bought in wrapped bales, can be useful for horses with respiratory problems linked to dust or mould spores. However, disposal can be a problem, and in some areas it may have to be collected and disposed of by a professional contractor. It can take longer to break down than some other types of bedding, and it is particularly untidy in windy conditions.

Rubber matting

This is a popular choice, but unless the system you choose is sealed to the floor so that no liquid can seep underneath it only works well in

Tying up

Although mucking out and grooming should be done with the horse outside the stable rather than inside, in order to minimize dust in its environment and thus help to protect its respiratory system, it is useful to have a tying-up ring inside as well as outside. If you feed hay from a haynet, you will also need a higher ring to tie it to.

combination with excellent drainage and scrupulous management. Rubber matting with a topping of highly absorbent bedding material is generally effective, and the matting will add warmth and a cushioning effect to a concrete floor.

Other bedding

New bedding materials are being developed all the time, including some made from wood fibre, flax

BELOW: *Straw bedding makes a warm bed, but it should be mucked out on a daily basis with the horse taken out of the stable.*

straw and elephant grass. Hemp is another common material, but care must be taken to make sure that the horse does not eat it. If this occurs, you should use another form of bedding to avoid digestive problems.

Disposing of manure

When choosing bedding, you should always take into account how you are going to manage and dispose of the manure. Some bedding materials are claimed to reduce the size of manure heaps to the extent that they can be disposed of more easily. To get rid of large heaps you may even have to pay a professional contractor, and

the cost will rise even further if you use a bedding material that does not rot down quickly.

Building a muck heap

The muck heap should be sited within easy reach of the stables. Ideally, it should have a concrete base with one side open and the other sides built up to a height of 1.8 m (6 ft). You can use railway sleepers or concrete blocks for this. It will need daily care, and the manure should be built in steps with a flat top to allow it to absorb rain and rot down. Keep the sides vertical and well raked down, and the surrounding area clean.

2.4 Bedding down

Stable bedding should be deep enough so that when a fork is stuck into it, the prongs do not touch the floor. You can build up the bedding around the sides of the stable in banks to keep out draughts, protect the horse from abrasions when lying down against a wall and prevent it becoming wedged when lying down and then unable to rise (being cast).

Some horses and ponies love to eat their straw bedding and others are allergic to fungal spores in the straw which can cause coughing. For them, wood shavings, chopped hemp, dust-extracted straw or shredded paper are much better bedding materials, although these are all more expensive than straw. To keep your horse healthy and happy, it is worth paying the extra for the right bedding.

1 Using a fork, pile the straw up against a wall. Once a week, disinfect the floor and leave it to air and dry for an hour or two before replacing the bedding.
2 When the floor is completely dry, bring the old straw into the middle of the box and spread over the floor. Use the new bedding to make banks round the walls.

3 Bank the bedding up against the walls of the stable, making it a little deeper around the sides. To test whether the bed is deep enough, turn the fork upside down and push onto the straw – you should not feel the floor.

4 When you are satisfied that the bedding is ready and of the right depth, you can allow your horse or pony back into the stable. However, you should keep an eye on him until you are happy that all is well.

2.5 Mucking out

Mucking out the stable is an essential daily job for the horse or pony owner. An important form of basic hygiene, it will help minimize the risk of poor health and ailments and will keep the horse's living quarters dry and comfortable. Make it part of your everyday routine – when it is done correctly, using the right equipment, it need not take long.

Equipment

For mucking out your horse or pony, you will need the following items of equipment: a wheelbarrow, a shovel or long-handled scoop, a yard brush and a stable fork. It is essential that you turn the horse out of the stable, and also that you remove any buckets or portable water containers while you are mucking out your horse's loosebox.

1 Start by shovelling out any visible droppings and then transporting them away to the muck heap, which should be sited away from the stable but within easy reach (see page 55).

2 Now sort out and separate the wet bedding from the dry bedding. With a straw bed, this is best done with a two-prong fork. Throw the dry straw to one side, and remove the wet bedding by putting it into a wheelbarrow. Use a four-prong fork for this job.

3 Finally, you should sweep the stable floor with a sturdy brush and then replace the straw, taking extra from one of the banks around the walls.

2.6 Horse-friendly housing

Horses are sociable animals and are much more relaxed if they can see their neighbours. They are usually much happier if the top half of a dividing wall between their stables comprises a metal grille rather than being blocked in – and this also helps with air circulation and light. However, it does mean that any neighbouring horses always need to be compatible and healthy.

Stable vices

Some horses and ponies dislike being confined in a stable, and this can result in unwanted behaviour which is traditionally known as 'stable vices' but now, more fairly, is often referred to as stereotypic behaviour. The three most common behaviour patterns that are associated with this are: weaving, crib-biting and wind-sucking. A horse or pony that crib-bites will often wind-suck as well.

A horse that weaves swings its head from side to side, usually over the stable door. In some cases, it may also shift from one front foot to the other, thus putting strain on its limbs. Crib-biters grab hold of a convenient surface, usually the top of the door or a window ledge, and hold on to it, taking in air at the same time, while windsuckers take in air without holding on.

It is now thought that horses may carry out this behaviour in order to create endorphins, natural substances which are produced in the body to relieve stress and to stimulate the production of saliva to try and soothe digestive problems; again, these may well be related to stress.

Remedies

The best remedy in these cases is to turn out the affected horse as much as possible, and if it has to be stabled to make the environment as horse-friendly as possible. This is where a barn set-up can help. Anti-weaving grilles are V-shaped metal frames that fit on top of the stable door and limit the side to side movement of the horse's head. They may prevent the behaviour in some cases but will probably not reduce the stress that causes it. Some horses will simply weave behind the grille.

In the same way, painting a really unpleasant-tasting substance on the stable door may help to deter the horse from crib-biting, but it will not take away the need to do so.

Anti-cribbing collars with a metal arch which digs into the horse's throat as it arches its neck to crib-bite are sometimes used, but in the light of modern research, many people prefer to minimize crib-biting by turning the horse out more. Your vet may also suggest feeding an antacid product.

Other remedies

All horses should have either some hay or haylage available when they are stabled in order to mimic their natural grazing behaviour; this is even more important with those that show any stereotypic behaviour. Specially designed stable toys may also help.

Stable toys

These may help to keep some stabled horses happier. The most successful seem to be those that, when pushed around the floor, release a small amount of hidden feed and thereby mimic the horse's natural foraging behaviour. They should not be used as a substitute for turning out and/or exercising your horse.

Danger spots

All stable yards, whether they are large complexes or smaller set-ups that are designed for two horses, should be equipped against emergencies, especially fire, theft and injury to horses and people. The best way to ensure that you are able to deal with the risk of fire is to contact your local fire service and ask for advice from the fire prevention officer. Many will arrange to visit you and will advise on what equipment is needed. Similarly, contact your local police station to be put in touch with a crime prevention officer and arrange for your house and yard to be assessed.

RIGHT: *Fitting anti-weaving bars to the door of your horse's stable may prevent him weaving but will not remove the cause of the behaviour.*

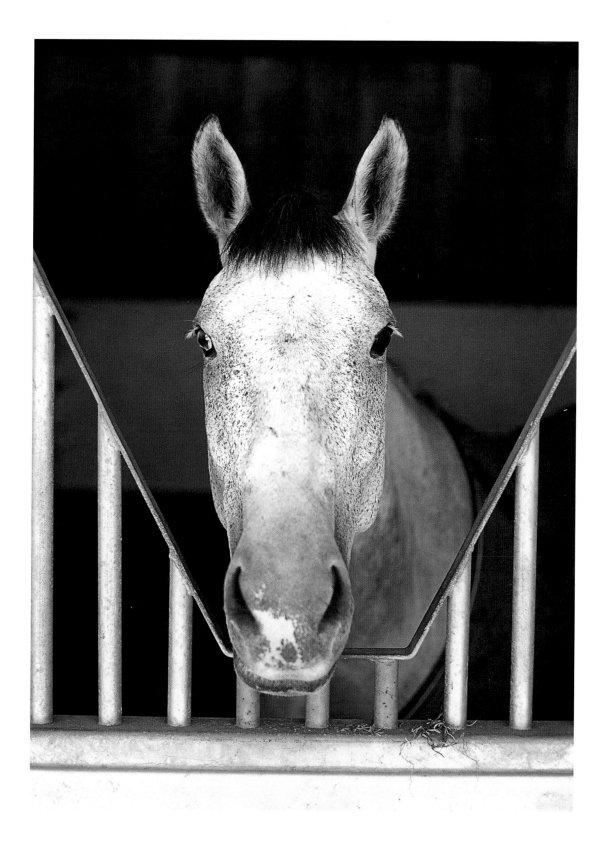

2.7 Storage space

As well as stabling for your horse, you will also need space to store his feed, clean bedding, hay or haylage, rugs and tack.

Storing feed

This must be kept under cover and stored in vermin-proof containers. Purpose-built feed bins which are filled from the top and then emptied from the bottom are ideal and easy to keep clean. Metal dustbins with securely fitting lids are a much cheaper and serviceable alternative. If you store bagged feed in a dustbin, leave it in the bag so you don't keep putting new feed on top of old.

Whilst stable yards and feed storage areas should always be kept as clean as possible and precautions taken against vermin, it is impossible to eliminate them completely.

Storing hay

A weatherproof building with good ventilation is ideal for storing hay. However, hay stores should be sited far enough away from stables that there is no danger of dust and spores, which are present even in clean hay, contaminating your horse's living space. Some American barn designs include overhead lofts, but these are not recommended as they are both an environmental and a fire risk. If you use straw bedding, then the same guidelines will apply.

Wrapped and bagged haylage can be stored outside the stable because the packaging will protect it.

Storing rugs

You will need somewhere to store rugs that are not in use and also to dry outdoor ones that have got wet. Clean rugs can be stored in trunks or similar containers to keep them safe; even a single mouse can do a lot of expensive damage. Storage racks installed under cover are ideal for rugs that are in use, and if you have an electricity supply in your storage space you may want to invest in heated storage racks – similar to heated towel rails – to dry off the outdoor rugs more quickly.

Storing tack

Tack theft has become a nationwide problem and if you keep your horse at home, then the safest option is to store at least your saddle and bridle in the house in a room where it cannot easily be seen from outside. If you are based at a livery yard, you may want to do the same, even though this means you have the inconvenience of transporting tack every time you ride, unless the yard has top-class security. Many large yards now have closed-circuit TV systems as

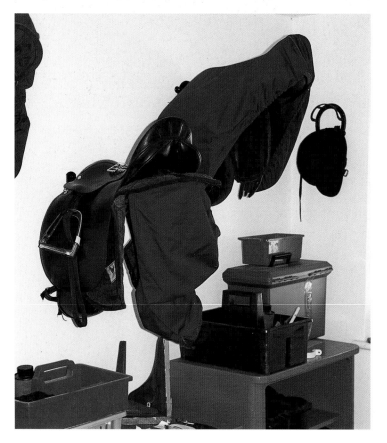

LEFT: *Keep your tack clean and tidy, and store it in a dry place which is not overheated to protect the leather.*

ABOVE: *In livery yards and stables with lots of horses, the saddles can be stored in a special tack room on specially designed saddle racks made of plastic or wood.*

ABOVE RIGHT: *You will need a shelving system, special boxes or dry, airy cupboards for storing rugs. Keep them clean and aired and always follow the manufacturer's cleaning instructions.*

well as burglar alarms and sophisticated locking systems. Individual tack storage units which look like large metal safes and bolt to the floor are another option, as are locking saddle racks.

Whatever type of building your tack is stored in, it should be kept dry, as damp conditions will encourage the growth of mould. Tack should not be stored directly over a heat source, such as a radiator, as this may dry out and damage the leather.

RIGHT: *Bridles should be hung up on semi-circular bridle holders in order to keep the top of the bridle rounded. If you have several horses, use slip-in holders for their names to avoid getting the bridles muddled up. The same advice applies to saddles.*

2.8 School time

Many riders regard an outdoor school as an essential rather than a luxury. If you keep your horse or pony at home and you want to build your own school, calling in a specialist contractor may seem expensive to start with but will usually save money and problems in the long run. Unfortunately, there is a lot more to it than most people realize.

Before you embark on constructing an outdoor school you should check with your local planning authorities to see whether you require planning permission. Basic planning is as vital for arenas as it is for stables. Even if you have little choice as to where you are going to site your school, there are still points to take into consideration. Lorries will need access at all stages of building the school, and if you want floodlights, you will also need electricity. Try to take the prevailing wind conditions into account; they may not make much difference in summer but certainly will in winter. The school should also be safely and securely fenced.

A good base is as important as a good surface. Your options include clean limestone, demolition hardcore and road planings, and your choice will depend on cost and availability. The separating layer between the base and surface is also vital, and a specialist arena builder will help you to achieve the right combination.

Outdoor surfaces

There are many types of surface, and your choice will depend on the intended use of the arena. They all have advantages and disadvantages and will need regular care. Picking up droppings rather than letting them get churned into the surface will help to maintain drainage qualities. It is important to keep the arena level, either with specialist levellers which are designed to be towed behind a four-wheel drive vehicle or tractor or by raking the surface by hand.

Most people opt for sand which is laid down on a properly prepared base. A starting depth of 8–10 cm (3–4 in) is recommended, and you can top this up as necessary. You can use clean sharp sand, black sand or, best of all, silica sand, which is dust-free, drains well and is less likely to freeze. The alternatives to sand are shavings, wood chips, plastic granules, shredded rubber or a combination of these. However, sand is the most widely used all-purpose surface.

RIGHT: *An outdoor school will prove helpful if you have regular lessons to improve your riding skills.*

BELOW: *As well as fencing, high hedges or trees can provide effective windbreaks around an outdoor arena.*

2.9 Daily routine

A horse is not usually kept in its stable night and day, unless the weather is particularly bad or the animal is unwell, or there are other pressing reasons for stabling it temporarily. Horses need plenty of space to exercise and to stretch their legs, roll around when they feel inclined and generally enjoy themselves outside in the open air.

Any horse or pony which is housed indoors permanently can become irritable and prone to stable vices (see page 58), leg swelling and digestive upsets. Stabling your horse at night and turning it out into a field or a paddock during the day is a good routine to get into. At the very least, a stable-kept horse should always have four hours outside, either being ridden or wandering free in pasture each day. This enables it to graze, to get essential exercise and to have important social interaction with other horses if there are others turned out in the field. Introduce a new horse into an established group carefully. If possible, turn him out with the quietest horse in the group in a separate field, or a fenced-off area next to the main group. When they have settled together, put them with the others.

In summer, you may have to provide your horse with a fly fringe to keep worrisome flies away from his eyes, whereas in winter he may need to wear an outdoor rug for warmth, especially if his coat has been clipped.

BELOW: *You should turn your horse out into a field to graze every day for a minimum of four hours.*

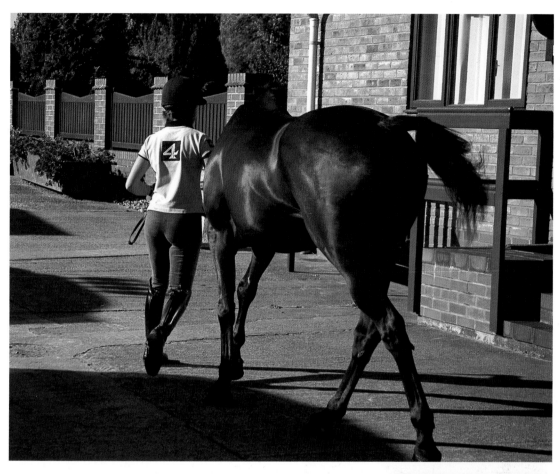

Time dedication

Even if your horse lives outside all the year round, you need to check on him every day and provide food and fresh water. You may also have to check his rugs, exercise and groom him, and pick out his feet. If your horse is stabled, he will need regular mucking out. Owning any horse is time-consuming and you need to devote time to caring for him and will have to adapt your daily routine in order to do so. A healthy horse needs routine, and this means that you will have to feed him at the same time each day as changes to his usual regime may upset him and may even predispose him to colic.

ABOVE: *Remember to warm up your horse before his daily exercise and cool him down afterwards. Riding him every day will promote bonding.*

RIGHT: *If your horse is stabled, you will have to provide feed and forage each day as well as fresh water.*

What you do on a weekday must be repeated at the weekend, too, so if you normally feed him at 6 am in the week before leaving for work, you will have to forego your weekend lie-ins and feed him early on those days, too. Things can and will go wrong if you are in a rush, and you must allow sufficient time to look after him.

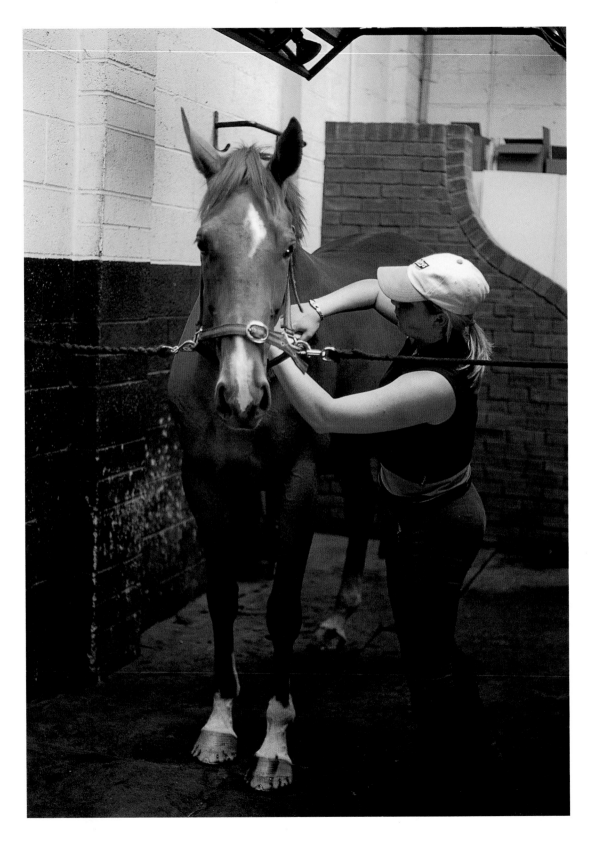

2.10 At livery

If you do not have room for a stable nor own a paddock, you may decide to keep your horse or pony at livery. This means basically that you rent the facilities for looking after your horse. There are several different systems, including full livery, do-it-yourself livery and working livery.

Choosing a livery yard

When deciding on a yard and which system you want for your horse, it is important to consider not only the stabling and grazing facilities on offer but also the general state of hygiene and cleanliness, the health and demeanour of the other horses, the friendliness of the staff and whether it is a working livery where your horse could be used in the school for lessons or ridden out. You will also need to check the livery owner's insurance.

Whatever you choose, it is vital that your horse is healthy and happy and has a regular routine of feeding and exercise. Check out the livery yards in your area to discover which is best for you and your horse.

Full livery

Under this system, you keep your horse at a stables where it is fed, groomed and even exercised for you by the staff. The advantage of this is that your horse should be well looked after and your duties are limited, making it an ideal arrangement for very busy people who want to own their own horse but do not have the time or the facilities to care for it themselves nor to ride regularly. Also, the horse can live and socialize with other horses. The downside is that it is an extremely expensive business to keep a horse at full livery.

Working livery

This is a more common arrangement for owners who keep their horses at a riding school as it is cheaper. It will be up to you to agree a system that works for both of you with the riding school, with clearly defined areas regarding responsibility and who pays for what. For instance, who will provide essential equipment for the horse and exercise it? Who will be responsible for such tasks as shoeing, clipping and repairing tack?

Do-it-yourself livery

Livery is much cheaper if you look after your horse yourself and perform the basic tasks of grooming, cleaning tack, mucking out and exercising. Again, you must clearly define the conditions in advance and agree them in writing, signed by both parties.

RIGHT: *If you opt for do-it-yourself livery you will have to care for your horse yourself. This will include such tasks as cleaning his tack as well as exercising him.*

LEFT: *If you choose full livery, your horse will be cared for by the yard staff but this is expensive.*

Chapter 3

Grass management

• •

If your horse could choose whether he lived in a stable or out at grass, he would certainly opt for a life at grass. Roaming about and grazing are what a horse is designed to do. Compared with keeping the horse in a stable it might also seem the easier option for you, the owner – and generally it is. Nevertheless, there is far more to keeping your horse at grass than simply turning him loose in a field and shutting the gate. You will have to manage the land, provide shelter against heat, cold, wind and rain, and maintain all the fencing and gates in a good state of repair.

3.1 Pasture care

In their wild state, horses are free to wander far and wide in their search for food. Nowadays, most domesticated horses have to be kept in very confined conditions – an acre or two is nothing in the equine scheme of things – and nothing will turn land into a dust-bowl or a quagmire more quickly than over-grazing by our equine friends. So, for the good of your horse and your land, make a point of discovering how to manage what grazing land you have in the most efficient way. Think of it as gardening – only on a larger scale.

Getting started

The first thing to bear in mind is that horses are very selective grazers. You can easily recognize a badly managed field by the presence of bare patches, where the occupants have grazed the palatable plants right down to the roots, and other suspect areas, where rampant, unpalatable grasses have taken over.

Before you do anything else, you must get the soil tested in order to see whether it needs treating for any imbalances or deficiencies. Samples should be taken from both the good and poor areas of the field. Your local Animal Health Divisional Office (part of DEFRA) will be able to advise you on seed and fertilizer merchants who are qualified to carry out this soil analysis. With a little effort, you can improve even the roughest pasture.

Harrowing and rolling

The regular use of a harrow can work wonders. Harrowing grassland in the spring – as soon as the land is dry enough – will have the same beneficial effect as raking a lawn: it will make room for new growth by removing dead matter, as well as aerating the soil. If there are badly poached (churned-up) places, these will need extra attention, especially if you want a level area on which to ride. The poached ground can be reclaimed by harrowing, re-seeding and rolling. Rolling the entire field in early spring (provided the ground is not heavy) can encourage early grass growth. If your soil test reveals that the ground needs fertilizing, have it harrowed before any fertilizer is applied.

Fertilizing

If your land has been well managed in the past, the soil may not require fertilizing. Applying too much fertilizer can be detrimental because it tends to produce over-lush grass. This may, in turn, lead to digestive-tract problems and even laminitis, which is a serious and painful inflammatory condition of the sensitive interior of the horse's hoof. Ponies are especially susceptible to this problem.

If the soil test does reveal a deficiency of any or all of the main elements required by plants (nitrogen, phosphate, potash and lime), then a suitable fertilizer or mix of fertilizers should be applied – in the spring and preferably while the field is being rested. The horses can go back on the land once the fertilizer has been either washed into the soil or, if dry granules are used, when these are no longer visible. However, the grass will benefit from a further period of rest if this is possible.

If your soil proves to be acidic, then this can be remedied easily by the application of a top dressing of lime. Have the land harrowed first and the lime applied on a still day to avoid wind-loss. Liming is best done in the spring or autumn. Keep your horses off the land until the lime has been washed in by rain.

If you prefer to use an organic fertilizer, farmyard manure – if you can get it – contains the requisite nitrogen, phosphate and potash and is good for improving soil texture. To ensure that it is free of infection, you must lay the manure aside for several weeks before spreading it and keep your horses off the treated field for several weeks afterwards.

Spraying

If some parts of your land have been entirely taken over by weeds, you may have to resort to spraying to kill them off. Take advice from a merchant and remember that there are specific laws which govern the use of weedkiller sprays. You can treat small areas yourself using a back-pack spray. For larger areas, you will need to bring in

RIGHT: *Whether your horse is kept at grass or turned out to graze each day for a few hours, you will need some well-managed pasture.*

heavy machinery. You should apply the weedkiller in the late spring while the plants are growing strongly. If you are planning to use fertilizer, then it may be possible to combine the two applications. Always spray on a still day to minimize any drift.

Remember that if you do use a weedkiller, you must keep your horses and ponies off the land afterwards for the full amount of time recommended by the manufacturers. You should always bear in mind that horses are particularly sensitive to weedkillers, more so than farm animals, so always err on the side of caution.

Topping

Some fields need topping (mowing) during the summer to prevent the grass sward becoming too leggy. Cutting helps prevent weeds and less palatable grasses from setting seed and spreading. It also encourages the more 'horse-friendly' grasses to grow. If it results in a substantial amount of waste material, this should be raked up, removed and burnt, or it will inhibit the growth of the grass underneath.

Re-seeding

Where the grazing land has been neglected so badly that it is beyond repair, the only solution may be to have it ploughed and re-seeded. However, this option should not be considered lightly as your field may be out of action for at least a year. Where possible, it is always better to improve what is already there.

LEFT: *Grazing land has to be kept in good condition. If you are unsure about which grass is best, check with your local seed merchant.*

The beauty of re-seeding is that it enables you to start off with the best 'horse-friendly' grasses. Nowadays it is possible to buy some specialist equestrian seed mixes. A good basic horse mixture will include plenty of perennial rye grasses and fescues, plus other varieties, such as smooth-stalked meadow grass. If you have land from which you intend to cut hay, the mixture should also include Timothy. As with a garden lawn, the denser the grass sward to start with, the less chance there is of unwanted weeds getting in on the act.

Bear in mind that different types of soil suit different grasses. For example, poor soil is no hindrance to crested dog's tail and common bent grass while dry, sandy conditions are tolerated by smooth-stalked meadow grass. Soil that is both rich and moist better suits the rough-stalked variety, which horses will find particularly palatable. If the fertility of the soil needs improving, you can add a little wild white clover to the mixture. Its root nodules contain nitrogen-producing bacteria. However, never use the farm varieties of clover; they will spread like wildfire and they can quickly overrun a whole field. This all sounds complicated, but a good seed merchant will advise you. They will have knowledge of local conditions, such as altitude, rainfall and prevailing winds, all of which may determine which grasses will thrive in your particular area.

Rotational grazing

The best way to prevent your land from becoming over-grazed or 'horse-sick' is to divide it up so that part of it is resting while part is being grazed. If you have two or more separate fields, you can simply graze and rest them alternately. If you have only one, then invest in some electric fencing – it is simple to erect and horses will respect it once they have touched it and realize what it is. You can use this to divide your land into two sections - one for grazing, one for resting - on a rotational basis. Better still, if you have the space, you can divide it into three and put your horse in one section, leave another to rest, and ask a local farmer to put a few sheep or cattle in the other. Sheep and cattle will help keep your pasture tidy by eating the rougher growth that horses avoid. Remember, however, that on wet ground, sheep are preferable to cattle since their feet cause less damage.

Drilling

Badly neglected fields can often be reclaimed by a process called direct drilling – you can hire a professional contractor to do this. Provided that the soil is suitable, drilling can be a very effective way of improving bad pasture. The drill creates channels in the ground into which grass seed is sown together with fertilizer, as necessary. The land is then rolled. The seed will germinate most successfully when the soil is warm and moist, so spring or possibly late summer is usually the best season for drilling. If the weed infestation is really severe, it might be necessary to eliminate all the old growth with a herbicide before drilling.

3.2 Making your own hay

If you have quite a lot of land at your disposal and the grass is suitable, you could consider using some of it for making your own hay. Bear in mind that you will not be able to use the land for grazing from around the middle of March until about six weeks after cutting. If the ground is wet, you may even need to rest it throughout the preceding winter.

The field should be harrowed and fertilized in the spring, and you will need to find either a local farmer or contractor to do the cutting and baling as it is not economical to buy special haymaking machinery for just a small acreage. There are two types of hay: meadow hay and seed hay.

Meadow hay is always made from permanent grazing land which has simply had horses taken off it.

Seed hay is made from fields which have been specially sown – the yield of hay will be heavier and of better quality than that from permanent pasture.

BELOW: *Horses and ponies love the freedom of a large field or paddock to exercise themselves. However, always check for poisonous plants.*

Check for ragwort

It is essential when using land for haymaking and grazing to check that it is totally free of ragwort before cutting begins. Remember that this highly poisonous plant is far more palatable to horses when it is dry.

Check the drainage

If your field is drained by ditches, you must be sure to check them regularly to make sure that they are working properly. If there are any obvious blockages, then you must clear them out immediately.

If the ditches are not blocked but the surface water is still not draining away, it could be that the ditches are blocked elsewhere – on the land of a neighbour, perhaps. If this is the case, you may have to do a little detective work in order to discover where the trouble lies.

Protect your horse from worms

It is no one's favourite chore, but the best way to control equine worm infestations is to remove your horse's droppings from his field on a daily basis. The smaller the field, and the more horses present, the more crucial this becomes. You can do the job with a wheelbarrow and poopascoop, though some form of motorized transport with a trailer will obviously make it easier and quicker.

Some people harrow the droppings on a regular basis if they are unable to pick them up. This comes in a poor second but is one step better than just leaving the droppings and doing nothing. Do not harrow droppings in the wet. Eggs and larvae tend to thrive in wet conditions so harrowing will merely spread them over a wider area.

Grazing cattle or sheep on your horse pasture will help if you have an over-abundance of grass because the livestock's digestive system, unlike that of the horse, destroys the worm larvae.

Drainage problems can also be caused by damage to the structure of the soil – for example, when heavy machinery is driven over the land while it is wet. If this is the case, you can get the soil professionally improved by breaking up the top layer. DEFRA can advise (see page 284).

Advantages

If you make your own hay, you will know it is good quality and will cost less than buying it. Your field will benefit, too, as good grass growth is encouraged and weeds discouraged. Giving the field a rest from grazing will help reduce the worm burden.

Disadvantages

The downside of haymaking yourself is that finding a contractor can be difficult and they may not be able to do the haymaking when you want it done. Also, your horse may not like and eat hay that has been made from pastures grazed only by horses.

3.3 Boundaries

Making sure that your horse is securely confined in a field is vitally important, not only for its own safety but also for the safety of others. If your horse does get loose and causes damage to property or injures someone, you will be liable. Always remember that a horse is, by nature, a nomad.

Fencing

Stout wooden post-and-rail fencing has traditionally been the material of choice for horse paddocks. The initial outlay may be high, but when it is properly constructed and maintained, this type of fencing looks terrific and is long lasting, with a life expectancy of over 20 years.

However, it can be damaged by chewing, rubbing and leaning, and you should check it at regular intervals. Broken rails will need to be replaced promptly as the split timber and any exposed nails can be hazardous to horses. As always, some maintenance is required and the posts and rails will need regular creosoting to preserve them. Do make sure that the fence posts are sawn off at an angle, flush with the top rail, to avoid projecting posts that could cause damage if a horse tries to jump out.

Stud rails are an alternative and cheaper form of fencing. Made of plastic strips, they will withstand considerable impact, but will stretch with time and require tightening.

Hedges

Hedges have one big advantage over fencing in that they provide shelter from the elements. However, they need to be really dense and strong (holly is particularly suitable) and, ideally, they should be free of any poisonous trees and shrubs. You must remove any poisonous growth by the roots if possible. Otherwise fence it off and keep it cut back so your horse cannot reach overhanging branches. Hedges will need regular trimming. Any gaps through which a horse could push his way must be blocked by strong fencing. Never be tempted to use a piece of flimsy wire which can cause severe injuries.

BELOW: *Stout three-bar fencing with the fence posts on the 'outside' of the field is expensive but ideal. You must regularly maintain the fence, repairing any broken sections quickly and weather-proofing the timber.*

Wire

Wire in any form is not an ideal type of fencing for horses and should be avoided if at all possible. If it has to be used, then it needs to be kept taut and have a line of electric fence put in front of it. Wire mesh of any sort should not be used for horses.

Fencing tips

■ Secure the rails of post-and-rail fencing to the paddock side of the posts to prevent horses loosening the rails or even pushing them off by leaning on them. This also prevents your horse from hurting himself on the edges of the posts if he bangs into the fence.

■ To help protect the wooden posts from wet weather, cut the tops on a slight slope so the rain drains off.

■ Fix the top rails of the fence level with the tops of the posts.

■ To protect it from the weather and deter your horse from chewing it, you should treat all timber with a non-toxic preservative.

■ Try to avoid having right-angled corners. Horses like to gallop about now and again, and coming to a sudden stop in a corner can jar their legs. Curved corners will not only help prevent this but they can also save a horse from becoming trapped by a bossy or hostile companion.

■ Always be sure to make electric fencing as visible as possible to both horses and humans. Plain wire can be seen more easily by animals if pieces of coloured plastic are tied between the posts.

■ The following are unsuitable: wire netting, sheep or pig wire, chestnut fencing and old iron rails.

Stone walls

Well-maintained stone walls make effective field boundaries for horses because they provide excellent shelter from bad weather and are stock-proof. They must, however, be kept in good repair and should be at least 1.2 m (4 ft) high – horses might try to jump out if they are any lower. If a wall is on the low side, you could consider fitting a rail above it or, in the case of cobs and ponies, one or two strands of well-tightened plain wire or an electric fence.

ABOVE: *Well-trimmed thick hedges make good field boundaries if kept at a height of 1.2–1.5 m (4–5 ft) and cut back annually to encourage growth. They also provide winter shelter.*

Safety first

■ Carefully check any new fields for dangerous 'foreign bodies', such as lengths of wire, fragments of old farm implements, baler twine, etc., and remove anything that has the potential to cause injury to a horse.

■ You should check on your horse regularly, preferably twice a day.

■ If there are rabbits in your neighbourhood, you should regularly inspect your field for holes, which are another potential source of injury. Also, fence off any areas that look unsafe.

■ If your field adjoins any roads or footpaths or has a path crossing it, it is important to make regular checks for possibly harmful litter. If it adjoins houses, you should check that people are not dumping their garden waste in the field – many cultivated plants are poisonous.

Electric fencing

This form of fencing is cheap and easy to erect. It can be used to keep horses away from a weakened fence or hedge; separate horses safely from others in adjoining fields; enable strip grazing of a field; or divide a field on a temporary basis in order to rest some areas. It should be positioned 1.5–1.8 m (5–6 ft) from the boundary fence, and can be run off a portable battery-powered unit or wired up to the mains electricity supply with a transformer to reduce the voltage to approximately six volts.

Avoid sharp corners and angles when erecting a fence, and never place it underneath or parallel to overhead electric cables. The posts must be well heeled in, and any attachments to hedges and gate posts must have a sound insulator to break the current.

The best electric fencing for horses is the thick white tape that is easy for them to see, cheap to purchase and simple to move.

Gates

Gateways need to be sited with care. In the interests of safety and security, avoid having a gate opening on to a busy road. However, bear in mind that

ABOVE: Electric fencing can help to prevent horses jumping out of their field, although a few horses will never respect it and will still jump!

you might occasionally need to turn large vehicles (such as a tractor with a harrow or roller attached or even, in an emergency, a horsebox or trailer) into your field. Make sure that the gateway is wide enough to take such machinery. Avoid siting gates on any naturally wet ground. You should choose the driest spot possible.

Wooden or metal?

Both are equally suitable for horse paddocks provided they are sturdily made, and both will need a certain amount of maintenance. Wooden ones should be treated with a non-toxic preservative, while galvanized metal ones need regular repainting. Rusty metal gates are dangerous for horses because they break easily and

can cause serious injury. Never use narrow gates: with anything narrower than 1.8 m (6 ft) there is a danger of the horse bumping into the gateposts as it passes through. Horses' hips can easily be damaged in this way.

Installing gates

Always get the gateposts and gates installed by a professional. A correctly hung gate will last for years and will be a pleasure to use. There is nothing more tiresome when you are leading a horse through a gateway than a gate that either flies open as soon as you unclip it, drags heavily on the ground and needs lifting, or swings shut of its own volition as you try to go through it.

LEFT: A metal sprung gate handle, which requires only one hand to open and close the gate, is ideal.

Field gates are heavy and the posts that support them need to be sunk 90 cm (3 ft) into the ground. Really strong hinges must also be used, plus catches that cannot be opened by a horse with his teeth. Gates should be hung to open inwards, so when you go to feed or catch your horse he cannot barge through the instant you open the catch. Invest in strong metal chains and padlocks and affix one to the gate's opening side and another to the hinged side. You need to make things as difficult as possible for would-be thieves. If you must, in an emergency, climb over a gate, always using the hinge-end. Otherwise, avoid putting extra strain on your gates.

Feed your horses well away from any gateways or the ground will soon become poached and getting in and out of the field in wet conditions will become really arduous. Having more than one gate will help.

ABOVE: *Remember to padlock a remote or isolated field to prevent other people accidentally leaving the gate open and for your animal's security.*

ABOVE: *Heavy-duty metal gates are suitable with metal or wooden posts. Treat with a rust-resistant solution.*

LEFT: *A sturdy wooden gate, with strong hinges, which opens into the field is recommended. Note the white electric strip along the fence to protect the saplings.*

3.4 Water

A horse kept at grass must have constant access to clean water. His consumption may vary from as little as five litres (nine pints) a day to as much as 45 litres (10 gallons) or more, depending on his size, the quality of the grass, the weather conditions and the time of year. In winter, for example, when he is being fed dried supplementary foods such as hay, a horse will drink more than when there is a plentiful supply of spring grass.

A galvanized metal or a concrete drinking trough, fed by piped mains water, is the most efficient method of providing water. The trough should be fitted with a ballcock to control the water level and this needs to be enclosed to prevent horses from damaging it. Troughs should be set on a firm brick or concrete base and the area around may need firming by ramming hardcore into the ground.

BELOW: *Keep any drinking troughs in your horse's field regularly topped up with clean, fresh water.*

However, if there is no piped water available, you can always fill your container by hosepipe, assuming that there is a conveniently located tap. If you only have to water one or two horses, you could use buckets, old stone sinks or plastic containers. These can be moved about the field to prevent the ground becoming poached but are knocked over easily and will need to be anchored in some way, such as by standing them in an old vehicle tyre. All containers that contain static water will need to be cleaned out regularly.

Siting water containers

■ Troughs should either be sited lengthways along the line of a fence or well away from the fence, at least 1 m (3 ft 4 in), to prevent a horse becoming trapped between the trough and the fence.

■ Troughs recessed into the line of the fence can be used by animals in the adjacent field, but make sure that there is a strong rail over the trough otherwise some horses might decide to jump over it.

■ All water containers should be placed well away from any trees in order to prevent leaves and other debris falling into the water.

■ Water containers should never be sited in the corners of fields because of the risk of a horse becoming trapped.

Natural water supplies

A stream or river in your field may seem like the perfect answer to your watering problems, but it is likely that the water, even if it looks clean, will be polluted as who knows what people may be putting into it upstream? Unless you are absolutely sure that natural water really is pure, fence it off and provide your own supply. Fence off stagnant ponds and boggy areas, too. If a stream or river is clean, ensure the approach to the drinking area is safe. It needs to be fairly flat, as steep banks will eventually collapse. If your horse could wander along a watercourse on to someone else's land, erect a fence across it.

RIGHT: *Buckets have the advantage of being easy to move about in a field to prevent the ground getting poached.*

3.5 Shelter

In bad weather conditions, horses and ponies like to take advantage of natural shelter, such as rocks or banks. In the heat of summer they will take refuge under trees. But since many fields lack these facilities you may have to provide a wooden shelter, which affords the best means of escape from bothersome flies, or a windbreak screen.

Field shelters

Fields certainly provide a more natural environment, but the horses in them still need all-year-round shelter. Thick hedging can form a natural windbreak but, in many cases, the best option is a purpose-built field shelter. Again, you will usually find that you need planning permission for one that is sited permanently, although several companies now make 'portable' shelters that are said to be exempt.

If you have the option, site your shelter on the highest – and thus the driest – part of the field so that the land surrounding it does not become waterlogged. The back should be facing towards the prevailing wind and there should be enough room between the shelter and the field fencing to prevent a horse being trapped by a more aggressive one.

Dimensions should be a minimum of 5.5 x 3.65 m (18 x 12 ft) for two horses, and it is usually best to leave one side completely open so that

BELOW: *A field shelter should be open-fronted to give the horse or pony protection from rain and winds.*

both horses can come in and go out of the shelter without any problems: sometimes even good-natured horses will become bad tempered if they think that another horse is encroaching on their space.

Structure and siting

If your horse or pony has one or more companions, then the field shelter must be large enough to accommodate them all without them squabbling. It should be open-fronted so that if a horse is picked on, he has a ready means of escape. To avoid the possibility of injury, there must always be plenty of head room, and, ideally, the roof

How to tell if your horse is cold

The best way to tell whether your horse or pony is cold is to feel his ears. If they feel very cold, it may well be best to bring the horse into the stable and 'thatch' him. This involves placing a layer of straw along his back and putting a rug on top; this creates an insulation layer.

should be sloped to the back to carry water away from the entrance.

Shelters should be strongly built and sited on well-drained ground to prevent the ground in and around them becoming poached. If this is not possible, you should provide a hard surface, such as concrete or hardcore, inside and in front of the shelter.

Position the field shelter with its back to the prevailing wind. However,

remember to ask your local council first whether you need to get planning permission to erect a shelter.

Windbreak screens

Windbreak screens are much cheaper to build than field shelters and they can either be incorporated into the fencing or may be positioned in the open. The screens should be about 2 m (6 ft 8 in) high.

3.6 Know your poisons

There are a great many trees, shrubs and plants that are poisonous to horses. You should learn to recognize them and check carefully a new field before turning your horse out in it. If you find any poisonous plants, dig them up and burn them immediately. Remember to wear gloves for this job. Trees and hedging material which are too big to be dug out must be cut well back and securely fenced off.

Remember that some very poisonous plants – most notably ragwort and foxgloves – are more palatable to horses when they are dead, so never leave cuttings from any poisonous growth lying around in your field. Inspect your land regularly; it may start off being poison-free, but toxic plants can spread all too easily from the adjacent fields.

Meadow plants

Among the most harmful meadow plants for horses are: ragwort, which causes serious liver damage; bracken; meadow saffron; foxgloves; hemlock; all the members of the nightshade family; and monkshood. Aconite, bryony, flax, horseradish, hellebores, lupins (especially the seeds), purple milk vetch, St John's wort, water dropwort and yellow star thistle are also dangerous.

Shrubs and trees

Poisonous shrubs include box, laurel, privet and rhododendron, while among trees the yew is one of the most lethal – even a relatively small amount usually proves fatal.

Horses should also be kept well away from laburnum, and care must be taken with oak trees, whose leaves and acorns, if they are devoured in large quantities, are harmful. If there is a good crop of acorns, then they should be raked up and removed from the field; alternatively, you could completely fence off the tree to prevent horses accessing them.

BELOW: *It is essential that you learn to recognize ragwort and remove any traces of it from your horse's field.*

Poisonous vegetation

Before putting a horse out to grass, or if you know which field is being used for haymaking, make sure that you check for poisonous plants and don't forget to watch out for poisonous bushes and trees that may overhang from the adjoining fields. Some dangerous plants will only be eaten by horses when other food is in short supply, or when the plants are dead and dried. Some have to be eaten regularly over a period of weeks or months to cause their ill effects; others can kill a horse after a single mouthful. Listed below are some of the most important poisonous plants to look out for.

Acorns and Crab Apples
(Malus)

Horses and ponies will eat ripe acorns and crab apples in the autumn so you should clear up and cart away any fallen fruits that land in their grazing pasture. Acorns in large quantities are poisonous although they are harmless in smaller amounts. Consuming crab apples can cause severe colic.

Bracken (Pteridium aquilinum)

Horses usually only eat this in late autumn or when other foodstuffs are scarce. It contains a chemical that destroys Vitamin B1. It usually has to be consumed over a period of several months before producing any recognizable symptoms.

Deadly Nightshade (Atropa belladonna)

This is rarely eaten by horses but the brown or purple berries are poisonous. It tends to grow in hedges on the edges of fields and should be pulled out and burned.

Horsetail (Equisetum spp.)

The effects of this plant, which is also sometimes known as Mare's Tail, are similar to those of bracken. It is usually eaten in hay.

Milkweed (Ascelpia spp.), Rhododendron (Rhododendron spp.), and Foxglove (Digitalis spp.)

All these plants contain chemicals that affect the heart and can cause sudden death in a horse. You must ensure that they do not grow in your horse's field. If you see them, dig them up and dispose of them.

Water Hemlock (Cicuta spp.) and Hemlock (Conium maculatum)

The symptoms of nervous system poisoning appear within two hours of being eaten by a horse.

Ragwort (Senecio spp.)

This common plant will cause liver damage if it is consumed over a period of weeks or months. It is usually found dried in hay, which makes it particularly dangerous. Its distinctive yellow flowers are in bloom between July and September, and mature plants can grow to a height of 120 cm (4 ft). You must pull up the plants and burn them.

Note: Similar effects are produced by Rattleweed (Crotalaria spp.), Salvation Jane (Echium spp.) and Fiddleneck or Tarweed (Amsinckia spp.).

Yew (Taxus spp.)

This tree is commonly found in English churchyards and all parts of it are poisonous, even when the tree is dead. Just a handful of leaves, twigs or berries can lead to fatal effects for a horse within a matter of minutes. Make sure that there are no yew trees bordering the areas where you turn him out to graze.

Beware!

Of course, there are many other poisonous plants that less frequently cause trouble for horses. If you are in doubt as to the identity and safety of any plant, you should take a specimen to your veterinary surgeon for identification.

Chapter 4

Safety and equipment

• •

A basic knowledge of tack and equipment is essential; the safety and comfort of you and your horse depend on it. Kitting out a new horse is a major expense, and you must work out what you need to get the best value for money. You will require specialist advice in areas such as saddle fitting. If you are not ready or do not intend to buy a horse, riding at a BHS approved school should ensure that all the equipment is appropriate and correctly fitted, but you should still be able to check for yourself. Buying poor-quality equipment is dangerous as well as a false economy. It won't last and could literally put your life in danger. Fit is as important as function: a badly-fitting saddle may damage a horse's back, and a hat that is the wrong size won't give adequate protection.

4.1 Saddles

A saddle is the most expensive item of equipment that you will buy for your horse. There are three key points to consider when you are choosing a suitable saddle: it must be designed for the activity or activities you want to do; it must fit the horse; and it must fit the rider.

Saddle design

There are many saddle designs for the various disciplines, which range from dressage to racing. The basic differences between them lie in the cut of the flaps and the position of the stirrup bar. These factors will influence the stirrup length and also the riding position. For instance, a dressage saddle has a straighter flap than a jumping model and the stirrup bars will usually be set further back. This is because dressage, or schooling a horse on the flat, will involve a deeper seat and longer leg than other styles.

For most riders, the best choice is a general-purpose saddle; it will give support and allow you to school, hack out and jump to a reasonable standard in security. A good general-purpose saddle has a forward enough cut to allow you to jump but is not so forward cut that you cannot sit in a more upright position on the flat.

Fit for the horse

It is crucial that a saddle fits well, or it will cause discomfort, pain or even permanent damage to the horse's back. Every horse should have its own saddle, with or without a tree – there are treeless saddles now – which is the correct width for the horse. It should always be fitted by a good professionally qualified saddler and should be checked and adjusted when necessary. Horses and ponies can change their shape as they gain or lose weight or as their muscles develop through work.

Every rider and horse owner needs to learn how to assess the basic fit of a saddle, and all this takes is some observation and attention to detail. It is essential that the saddle distributes your weight evenly and contours the back of the horse or pony so as not to inflict pain or discomfort.

If you start off with a well-fitting saddle which is the correct width for the horse and check it thoroughly every month, you will know when there is a possible problem that needs professional attention from a saddler.

Synthetic saddles

A leather saddle will last for many years but if you're on a tight budget, a good synthetic saddle may be a more affordable option. Although these are usually lighter than leather saddles, it is just as vital that they are fitted and maintained by an expert, as even a lightweight saddle can cause muscle problems if it creates pressure points on the horse.

RIGHT: *Always tie up your horse securely or get an assistant to hold him before preparing to saddle him up. Make sure that you approach him safely and talk reassuringly and gently to him as you approach.*

Parts of the saddle

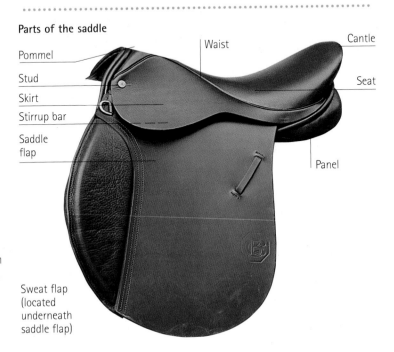

Pommel
Stud
Skirt
Stirrup bar
Saddle flap
Sweat flap (located underneath saddle flap)
Waist
Cantle
Seat
Panel

Basic points to look for

When you are considering buying a saddle, whether new or second-hand, you should consider the following:

■ The saddle should always be level from the front to the back and the rider should be balanced – neither tipped forwards nor backwards.

■ The saddle should sit evenly on the horse, not over to one side.

■ The gullet should clear the horse's back all the way along, especially when the rider is mounted.

■ The panel should always be in contact with the horse, without pinching it anywhere.

■ The pommel should clear the withers and the cantle should clear the back. The amount of clearance needed will depend on the work you are doing. Stand up in the stirrups and ask a helper to put two fingers between the pommel and the horse's withers. If their fingers get pinched, then the saddle will come down too low as you ride.

■ When you ride, your saddle will move slightly with the horse, but there should not be any rocking, either from side to side or backwards and forwards, and the back of the saddle should not bounce up and down.

Mounting

Whenever possible, it is best that you mount your horse from a mounting block rather than from the ground. This will help to prevent the saddle from being pulled over to one side, which is not only uncomfortable for the horse but may also lead to the tree of the saddle becoming twisted over a period of time. Saddles are very expensive items and it is well worth looking after them.

BELOW: *When choosing a numnah or saddle pad, it is wise to get expert advice before you buy one.*

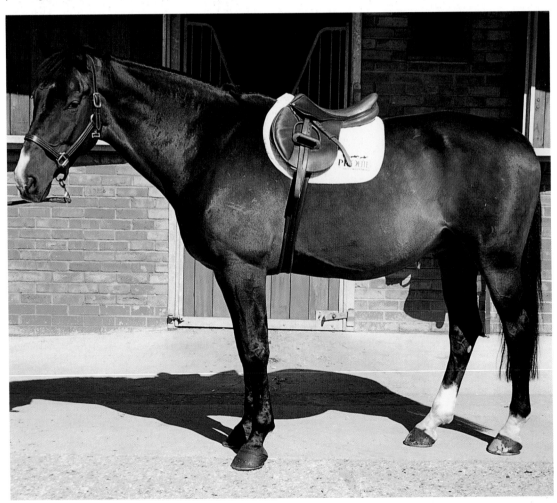

Fitting a saddle

A correctly fitted saddle will spread the rider's weight properly over the horse's body. This is essential both for your horse's health and your safety. You should always ask a member of the Master Saddlers Association to fit your saddle for you. A comfortable saddle that fits properly is a must if you want your horse to perform well and also to avoid some of the most common fitting problems.

ABOVE: *The front arch of the tree is too narrow.*

ABOVE: *The front arch of the tree is too wide.*

ABOVE: *The front arch is the correct size.*

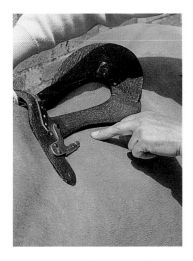

ABOVE: *The tree of the saddle (with the front arch) must conform exactly to the horse's shape, as shown here, so as not to inflict any discomfort or pain and to avoid pressure.*

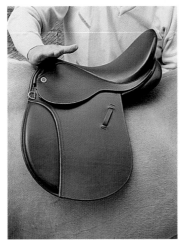

ABOVE: *This saddle is too wide. If your weight is over the front arch, the saddle drops to the wider part of the horse and the frame lifts off at the back, transferring weight to the front.*

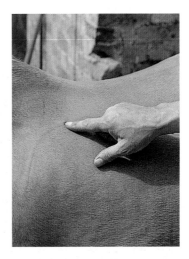

ABOVE: *After riding and removing the saddle, if it is fitted correctly, the hairs of the horse's coat along its back should lie in a natural line. This can be checked easily as above.*

Fit for the rider

Although priority will be given to fitting the saddle to the horse, it is important that it also fits the rider and encourages a correct, balanced position. A rider who is off-balance will be an uncomfortable burden on the horse. Therefore you must also check the following points before you decide on a saddle:

■ The saddle seat will need to be large enough to accommodate the rider comfortably without putting pressure too far back on the horse, as can happen if a large rider tries to ride a horse or pony that is too small for them.

■ The saddle flaps should be the right length; if they are too short, they will catch on your boot tops, and if your thighs hang over them at the back, then your security and comfort will be affected when you are riding.

■ The knee rolls should be sited so that when your stirrups are adjusted correctly, your knee sits just behind them. Some saddles have movable knee rolls, which are fastened on with a special sort of Velcro to allow you to customize the fit.

4.2 Saddle fittings

In addition to a good well-fitted saddle, you will need some fixtures and fittings, such as stirrup leathers and irons and a girth. Again, these should be the best quality that you can possibly afford and should fit correctly.

Stirrups

Stirrups should be made from stainless steel for strength and they must be the right size for the rider. When the widest part of your foot rests on the tread, there should be 1.25 cm ($^1/_2$ in) clearance either side – no more, or your foot could slide too far in to the stirrup, and no less, or your foot could become trapped. Most riders use rubber treads for extra comfort and security.

Safety first

Many saddles still have stirrup bars – the metal fixings that hold the stirrup leathers in place – with traditional hinged ends. These must *always* be pushed down and must allow the leathers to slide off when they are pulled hard. In the unlikely event of your foot becoming trapped in a fall, the leathers will be released.

Safety stirrups

There are several designs. Those with rubber rings on the side are fine for lightweight small children, but older youngsters and adults tend to use the 'bent leg' designs where the metal takes the stress of heavier weights.

You should always run the stirrups up the leathers when you are leading or holding a tacked-up horse; this will prevent them flapping about or getting caught up. Never lead a horse out of the stable with the stirrups down, or they could catch or bang on the door. If you are lungeing a horse with the saddle on, secure the run-up stirrups with the leathers turned up. Pass the end of the leather through the loop before slotting it through and securing the loop on the flap. You can use an overgirth or an elastic surcingle to prevent the flaps flying up and down.

Stirrup leathers

These can be made from leather or synthetic materials. Most riders put more weight in one stirrup than the other, even if they do not realize it, so if the leathers have the capacity to stretch it is a good idea to swap them round each time that you ride

to try and keep them even. Regular riding lessons will help you to keep your position and weight level.

Girths

Girths can be made from synthetic materials or leather. Those that 'give' a little as the horse breathes out, thanks to some elasticity in their construction, are presumably more comfortable for the horse. Leather girths, in particular, are often shaped behind the elbow, where the skin is thinner than in many other areas and therefore more prone to rubbing. Girths must be kept clean to ensure that they do not rub and chafe your horse, causing 'girth galls'.

Numnahs and pads

These come in many designs and materials, including sheepskin, cotton and even models incorporating airbags. Some are said to relieve pressure or help prevent the saddle slipping. Ask your saddle fitter's advice if necessary and make sure that whatever you use stays up in the saddle gullet and does not pull down on the withers, leading to rubs or pressure points.

Numnah

RIGHT: *It is important to saddle up your horse correctly and to check the girth is tight enough to keep the saddle in place when riding.*

Stirrups

Peacock irons

Rubber quick release

Rubber treads

Irons

4.3 Putting on a saddle

Before you saddle up your horse, collect everything that you will need and have it to hand. You should tie up the horse securely but comfortably – the rope should not be too tight nor too loose – and talk to him soothingly all the while, patting his neck and generally putting him at ease.

Start by checking that the stirrup irons are run up, the numnah or pad is pulled up into the gullet and the girth is folded over the saddle seat.

Lower the saddle gently well forward of the horse's withers, and slide it back into the correct position so that the coat hairs on the back lie flat.

Go to the other side of the horse to release the girth so it rests down the horse's side. Check that all is safe under the saddle flap. Go back to the near (left) side, reach under the belly and fasten the girth, loosely at first. Tighten, a hole at a time, until it's tight enough to keep the saddle in place but does not cut into the horse. Check it again before moving off and after riding for a few minutes. Gently pull each foreleg forward in turn to release any wrinkled skin. Before you mount, double check that the bridle, bit, saddle and numnah are adjusted correctly.

Saddling up your horse

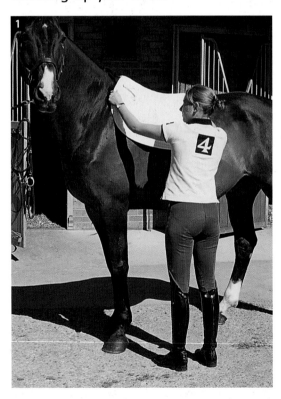

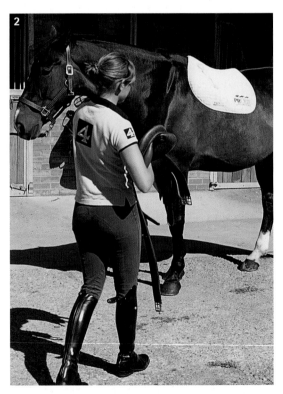

1 Always approach the horse's nearside steadily, talking gently and reassuringly to him all the time. Make sure that he is tied up securely. Place the numnah or saddle cloth well forward over the horse's back and smooth it out.

2 Always hold the saddle with your right hand, with your left forearm positioned under the pommel. Pat the saddle area and then place the saddle gently on top of the numnah. Pull the numnah up into the gullet of the saddle.

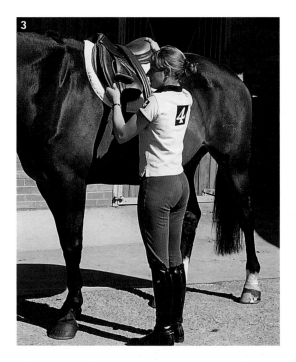

3 Gently slide the numnah and saddle back together into the correct position on the horse's back.

4 Check again that the numnah is positioned well up into the gullet of the saddle.

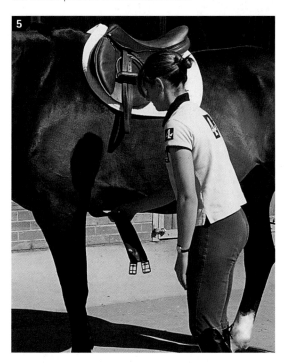

5 It is advisable to go to the horse's offside to check the girth before reaching down and doing it up on the nearside.

6 Fasten the back girth to the third girth strap and then adjust the buckle guard.

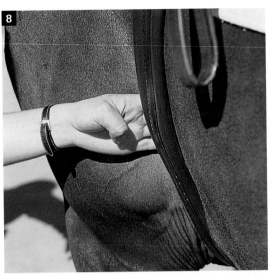

7 Pull the buckle guard down over the buckles to prevent them moving and rubbing, damaging the saddle or rubbing against your legs when you are riding.

8 Give the girth a final check to ensure that it is tightened correctly and that no skin is wrinkled below. You don't want the saddle to slip round when you are mounting.

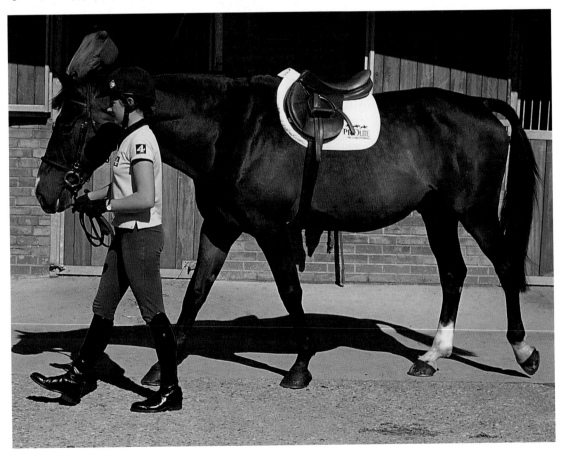

4.4 Removing a saddle

There are several accepted methods of unsaddling a horse but the one featured below is the normal procedure. After use, take the saddle to the tack room for cleaning and storage.

If the saddle is dirty and is spattered with mud after riding, it is best to clean it immediately as any mud will come off more easily if it is sponged when still wet. If the horse is wet, after removing the saddle you should put on a sweat rug or, alternatively, you can place some straw underneath the rugs and then walk him dry. Pick out his feet and wash them if they are muddy. Check his legs and sponge or brush off any sweat marks. Groom him, checking for telltale signs of rubbing in the saddle, girth and mouth areas. Put him back in his box and tie up the haynet and refill the water bucket or trough. Replace all his rugs before bolting the door.

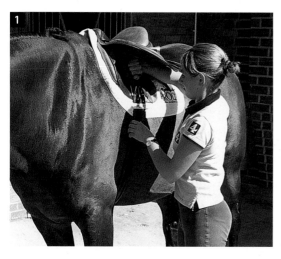

1 As soon as you dismount, tie up the horse securely and run up the irons on the leathers.

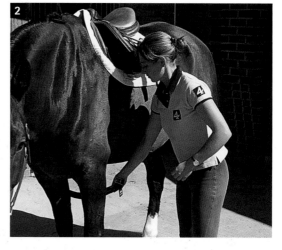

2 Your next task, still standing on the horse's nearside, is to unfasten the girth.

3 If the girth is wet or muddy, leave it down; otherwise, put over the top of the saddle. by going to the offside.

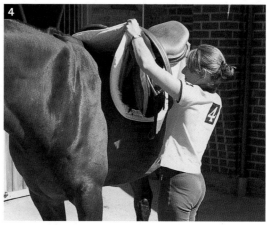

4 Lift the saddle and numnah sliding slightly backwards, then drawing them gently off and placing them on your right arm.

4.5 Bits and bridles

The right choice of bit and bridle is vital for a horse's comfort, to enable him to work correctly and for the rider to control him. As with saddles, bridles must always fit correctly.

Bits

There are literally hundreds of types of bit, but they can be divided into groups. For most riders, the three important ones to know about are:
- Snaffles, with a single rein
- Double bridles, which have two bits and two reins
- Pelhams, with bits that can be used with a single or double rein and are more severe than a snaffle.

All bits rest on the bars of the mouth and, depending on their design, act on some combination of the bars, tongue, corners of the lips, curb groove and poll. Their purpose is to help you to control your horse.

Snaffles are relatively simple to use and fit, and most horses that have been correctly trained go well in them. Most riding school horses are ridden in snaffles.

Bit guidelines

There is such a wide range of mouthpieces and cheekpieces available that it is best to get advice from an experienced trainer who understands the theory and practice of bitting. If you have to choose a bit for your horse or feel that you need to change the one he is currently ridden in, the following guidelines should help you.

- Thicker mouthpieces are usually said to be kinder than thinner ones, but for some horses they are literally too much of a mouthful and a slightly thinner mouthpiece can actually be more comfortable in these cases. The rider's ability has a big effect on the action of a bit – thus a novice rider with unsteady hands will not be as sensitive with the rein aids as, say, a balanced, more established rider.
- Different mouthpiece designs will act in different ways. For instance, a straight bar acts more on the tongue; a single-jointed bit works on the bars; and a double-jointed French link has a less direct action on the bars and reduces tongue pressure.
- Different mouthpiece materials also have varying effects. For example, bits coated in special plastic are often used for young and sensitive horses, whilst bits that are made from sweet iron and those containing copper may encourage a horse to salivate and relax his jaw.
- Some snaffles, such as the gag snaffle and snaffles with a lever action, have a potentially more severe action and should not be used by novice riders. They are only used when other methods of control have failed.

Snaffles

- The eggbutt snaffle will stay still in the horse's mouth and the smooth sides will minimize the risk of pinching. It's a good bit to discourage horses that are 'mouthy' and tend to play with the bit.
- The loose-ring snaffle will make constant tiny movements in the mouth and encourages a horse who is 'set' in his mouth to relax his jaw.
- The French link snaffle has a less direct action and many horses like it.
- The three-ring snaffle is potentially a powerful bit – the rein can be fixed to any of the rings and the lower it is positioned, the greater the possible leverage and control.

Eggbutt snaffle

French link

Loose-ring hollow mouth snaffle

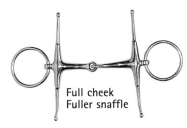

Full cheek
Fuller snaffle

Continental
3-ring snaffle

Double bridles

The double bridle comprises two bits: a thin snaffle with small rings called a bridoon and a curb bit with cheekpieces of varying lengths called a Weymouth. The Weymouth is fitted with a curb chain, which rests in the horse's curb groove and applies pressure there when the curb rein is used.

The double bridle allows a good, experienced rider to establish greater communication with a well-schooled horse. However, it should not be used by inexperienced riders or on horses that are not well established in their basic education.

Pelhams

Pelhams try to combine the action of a double bridle in one mouthpiece and are used with a curb chain. They, like the Weymouth of a double bridle, act on the poll and curb groove as well as on the mouth.

Many horses go well in pelhams. There is a wide variety of mouthpiece designs and materials. Pelhams are

Mullen-mouth pelham

Pelham roundings

ABOVE: *This pony is wearing a simple snaffle bridle and cavesson noseband.*

not allowed in dressage tests, but they are popular in showing classes.

Ideally, a pelham should be used with two reins; the one on the top or 'snaffle' ring gives less leverage than the one on the bottom or 'curb' ring. At first, holding two sets of reins and using them independently of each other may seem confusing for the rider, but the skill will come with plenty of practice and the help of a good instructor.

Some riders prefer to use a single rein and couplings, which are called pelham roundings, attached to the top and bottom rings. This is quite a popular option for jumping.

The Kimblewick also has a curb chain and is less subtle in its action than a pelham. It has a single rein

and is another bit that acts on the curb groove and poll. Nowadays, it is not seen as often as it used to be, as a horse will tend to set its jaw against the action.

Going bitless

There may be times when a horse cannot be ridden in a bridle – for instance, when a youngster is cutting teeth. There are also some trainers and riders who believe that a bit should only be introduced when a young horse has learned to carry his rider. In these instances, a bitless bridle can be used. There are several designs and anyone intending to use one should get help and advice from someone experienced in their fitting and use. They can be, and are, used in all disciplines except dressage.

4.6 Fitting a bridle

For a bridle to fit correctly, the different components must be the correct proportions for the horse's head and they should be adjusted so as not to pinch or rub anywhere.

The main things to remember are that:
■ The headpiece and browband must not pinch the horse's ears.
■ The throatlatch (pronounced throatlash) must not be too tight.

■ The noseband must not rub the horse's facial bones and, if it fastens below the bit, it must not interfere with the breathing or be so tight that it prevents the horse mouthing on

the bit and flexing his jaw.
■ The reins must be long enough to allow the rider to lengthen and shorten them, but not so long that there is a danger of the rider's foot catching in the loop. This can happen if children on smaller ponies ride with reins designed for horses.

Types of bridle

A snaffle bridle is used with one pair of reins. Many riders like to use different designs of reins to give a better grip, such as ones made from

Fitting a bridle

It is important both for the comfort of the horse and for your safety that the bridle fits correctly – it should be neither too big nor too small, too loose or too tight. It is easy to check whether a bridle is fitted correctly as shown here. The best bit is the one that is kindest in allowing the horse to go forward under your control; the type used will depend on the horse's schooling and temperament.

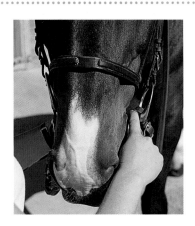

ABOVE: *There are 5 mm (^{1}/$_4$ in) between the side of the mouth and the bit.*

ABOVE: *Your hand should fit sideways under the throatlatch.*

ABOVE: *Two fingers should fit between the browband and the horse's head.*

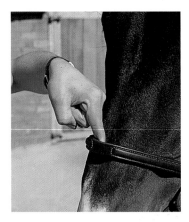

ABOVE: *If you cannot put a finger or two into the noseband, it is too tight.*

ABOVE: *Insert a hand under the headpiece to check the mane is flat.*

laced or plaited leather or which incorporate rubber or other synthetic handgrips. Double and pelham bridles are used with two pairs of reins, usually plain leather with the top rein wider than the bottom one. Some riders like top reins made from laced or plaited leather or with rubber grips inside.

Bridles and headcollars can be made from leather or a synthetic material. Leather will look best for bridles, but washable synthetic designs can be useful for wet and muddy conditions. Leather headcollars are always better than nylon headcollars, which can be used in situations where the horse is under supervision.

Safety

For safety reasons, always use a leather headcollar when travelling and either a leather or 'safety' design with a breakaway section to prevent the horse getting caught up out in a field. However, it is always better to turn out a horse without a headcollar on. Designs marketed as 'pressure' or 'controller' headcollars should only be used by experienced riders and should never be used to tie up a horse.

On the nose

The simplest type of noseband is the cavesson, which fits under the bridle's cheekpieces and will give a 'finished' look to the horse's head. Many horses will perform well in a plain cavesson noseband and a snaffle bit.

Different types of noseband are used to give more control, usually by preventing the horse from opening its mouth too wide and/or crossing its jaw, and by applying pressure to the nose. Flash nosebands are most

Neckstrap

If your horse does not wear a martingale, it is often a good idea to use a neckstrap – especially if he is young and/or lively. This gives you something to hold on to if he misbehaves. A simple method of making a neckstrap is to buckle a spare stirrup leather round his neck.

commonly used but drop and Grakle (crossed) nosebands are suitable in some cases. A good instructor will help you to decide which is the best choice for your horse. However, the cavesson is the only noseband that should be used with a double bridle or pelham. There are many other types of nosebands with specialist uses, but those outlined above provide enough choice for most riders.

Martingales

These give extra control, often when you are hacking or jumping. Designs in common use are the running, standing and bib martingales. They should be fitted in such a way that they are just tight enough to prevent a horse

raising its head above the point of control but not so tight as to try and hold the horse's head down.

Whereas the running and bib martingales attach to the reins, the standing martingale attaches to a cavesson noseband or the cavesson part of a Flash. It should never be used with a drop noseband or any part of a noseband which fastens below the bit, or it will interfere with the horse's breathing.

Breastplates

Breastplates and breastgirths are used as a safety precaution to prevent a saddle slipping back, especially in cross-country competition. However, they are not an adequate substitute for a correctly fitting saddle.

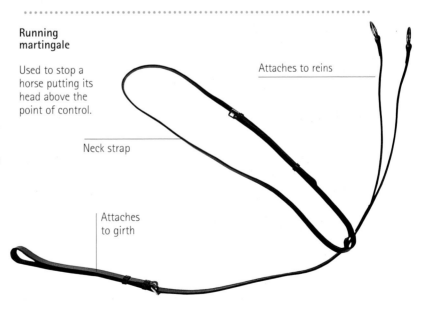

Running martingale

Used to stop a horse putting its head above the point of control.

Attaches to reins

Neck strap

Attaches to girth

Putting on a bridle

A bridle must always fit properly and effectively. It should be kept in good condition for the horse's comfort and wellbeing and also for your safety.

When putting on a bridle, check that the noseband and throatlatch are undone. Put the reins over the horse's head and, if he is tied up, loosen the quick-release knot and remove the headcollar. Fasten the headcollar round his neck to prevent him from walking off. Always hold the bridle in one hand and support the bit with the other. It is important to present the bit to the horse's mouth gently, although many horses will take it of their own accord. If not, press lightly on the bars with your thumb.

Checking the fit

■ The browband must always be comfortable and not too tight or it will pinch the horse's ears. If it is too loose, the headpiece may slip back.
■ The cheekpieces should be an even height on both sides, with the buckles positioned just above eye level.
■ The snaffle bit should slightly wrinkle the corners of the mouth (make the horse smile) and not protrude more than 5 mm (^{1}/4 in) each side. It should be high enough in the mouth to clear the tushes.
■ The throatlatch should be buckled so you can insert four fingers between the leather and the horse's jaw.
■ The noseband should be two finger widths or 2.5 cm (1 in) below the cheekbone. You should allow at least one finger's width between the leather and the horse's jaw when it is fastened at the back.
■ The reins should have 43–51 cm (15–20 in) spare when they are held.

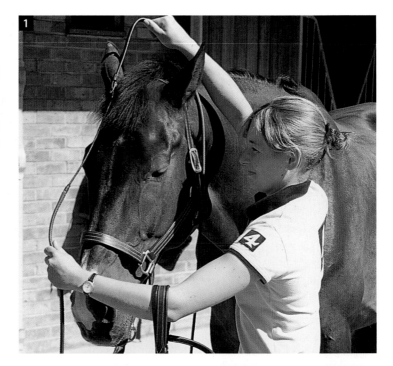

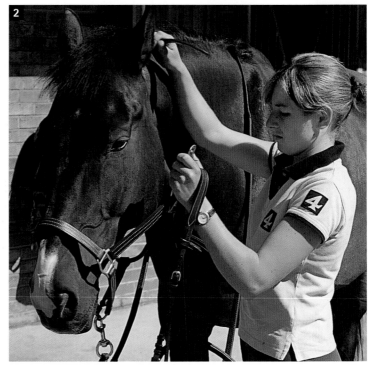

1 Approach your horse, talking to him gently and reassuringly, and then slip the reins over his head.

2 Undo the headcollar and put it round the horse's neck. Fasten it to ensure control of the horse.

3 Hold the bridle in one hand in front of the horse's face and, with the other hand, guide the bit gently into his mouth without banging it on his teeth.

4 Bring the headpiece up over one ear and then over the other ear. Make sure that you tidy the mane under the headpiece and pull out the forelock from the browband.

5 Try to be as quick and efficient as possible when getting the bridle over the ears so that the horse does not 'spit out' the bit. Do up the throatlatch, leaving enough space for four fingers to fit easily between the horse's cheek and the strap. The noseband should be taut – you should be able to put at least one finger between the nose and the leather.

4.7 Rugs

Rugs can be used for several reasons, including providing protection from the weather, when travelling, to dry off a wet or sweating horse, and to keep the back muscles warm and dry when exercising the horse in bad weather.

Types of rug

There are many different types of rug of which the main ones are:

■ Turn-out (or New Zealand) rugs of various weights to suit different conditions. Modern materials make them waterproof, breathable and lightweight. Some have built-in or detachable neck covers. They are worn by horses living out in winter, and by stabled horses that are turned out during the day.

■ Stable rugs will keep a stabled horse warm and snug at night. They can be made of hemp, canvas, jute or various synthetic materials.

■ Summer sheets come in lightweight designs, usually made from cotton. They keep the horse's coat clean and provide some protection from flies. In warm weather they can be used for horses travelling to competitions.

■ Outdoor fly rugs are designed to protect against flies and insects.

■ Thermal rugs and coolers will help dry off a wet or sweating horse.

■ Exercise rugs will keep the horse's back warm and dry.

Which size?

To find out which size rug a horse will need, you should measure from the centre of his chest along his body until you reach an imaginary perpendicular line dropped from the top of his tail. Most rugs fasten at the chest with cross surcingles under the belly; there should be one hand's width between the surcingles and the horse. A well-fitting rug will come just in front of the withers, will fit at the neck and chest without gaping or pulling tight and will not restrict the movement of the horse's shoulders.

RIGHT: *Modern rugs designed to protect a horse from fly and midge bites are becoming very popular during the warm summer months.*

BELOW: *Turn-out rugs protect against wind and rain and also help to keep horses and ponies clean.*

Putting on a rug

First, make sure that the rug is the right size for your horse or pony. It should be deep enough to cover the belly, elbows and stifles and should be sufficiently long to cover the dock and buttocks. It should also fit neatly over the shoulders, withers, ribs and croup. It should fit snugly – not too loose nor too tight – around the neck. If it is too loose, it may slip back over the withers and cause a sore. Also, the horse might get a foot caught in the neck when he is getting up and tear the rug or even injure himself. However, if the rug is too tight in the neck, it may put pressure on the horse's windpipe. Horses with high withers may benefit from rugs that are fitted with comfortable sheepskin pads inside part of the neck. Note that rugs worn next to the skin must be cleaned regularly.

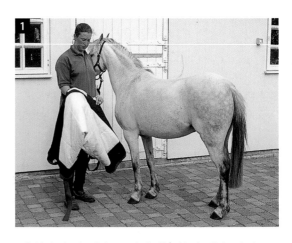

1 Fold the back of the rug in half (with the lining facing outwards) and approach the pony at the shoulder.

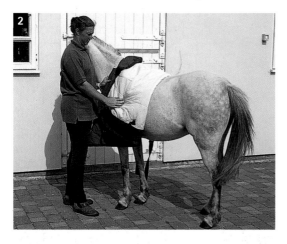

2 Gently put the folded rug on the pony, talking reassuringly, with its forward edge well in front of the withers.

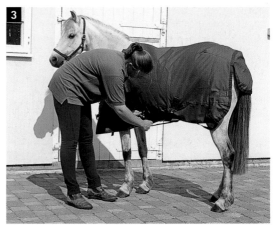

3 Fold the rug back, pulling it slightly towards the rear, and then fasten the belly straps without pulling forwards.

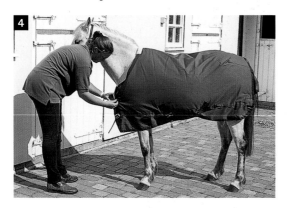

4 Fasten the front straps, still taking care not to pull the rug forwards over the pony's coat.

5 Carefully go behind the pony so as not to alarm him and then fasten the hind leg straps by linking them.

4.8 Booting up

Boots are worn to protect horses' legs, especially when they are jumping or travelling. Use them when working a young or unbalanced horse or one that tends to brush or overreach.

There are many types of boots for horses and ponies, of which the most commonly used are the following:

■ Brushing boots protect the inside of the cannon bone and fetlock if the horse brushes (hits one leg with its partner on the other side).

Brushing boots

Overreach boots

■ Overreach boots protect the front heels from being struck or trodden on by a hind hoof.

■ Tendon boots are designed to protect the tendons down the back of the front leg from being struck by a hind hoof.

■ Travelling boots prevent the horse from knocking his limbs when he is travelling. Some are designed to protect the limbs from the knees and hocks down to the coronary bands. Bandages can be used instead but boots will save you time and labour.

Designs and fit

Most boots are designed so that each fits on a particular leg, though some of the latest brushing boots can be used on any leg. They must be the right size and adjusted so that they stay in place without putting any pressure on bones or tendons.

Travelling boots

Fitting boots

1 Always fasten the straps of the boot on the outside of the leg, taking the straps from front to back.

2 Boots should fit snugly but not too tightly. You should be able to slip a finger down inside them. These boots are a bit too long, as indicated.

General handling

Whenever you examine your horse or pony, stand close to him. The closer you are to the hind leg, pressing on it, the less risk you run of being on the receiving end of a kick that has got some impetus behind it. You should accustom the horse to being touched. Firmly run your hands, regularly and frequently, over his head, neck, body and, very importantly, legs. Apart from getting the animal used to your touch, this will also enable you to detect any abnormal lumps and bumps under your hands.

4.9 Bandages

Bandages are used to protect a horse's legs from injuries and to keep the tail tidy and protected when travelling. There are several types of bandages but it is important to apply them correctly. Badly applied leg bandages can do more harm than good to a horse's legs and may actually damage them. You must learn the correct techniques for bandaging a horse.

Leg bandages

These can be used to protect your horse's legs, either when working or travelling, to keep an injury clean, or to give warmth and support.

Stable bandages

These protect the legs, provide warmth, keep the circulation active and help dry off wet legs. They are useful to support the opposite leg of a horse that injures a leg and puts more weight on the sound one. Travelling bandages are similar to stable bandages but tend to come lower down the leg to ensure protection for the coronary band. Exercise bandages for working horses should only be applied by experienced owners with expertise in bandaging.

Surgical bandages

These cover and protect wounds and are usually made of a synthetic stretch material. Special cohesive bandages, where each wrap sticks to the one underneath, are often used over dressings or poultices.

RIGHT: *A tail bandage should be firm but not pulled too tight. The tapes should not be tied tighter than the bandage itself. Only leave it on for a few hours as it can cause discomfort.*

Tail bandages

These are used in the stable to keep the tail tidy and to prevent the tail hair being rubbed when travelling, perhaps with a tailguard on top for extra protection. They encourage the hairs in a pulled tail to lie flat.

Putting on bandages

Bandaging is a skill that will take practice and the best way to learn is to get someone experienced to show you how to do it. The vital points to remember are as follows:

■ Leg bandages should always be used over padding.

■ Do not wet bandages, or they will tighten on the limb or tail as they dry.

■ The tension should be even and the bandage should not be too tight – as firm as necessary to keep it in place and prevent it from slipping.

■ Fastenings should be secured on the outside of the leg so they do not put pressure on bone or tendon.

■ Bandages should be rolled firmly and applied without any wrinkles.

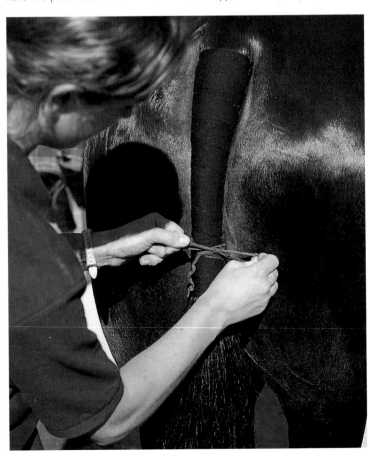

Bandaging

Applying a stable bandage must be done properly so as not to damage the horse's legs. Start with the bandage rolled with the tapes or fastening inside the roll. Put the padding round the leg. Holding the end of the bandage against the leg with one hand, go round and round with the other hand, overlapping each turn by at least half to two-thirds of the breadth of the bandage. Always bandage from the front to the back of the leg. Finally, tie the bandage around the leg with a neat, tight bow on the outside and tuck away the loose ends.

1 Always put a layer of padding under a bandage. Check that it fits well and lies smoothly before covering it.

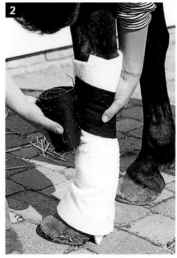

2 Make sure you have the bandage ready and firmly rolled before you begin to bandage the horse's legs.

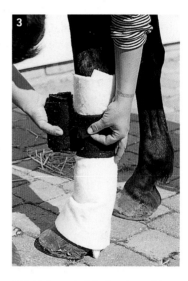

3 Hold the end of the bandage with one hand and then slowly begin to unroll it around the leg, pressing firmly.

4 Start at the top of the padding and then work downwards. When you reach the bottom of it, you should go back up again.

5 Each turn should overlap the previous one by two-thirds of the breadth. The lining should show at least 1 cm ($\frac{1}{2}$ in) above and below the finished bandage.

6 Fasten the bandage with the same tension, with tapes or Velcro. You should be able to slip a finger down inside the bandage. Fold in the tapes.

4.10 Looking after tack

It is important that you look after your tack and equipment and check it regularly for any signs of wear. Get into the habit of running a quick visual check over it before you get on a horse, whether it is your own or someone else's.

Tack

You should check stitching regularly, especially on reins, girths, girth straps and stirrup leathers, for signs of wear and get any repairs made immediately. Keep a close eye, too, on areas where the metal rests on leather.

In an ideal world, where our time is limitless, tack is taken apart and cleaned thoroughly after every use. However, most saddlers say that as long as the mud and sweat are wiped off after riding and the tack wiped over with a cloth that has saddle soap on it, then a thorough clean once a week and an occasional 'feeding' with a good leather dressing will be sufficient to keep leather items supple. Only if the leather is encrusted with heavy mud should you use a wet cloth and water – too much water will cause leather to become hard and brittle. Use a dry cloth or chamois leather to dry it off.

To clean a saddle, you should put it on a saddle horse, with the girth, leathers and stirrup irons on hooks. Next wash the leathers, girth, stirrup irons and treads.

With the saddle up-ended, rub the underneath clean with a damp cloth. Rinse the cloth and clean the rest of the leatherwork. Do not over-wash any clean leather, such as the seat of the saddle. Rub the saddle soap with brisk circular movements into the flaps, girth and leathers. Do not put too much saddle soap on the seat and flaps.

You also need to clean the irons regularly. Use a dry cloth to buff stainless steel irons and clean with metal polish. Nickel stirrup irons should not be used.

If a saddle has been used only on a clean horse with a numnah, it will not need frequent cleaning. However, the girth and leathers should always be cleaned carefully after use.

Leather girths should be soaped or oiled after cleaning, whereas nylon, string, webbing or lampwick girths may be brushed clean if dry, or soaked in warm detergent and then scrubbed if muddy or stained. Use pure soap flakes if your horse is allergic to detergents. Hang them up to dry by the buckle ends.

Synthetic tack should be cleaned according to the manufacturer's instructions. Some is designed to be wiped clean whilst other products can be washed in a domestic washing machine. Check the instructions.

LEFT: *Looking after and cleaning your horse's saddle is an important task not only for its appearance and durability but also for safety reasons.*

ABOVE: *You should use a sponge or cloth when you are transferring saddle soap to the tack.*

ABOVE: *Rub in the saddle soap with brisk, circular movements but be sparing and don't use too much.*

Rugs

These should be cleaned according to the manufacturer's instructions. There are many high-tech fabrics on the market and some may well lose their waterproof qualities if washed with the wrong cleaning agent. Large or bulky rugs are often difficult to fit in ordinary washing machines, so many saddlers and specialist companies now offer rug washing services, or you can try using a small power washer, such as those sold in garden centres. Using a thin, easily-washed cotton or thermal rug under a bulkier one will help to keep the lining of the thicker rug clean and means that it does not have to be washed so often.

Before rugs are put away in store, they must always be washed or cleaned or the ingrained manure will

ABOVE: *Hanging a bridle from a special bridle hook will make it much easier for you to clean.*

rot the material. Before washing, oil all the leatherwork or remove the fittings and sew them back on later. Put more oil on the leatherwork and buckles after washing. Hang rugs up to dry thoroughly before putting them away. Webbing rollers and surcingles should also be washed at home. Take care not to soak the leather fittings in hot water or they will become brittle and break; they should be oiled regularly. Leather rollers should be washed clean and then treated with neatsfoot oil or leather dressing.

Always give all rugs and blankets a thorough shaking, well away from the stable, at least once a week.

Numnahs and boots

Numnahs and boots must be kept clean in order to avoid the risk of rubs and skin infections. With all washable items, you should avoid biological washing powders as these irritate some animals' skin. Sheepskin numnahs can be washed by hand in pure soap flakes, then rinsed and some warm glycerine or neatsfoot oil applied to the skin side to keep them soft and supple and in shape.

4.11 Riding clothes

You, like your horse, need to be equipped for comfort and safety, whether you are schooling at home, hacking out or competing. There is so much smart casual clothing available that every rider can find something suitable, regardless of age, size and personal taste, but the golden rule is that you must wear proper headgear every time you get on a horse.

RIGHT: *This rider is dressed smartly for competing in the show jumping ring. Always wear sensible clothing, gloves and a hard hat or helmet.*

Hard hats and helmets

No matter how well you know the horse, how quiet it seems and how short a time you will be out riding, it is essential that you wear a hard hat or helmet that meets the most up-to-date safety standards, fits properly, is adjusted correctly and has not suffered an impact. If your headgear receives a blow, which usually happens if you have a fall or are kicked, throw it away and buy a new one. You must never buy a second-hand hat; the protection it offers may have been compromised by a previous wearer's fall even if there is no outward damage.

For most people, the best way to buy a hat or helmet is from a retailer who is a British Equestrian Trade Association member and who has attended its course on fitting hats and body protectors. Someone with this experience will also be up to date on the latest safety standards.

For everyday use, you can choose between a velvet-covered hat or a safety helmet. Helmets are available with a wide choice of features, including really bright colours, ventilation slots and washable linings. It is also sensible to wear protective headgear whenever you are lungeing or clipping a horse, as well as riding. In some cases, such

BELOW: *Even when you are riding at home or hacking out, you should always be suitably dressed and wear a hard hat or safety helmet, proper riding boots and gloves.*

as when you are handling a young horse, it is safer to wear a hard hat or helmet at all times.

Footwear

Proper footwear keeps you safe and comfortable not only when you are riding but also on the ground in the yard, field or stable. The one time that you decide to take a chance and lead your horse to the field wearing soft shoes is the time that he will stand on your foot!

Leather boots will give you more protection than rubber riding boots but, if you are on a tight budget, rubber ones are fine. However, they must be made specifically for riding: it is not safe to ride in Wellington boots, as the heavily-ridged soles may lodge in the stirrups.

Long leather boots look good but are expensive and they are often kept for competition use. For everyday use and also for young riders who are still growing, short boots, either the traditional jodhpur boots or ones that zip up, are often a much better option. They can be teamed up with half-chaps or gaiters which are designed to give the appearance of long boots and which can give extra support and protection.

Boots that are designed specially for use on the yard may not be suitable for riding, again because of the construction of their soles. In both cases, it is possible now to buy designs with safety toecaps which will minimize the risk of injury if a horse steps on your toes; again, a good specialist retailer will be able to help you to choose some boots that meet the latest and most appropriate safety standards.

Body protectors

These are a sensible precaution when you are jumping and are compulsory for cross-country events. Body protectors must be fitted and adjusted correctly. It is also sensible to wear one whenever you are riding a young or excitable horse, even if you are schooling or hacking.

If a horse is nervous of being clipped, a body protector offers some protection from kicks. Even the most experienced and agile handler can be caught unawares by a quick 'cow kick', when the horse kicks forward, usually when the belly is being clipped.

Gloves

These are another simple safety precaution. They should always be worn for riding, lungeing and leading a horse. Modern designs mean that there are gloves for all weathers and jobs: stretch cotton with grip palms are comfortable in warm weather and lined leather or synthetic materials are suitable in less pleasant conditions.

The comfort zone

It is impossible to ride well if you are uncomfortable, so stretch jodhpurs or breeches are always a better bet than trousers. Jeans should not be worn because the inner seams will rub your legs. Good-quality, wet-weather gear is a great investment, and many of today's riding jackets are machine washable and smart enough to wear when there is not a horse in sight. Again, follow the manufacturer's care instructions for washing and cleaning high-tech fabrics. Waterproof chaps or overtrousers will make riding and working in the rain more bearable.

Be seen, be safe

Both riders and carriage drivers need to be seen to be safe, all year round. BHS statistics show that there are at least, on average, eight horse-related accidents a day, with no difference between summer and winter accident rates. Research shows that drivers spot riders and horses equipped with reflective fluorescent equipment three seconds earlier than those in 'plain clothes'. As braking distance at 60 mph (40 km/h) on a dry road is 74 m (240 ft), wearing high-visibility gear can help to save lives.

There are many products now available, including rugs, boots and rider clothing. Research for the BHS has shown that the combination of a fluorescent, reflective hatband for the rider and boots all round on the horse make an effective combination. The rider's head can be seen at high level and the horse's movement is immediately eye-catching.

Riding in rain and poor light is inevitable for most of us. This is when materials that are reflective and fluorescent are best, as they show up in headlights. They should also be used when you are leading a horse on the road – for example, when taking him to or from the field.

RIGHT: *You and your horse must be easily visible to motorists and other road-users when you are out riding on the road.*

ABOVE: *This horse and its rider are visible in all weathers.*

LEFT: *Notice the difference between the rider on the left wearing high-visibility clothing and the rider on the right who is merging into the dusk and hardly visible.*

Chapter 5

Handling your horse

• •

Building a partnership with your horse means paying as much attention to the way in which you handle him as you do to your riding skills. Many of the keys to success in communicating effectively with your horse are the same: consistency, kindness coupled with firmness, patience and establishing mutual respect. These ground rules will always apply, whether you are dealing with a horse that has plenty of experience and a quiet temperament or one that is more sensitive and quick to react.

5.1 Think like a horse

The biggest compliment you can pay someone is to say that he or she is a true horseman or horsewoman. Some people have more of a natural affinity than others, but handling skills can be learned and they will grow with practice and confidence. This means learning to think like a horse.

Horses are naturally prey animals rather than hunters. If a horse thinks that it is in danger, perhaps because it is startled by a sudden noise, its instinctive reaction is to run away rather than stand and fight – the 'fight or flight' instinct. This means that the horse feels vulnerable when placed in a position that prevents it escaping unless it has been taught to accept that this is safe, such as when you pick up one of its feet.

A horse's senses

These are honed towards survival. Horses can hear things from much further away than we can and can also hear sounds in lower and higher registers. This is why they dislike and can be frightened by loud noises, such as fireworks and revving cars.

As a prey animal, a horse has eyes that are set at the side of his head (as opposed to humans, who, as hunters, have them set in the front). This gives the horse a much wider field of vision than us, but it has to alter its head position to see things that are near or far away.

If your horse appears to hear or see something that you cannot hear or see, it is not because he is being stupid or awkward but because his senses are more finely tuned.

LEFT: *The horse's eyes are widely set and positioned on either side of the head, giving him a wider field of vision than humans. A horse's expression is the key to its temperament and should be bold and generous.*

Body language

Horses are incredibly responsive to body language, which means that we have to be, too. Used in the right way, body language can help you to handle a horse more easily, but if you inadvertently take the wrong stance, you will often experience problems. Squaring your shoulders, making yourself look as big as possible and looking a horse directly in the eye will make it move away from you, whereas lowering your gaze and turning away from the horse will encourage it to come towards you, because it will not feel dominated or threatened by you.

These principles can be useful in all areas of handling a horse, from catching it in the field to loading it into a trailer or a horsebox. For instance, a common mistake when trying to load a reluctant horse is to stand on the ramp in front of and above it. This stance actually sends out the opposite signals – the horse is more likely to try and back off and will not step into a space that you are blocking.

The power of the voice

Horses are very responsive to the voice, as long as it is used correctly. If you babble away all the time, then a horse will often switch off, but a quiet, soothing word will help calm an excitable or worried animal. Just as important, it will also help to keep you calm. Similarly, it helps if you take slow, deep breaths whenever you are worried or nervous.

RIGHT: *Over time you will build a good working relationship with your horse and will learn to communicate well.*

Any horse can learn simple verbal commands, such as 'Walk on', 'Trot' or – when you want him to move away from you in the stable – 'Over'. However, your tone of voice is vital: a drawn-out word ending on a descending note will have a slowing down or soothing effect whilst a quicker command ending on an upward note will encourage him to go forward.

Whenever you are going to approach or touch your horse, speak quietly to him first so he knows you are there. If his attention is elsewhere, either because he's looking at something or dozing, touching him without warning may startle him. It is then that accidents happen. Be polite to horses in the same way you expect someone to be polite to you. A quiet 'Good boy' is the equivalent to someone saying 'Excuse me' before approaching you, rather than marching up and prodding you in the back.

It is often said that horses can smell fear. This may indeed be true to the extent that fear or nervousness stimulates the production of adrenaline and alters your body chemistry and smell – but it also means that if you can use physical techniques, such as deep breathing, and keep your

Left: *It is important to build a good working relationship with your horse; this will happen naturally over time.*

muscles relaxed rather than tense, your horse will pick up on your state of calmness and be reassured by it.

The learning process

Horses learn through repetition and positive reinforcement, whether they are being handled or ridden. This means that your instructions must always be the same and your reactions must be consistent. Inconsistent behaviour on the part of the handler may well lead to a confused and even a bad-tempered horse.

Be consistent

It is your job to set the ground rules and to see that you both stick to them. For instance, if you expect your horse to take a step back when you open the stable door to let you in, then insist quietly that he does this every time. If you ask him to do it one day but do not bother the next and get cross with him on the third day because he does not do it, you are creating confusion.

Stay calm and focused

Most of us have to fit in looking after and riding horses around work and family commitments and there are inevitably times when demands conflict. One of the most important things to appreciate is that no matter how stressed, fed up or hurried you may be, you need to switch off any

external stresses and switch on your calmness and concentration before you go near your horse.

Positive reinforcement

Reinforcement must always be positive, not negative. If you punish your horse for shying when you are leading him, you are carrying out negative reinforcement by confirming there is something to be frightened of. Similarly, a quiet word of praise and a scratch on the neck will confirm that he has done what you asked.

Correcting your horse

There will be times when you will need to correct your horse, but this must always be done immediately, so that he associates the correction with what he has just done – and never in temper. At the subtlest level, you can correct a horse by repeating an instruction that he has ignored or misunderstood. Any correction should be made immediately, or the horse will not be able to associate it with the behaviour it relates to.

Be calm and quiet

If you are calm, confident and quiet around horses, they will behave in the same way. Horses like people who behave quietly and make smooth, unhurried movements. They are worried by loud noises and jerky, sudden movements, and many are disturbed by hesitant handlers. If you walk into your horse's stable and hesitate because you are wondering whether or not he will let you put on his headcollar, you may find that he senses your concern and moves away from you – but if you behave quietly and calmly, he will follow your lead.

Using treats

The way to a horse's heart is through his stomach, according to the old adage, but feeding titbits indiscriminately is not a good idea. It encourages horses to nip at your clothing – and at you – and they will then be understandably confused when they are punished. The only time that it may be a good idea to reward your horse with a single food treat is when you have caught him, so that he associates it with something pleasant.

5.2 Catching a horse

All horses and ponies should be taught from an early age to be caught, led obediently, have their feet picked up and be tied up.

Training young horses is a subject all on its own – but even when you are dealing with experienced animals, it is important to handle them safely and keep all communications clear. As long as you do it the right way, most horses are reasonably easy to catch. Unless there are any special circumstances, such as when a horse is known to be very difficult to catch and runs the opposite way, they will usually not be wearing a headcollar.

Good rapport

It is easy to tell if there is a good rapport between a horse and its owner, not least when it is time to catch the horse. This should never be a haphazard, unpredictable confrontation but rather a quick, quiet, controlled and trouble-free coming together of good friends.

Putting on a headcollar

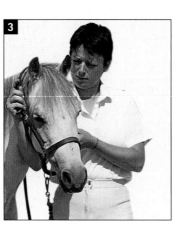

1 Approach from an angle, calmly and quietly, and talking gently to the horse or pony, with the headcollar hidden from view behind your back.

2 Pass the lead rope round the pony's neck to keep control if necessary. Bring the headcollar slowly up to the face – not in a rush or jerkily.

3 Gently slide the noseband up over the pony's muzzle. Talk to him quietly and calmly while you do this to put him at his ease.

4 Do up the head strap and check that all the parts of the headcollar are properly seated and that they are neither too tight nor too loose. Tidy the mane at the poll.

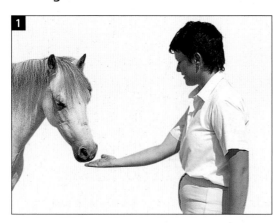

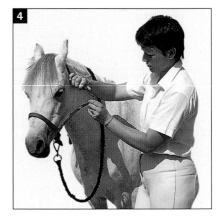

Guidelines

Like children who enjoy playing outdoors, some horses and ponies would sometimes prefer not to be caught, and it may take you some time and effort. However, if you get your horse accustomed to coming over to you to be fed or just to be talked to and patted, this will not be a problem as he will soon learn that being caught leads to a treat. Never try to chase or corner your horse. He will only enjoy the game and will be much quicker and more nimble than you. Instead, be patient and offer him rewards in the form of carrots or mints. Always praise him and fuss over him when you succeed in catching him.

Warning

If you are going to the field with the intention of catching your horse and tacking him up and you find him standing conveniently by the entrance, do not, in a fit of laziness, attempt to put on the bridle or headcollar by simply leaning over the gate. That way accidents happen!

Catching a horse

1 Enter the field and approach the horse at an angle to his shoulder, holding the headcollar behind you.

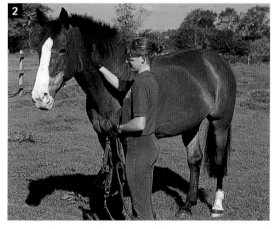

2 Talking gently all the time, approach the horse steadily and run your hand down his side.

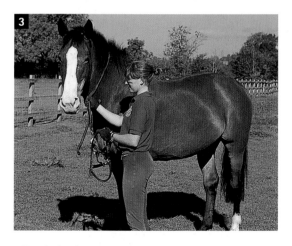

3 Put the lead rope around his neck and raise the noseband over his muzzle. Slide on the headcollar.

4 Adjust the head straps so that the headcollar fits properly, and then pat and reward the horse.

5.3 Leading a horse

It is very important that horses are handled equally from both sides, not only from the traditional near (left) side. Not only is this safer and more convenient, but it also helps to ensure that the horse is always comfortable and controllable wherever the handler is positioned.

Basic guidelines

To lead a horse in a headcollar in the accepted way, you should stand at his shoulder. If leading from the near side, your right hand will hold the lead rope near his head, close enough to the clip to give control but not so close that his natural head movement is restricted, whilst the free end rests in the other hand. Do not ever put your fingers through the headcollar rings or wrap the rope round your hand; if the horse spooks or takes off, you could be injured.

Look ahead and then take a step forward, if necessary giving a short verbal command such as 'Walk on'. An educated horse will keep pace without pulling. To turn him, move the hand nearest his head slightly away from you so that the horse also turns away.

Turning him away from, rather than towards, you lessens the risk that he will tread on you.

Sometimes, you will need to lead a horse in a bridle. If this is the case, pass the reins over his head and position your hands in a similar way to when you are leading him on a headcollar rope, but separate the reins with your index finger to give you more directional control.

Turning a horse

You will often have to turn a horse in one direction or the other, especially if you are checking it over for soundness. As with everything to do with horses, there is a way to make this as safe as possible. Look carefully at the photographs below and opposite to see the correct way to turn your horse or pony.

Leading a horse through a gate

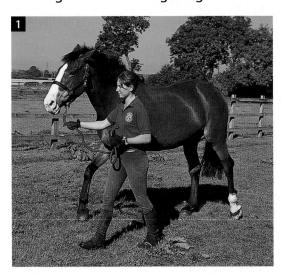

1 Encourage your horse to walk forward towards the gate out of the field – talk gently and reassuringly to him. When turning your horse, you should always hold the headcollar or bridle quite close to the mouth.

2 Always turn the horse away from you. You are likely to get trodden on if you try turning him towards you. He will have to bend his neck as you turn his head away from you. He will then walk beside you through the open gate out of the field.

Trotting up

There will be times when you need to lead a horse in trot, which is known as 'trotting up'. For instance, if your horse is lame, the veterinary surgeon will usually ask for him to be trotted on a straight line so that the lame leg and the severity of the problem can be assessed. A judge in the show ring or a potential buyer will also want to see a horse trotted up to assess the quality of his movement. Again, an educated horse will respond to the handler looking ahead, preparing to move into a jog trot and stepping out. You may also need to use a verbal command or a click of the tongue, but horses soon learn to respond to subtle signals. Before you trot, make sure that the horse is balanced. If you are asked to walk away and trot back towards a judge, then walk a straight line, turn a small half circle and straighten the horse again before asking him to trot. A vet may ask you to keep trotting on the turn, as some lamenesses are more easily identified this way.

Turning out a horse

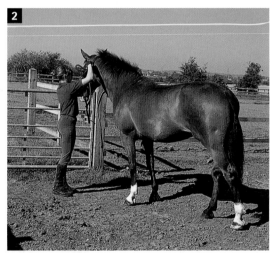

1 To bring your horse back into the field and let him loose, lead him in hand through the open gateway.

2 Make sure that you close the gate behind you. Turn the horse so his head is at the gate with his body straight behind. Quietly undo and take off the headcollar.

3 After removing the headcollar, pat the horse. Do not turn your back on the horse. You need to keep a careful eye on him to ensure that he does not turn quickly and kick up his heels.

5.4 Basic handling

When you need to hold your horse so that he is kept still, perhaps for the vet to administer treatment, for shoeing or for clipping, you should always stand on the same side as the person who is doing the job. Again, this is for safety reasons – if the horse objects to a needle or clippers, then he will move away from you rather than on top of you.

Tying up

There are often times when a horse needs to be tied up: for instance, when he is taken out of his stable in order to be groomed, or for it to be mucked out. Although he must be tied securely, there must always be a breaking point, so tie the lead rope to a loop of strong string or sisal baler twine (nylon baler twine does not break), rather than directly to a tying-up ring or a rail. If a horse is startled and runs backwards, the string will break, but if he is tied to a ring or rail without this buffer, he could end up trailing a large piece of broken wood at the end of a flapping lead rope with the obvious potential for injury. Always use a quick-release knot.

Picking up feet

Before you ask a horse to pick up a foot, check that he is standing with his weight evenly distributed so he can adjust it easily as he needs to. It is a good idea to use a simple verbal command such as 'Up'. Horses soon understand this. If you always move round the horse and pick up the feet in the same order, he will often do it for you without you having to do any more than support the toe as he lifts a foot off the ground.

Quick-release safety knot

1 Start off by putting the loose end of the rope through the string.

2 Make a loop with this piece of rope close to the string.

3 Put this loop across and on top of the other part of the rope.

4 Hold the loose end near the loop; pull it through the loop to make a 'U' shape.

5 Now you should pull the rope really taut.

6 Put the loose end through the loop to complete the quick-release knot.

To pick up a front foot

1 Speak to your horse, then touch or pat him on the shoulder so that he tunes in to your presence and stays relaxed; if you simply take hold of his leg, he may not be properly prepared. Run your hand down his foreleg.

2 Keeping in contact with him, run your hand down the back of his leg, towards the outside rather than the inside, until you reach the fetlock. Meanwhile, talk reassuringly and quietly to him all the time.

3 A gentle squeeze will encourage the horse to lift his leg for you and you can then either hold the fetlock or grasp the foot a little lower down. Make sure that the horse is tied up or held by someone while you do this.

To pick up a hind foot

1 Approaching from the horse's head, run the hand nearest to him along his back and down his hindquarters and outside of the leg to the hock.

2 Keep your hand on the outside; when you reach the hock or halfway down the cannon bone, run it down the front of the hind leg to the fetlock.

3 Now squeeze the fetlock, lifting it forwards and upwards so that the leg joints bend, and then catch hold of and support the hoof rim.

5.5 Safety measures

Whatever you do with a horse, whether you are leading him or riding on the roads, safety must always be a high priority, for your sake and that of other people around you as well as for your horse. Just a few seconds spent putting on a pair of gloves could later stop you from getting rope burns.

Safety on the ground

More horse-related accidents happen on the ground rather than in the saddle, and many of these mishaps can be easily avoided just through taking some common-sense safety measures, such as those that are outlined below.

■ Never take a horse for granted, no matter how well you know him. For instance, the quietest pony may spook if a bird flies out of a hedge when you are leading him, so always be aware of your surroundings.

■ Don't get sloppy because you are short of time. The day on which you take your horse down to the field in soft shoes rather than boots offering greater protection is the day that he will tread on your foot and leave you with broken toes.

■ Always wear gloves and a hard hat when leading, long reining, lungeing or loading a horse. Never wrap ropes or reins round your hand or you run the risk of being injured or dragged.

■ If you are clipping a horse that might be ticklish, wear a hard hat, especially when you are bending over to deal with the belly and legs.

■ Never kneel down at the side of a horse; always crouch down, so that you can jump out of the way if it is necessary to do so.

Testing times

Most riders will have to ride on roads much of the time and although the BHS works tirelessly to educate car drivers as well as riders and carriage drivers, there are many people who do not understand the nature of horses and the fact that even the quietest can occasionally behave unpredictably. Riders must also remember this and not fall into the trap of ignoring what is going on around them.

BHS riding and road safety test

One of the very best ways there is of appreciating the skills and techniques of riding on the road and giving yourself the confidence to cope with situations that need quick thinking and correct riding is to take the BHS riding and road safety test. This will reinforce the need for observation and show you how to make motorists aware of your intentions. It will also help you to ride in a way that encourages drivers and other road users, such as cyclists and pedestrians, to look on riders as responsible road users with as much right to be there as any other group.

Your local BHS Riding and Road Safety officers will help you prepare and take the test at a local venue, along with other riders. All the issues covered relate to the Highway Code; they include observation and signalling, your positioning at road junctions and roundabouts, passing stationary vehicles and coping with hazards.

Be courteous

It is vital that you show courtesy to other road users whether you are riding or leading a horse on the road. If drivers slow down or give you priority, always thank them. It is not always safe to take a hand off the reins to signal your thanks, but it should always be possible to smile and nod to indicate your gratitude.

Alternative approaches

The past few years have created enormous interest in different systems and methods of handling and building partnerships with horses. Many are of value and some practitioners have a gift for explaining how and why their methods work. We all need to realize that we never stop learning and should try and stay open-minded. By definition, that means not following a particular philosophy slavishly if it contains techniques with which you are uneasy.

Unfortunately, the often heard and frequently misused term 'horse whisperer' encourages the idea that there are people with almost mystical skills. In fact, all great horsemen and women follow the same principles of handling and training horses according to the horse's nature and being fair and consistent. Some are just better than others at communicating with people and passing on their knowledge.

Passing stationary cars

1 As you approach a car parked on the side of the road, look behind you to check whether any other road users are approaching. Both you and your horse should be wearing high-visibility equipment – this is an essential all year round, not just in rain and gloomy conditions.

2 Signal your intention to move out around the stationary vehicle only when it is safe to do so, and then take back the reins. Do not attempt any manoeuvre with only one hand on the reins as you will not have sufficient control of your horse.

3 After checking that the road is clear ahead and behind you, move the horse out to go round the car. Allow enough space between the horse and the car to ensure that a driver who

Leading on the road

A bridle should always be used when leading on the road, as a headcollar does not give enough control. You should be on the appropriate side of the road to allow you to face oncoming traffic – for example, on the left-hand side in the UK – and the handler should be between the horse and the traffic. This is safer, as horses move away from anything that frightens them rather than towards them, and taking up this position also makes it less likely that the horse will swing his hindquarters out into traffic approaching from behind. Both the handler and the horse should wear fluorescent, reflective equipment so that they are more visible to drivers.

starts approaching from behind will not try to overtake you when there is not enough room.

4 As soon as you can do so safely, move back to your correct position on the road. Remember, if you are leading, that in order to put yourself between the horse and the traffic, you will have to lead from the off

(right-hand) side. The horse will see you more and the traffic less.

BELOW: *Always be seen and be safe. The combination shown where both the horse and rider wear fluorescent, reflective materials, regardless of the time of day or weather conditions, makes them visible to motorists.*

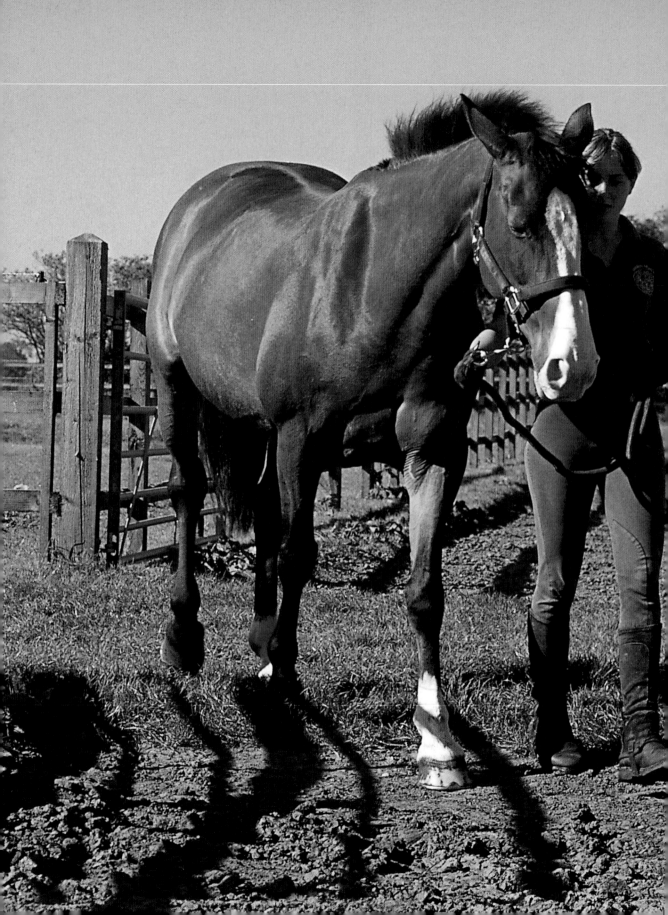

Chapter 6
Grooming and shoeing

··

Grooming is an important part of equine management, particularly for a horse that is fit and in hard work. When your horse is doing strenuous work, his skin excretes waste matter in the form of sweat. Brushing him helps keep him healthy because it removes the dried sweat, dead skin, hair and dust that accumulate, thereby keeping his pores clean and open. Making sure that your horse is clean where his tack fits helps to prevent chafing and sore spots, and, of course, the cleaner the horse, the cleaner your tack and rugs will be. Grooming also provides you with an opportunity to check your horse all over for cuts and bumps, heat or skin problems. Small problems spotted at an early stage can often be nipped in the bud before they develop into something more serious.

6.1 Grooming basics

The amount of grooming that your horse needs will depend on his regime and how much work he is doing. A horse kept at grass and not working will need minimal grooming.

The accumulation of grease and dirt in a horse's coat is nature's way of helping him to stay warm and dry. However, if you ride your horse off grass, you will need to tidy him up before putting his tack on. Removing the worst of the mud and cleaning and checking his feet will probably be sufficient. After exercise you should always make sure that he is quite cool and dry before turning him out again into his paddock.

The stabled horse is a different matter. He should be groomed both before and after exercise. Before exercise he needs just a quick brush over or 'quartering'. The best time to give him a thorough grooming session is immediately after exercise, when he is still warm and the pores of his skin are open. The whole session need not take long – usually only about 30–40 minutes in total and you will enjoy this time with your horse.

Safety first

■ Before you begin grooming, always tie the horse up, using a headcollar and rope. When tying a horse up, use a stable ring fixed to the wall but never tie the rope directly to the ring – attach a loop of string to the ring and attach the rope to that (see page 132). If you tie the horse directly to the ring and he takes fright and runs back, he may break his headcollar or, even worse, slip up and injure himself.
■ Always tie the rope with a quick-release knot (see page 132). Put the end of the rope through the loop to deter the horse from undoing it with his teeth. Never use a frayed rope because it may not come undone easily.
■ When brushing your horse's legs, adopt a crouching position so that you can get out of the way quickly if he makes a sudden movement. You must not kneel or sit when grooming the legs.
■ When grooming the legs, put aside the metal curry comb (well away from the horse and teeth downwards) and use the body brush instead in whichever hand is nearest the horse. Holding his leg with the other hand will help prevent him from fidgeting.
■ When brushing his hindlegs, stand close to your horse's body and use one hand to hold his tail to keep it out of the way while you brush with the other. This helps to steady a restive horse and you can also feel if he shows any signs of flexing his hock with the intention of kicking.
■ Lastly, never stand directly behind a horse – you might get kicked.

Equipment

You will need the following basic items of equipment for grooming your horse or pony.

Dandy brush

The long, stiff bristles of the dandy brush are used to remove any dried mud and sweat. The dandy brush may be used on the horse's body if he has not been clipped, but it is too harsh for a thin-coated horse, one that has sensitive skin or for use on the horse's head. It is not suitable for the mane and tail as it will break the hairs.

Body brush

The short, fine bristles of the body brush can be used all over the horse, including his legs, head, mane and tail. It is fitted with a loop through which you can slip your hand.

Metal curry comb

The teeth of the metal curry comb are used for cleaning the body brush. You simply draw the brush over the teeth after every few strokes and tap the dirt out of the curry comb at regular intervals well away from the horse. The metal curry comb should *never* be used on the horse.

Plastic curry comb

The teeth of this type of curry comb are suitable for removing dried mud from the coat of an unclipped horse.

Rubber curry comb

Use for removing mud, sweat and any loose hairs and for massaging the horse.

Cactus cloth

The coarse-weave cactus cloth, which originates from Mexico, can be used instead of a plastic curry comb for removing mud and sweat.

Hoof pick

The hoof pick, which must have a blunt end to avoid causing injury, is used to clean soil, droppings, stones, etc. from the horse's feet.

Hoof pick with brush

Hoof pick

Water brush

The bristles of the water brush, which are shorter and softer than those of a dandy brush, are used for dampening the mane and tail. It can also be used to remove stable stains (where a horse has lain in its droppings). A dry water brush can be used to remove mud and sweat from a sensitive-skinned horse.

Sponges

These are used for cleaning the horse's eyes, nostrils and dock (area under his tail). Always keep separate sponges for the head and dock.

Stable rubber

A cloth stable rubber is used slightly damp to remove the last vestiges of dust from the horse's coat and to give it a final gloss at the end of grooming.

Sweat scraper

The scraper's rubber blade, which is attached to a metal frame fitted with a handle, is used to remove excess water from the horse's coat after he has been washed down. You must be very careful when working round the horse's bony areas.

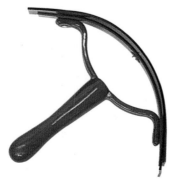

Mane/tail combs

These metal or plastic combs are not required for grooming but are essential items when you want to pull (thin and trim) or plait your horse's mane or tail

(see pages 157 and 158).

Bucket

A bucket is useful for washing your horse's feet, and wetting sponges and water brushes. Never use his drinking water for such purposes.

Other equipment

There are also some other items of equipment that might prove useful when grooming your horse, and these include the following:

Pulling comb

This is used both to tidy and shorten manes and strip out long hairs.

Hoof brush

Small brush to get into the hoof grooves

Hoof oil brush

This is good for painting on hoof oil.

6.2 How to groom

Grooming is not difficult and you will soon develop a routine that suits you and your horse. It is a good opportunity for you to check for warning signs of potential health problems, build a relationship and improve the horse's appearance.

Quartering stabled horses

This is done in the morning and takes about 15 minutes, depending on the size of the horse and how dirty he is.

Some horses lie down at night more than others; some have the unhelpful habit of always choosing the dirtiest part of their bedding.

A rugged-up horse is groomed a quarter at a time. You can do this before exercising your horse and it only involves picking out the horse's feet, brushing off any stable stains with either a sponge or water brush, sponging the eyes, nose and dock, and brushing the mane and tail.

If the horse is dirty, you may also need to wash clean any specific areas and then towel them dry. When you are doing this, you should pay special attention to the hocks, knees, flanks and under the belly.

1 Pick out the horse's feet into a skip (not into his bedding). Use a hoof pick from the heel towards the toe, taking care not to damage the frog.

2 Unfasten the rug and turn it back carefully over the horse's loins so that you can give each side of his front half a quick brush over.

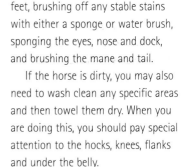

3 Brush the coat lightly with a body brush. Use a brush or a damp sponge to remove any stable stains and then dry off with a cloth or towel.

4 Remove any hairs from the body brush by regularly drawing it over the teeth of a metal curry comb.

5 Now turn the rug forward over the horse's withers and then brush his hindquarters.

6 Always make sure that you brush in the direction of the lie of the coat. Lastly, brush out the mane and tail.

Grooming a stabled horse or pony

A stabled horse will usually also need a full grooming session as well as quartering. This will remove any dirt, sweat and waste products from his coat and help to massage his muscles as well as his skin. When you are grooming your horse, you should always face his quarters, never away from them. Nor should you stand directly behind him or you may receive a shove or a kick! It is best to groom your horse outside the stable where it is less dusty.

RIGHT: *Before you start grooming, put on a headcollar with a rope and tie up the horse, using a quick-release knot. Never tie him directly to the stable ring.*

Pre-grooming clean

1 Start by removing any mud with a rubber or plastic curry comb. Brush in firm strokes with the dandy brush.

2 Beginning at the horse's neck and working downwards, rub in circular motions with the curry comb.

143

Checking the hooves

 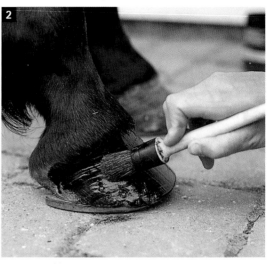

1 Pick out the sole of the hoof. Remove any foreign bodies and check the frog. Look for any smelly areas of rot.

2 For special occasions, you can paint on some hoof oil to keep the wall strong and in good condition.

Grooming the mane

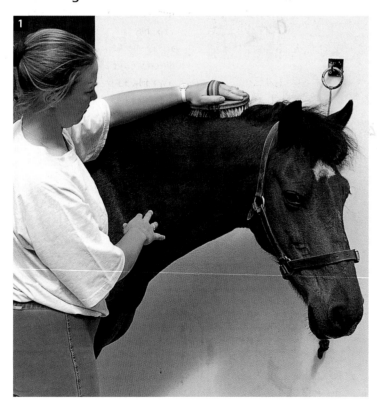 

1 With the body brush, brush the mane over to the other side so that the brush goes right through the hair down to the roots where grease can accumulate.

2 Brush the mane back over again to the original side, a little at a time. Next, brush the horse's tail, standing to the side of the horse. Brush gently, a section at a time.

Using a body brush

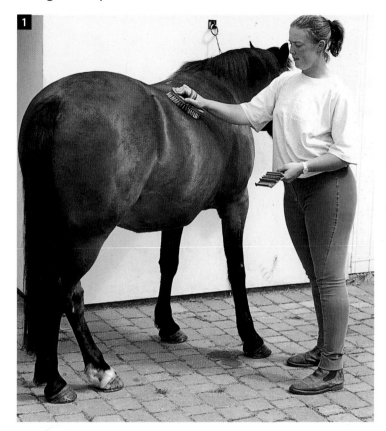

1 Beginning at the top of the neck and working down, use the body brush, working in the direction of the hair and using straight movements.

2 After two or three strokes, scrape the brush on the teeth of a metal curry comb to clean out the bristles.

3 Tap the curry comb on the floor (away from the horse) to loosen any hairs frequently during grooming.

Useful tips

■ Never try to groom a sweaty horse. If the weather is suitable, walk him about after exercise until he has dried off.

■ You can speed up the drying-off process of a wet horse inside his stable by covering him with a sheet that is made of breathable material. A traditional method is to place a layer of straw along his back and the hindquarters with an inside-out rug over the top. This is called thatching (see page 85). The rug keeps him warm; the straw absorbs moisture and allows the air to circulate.

■ In cold weather, you can keep a thin-coated or clipped horse warm during grooming sessions by turning his rugs back and then forward, as you do during quartering (see page 142), rather than removing them altogether.

■ You should wash all your grooming tools in detergent regularly. To prevent the bristles becoming loose, avoid over-wetting the backs of brushes and lie them on their sides to dry, away from direct heat.

■ You can get your horse accustomed to being hosed by trickling water gently around and over his front feet. It is best if an assistant holds him when you first do this. Now very gradually work up his legs and then on to his body. You must only increase the water pressure when you are sure that he is not frightened. Most horses will accept being hosed and even seem to enjoy it in warm weather.

Sponging the head

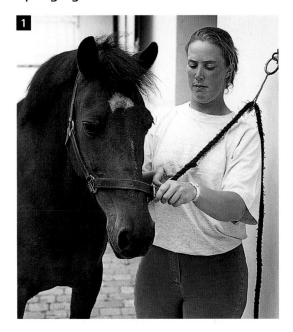

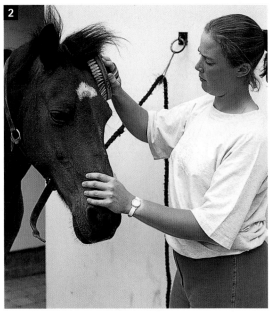

1 Put the headcollar round the horse's neck before brushing the head. The lead rope should be through the string but not in a quick-release knot.

2 With the body brush, gently brush the face, steadying the head with one hand. Do not forget to brush under the jaw and gullet and around the ears. Do not be rough.

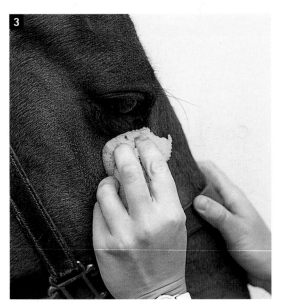

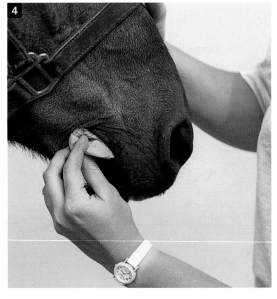

3 Put the headcollar back on and, with a damp sponge, which is kept specifically for this purpose, sponge the eye area with some clean, preferably warm, water. It should not be so wet that it gets water into the horse's eyes.

4 Rinse out the sponge in some clean water and then gently but firmly sponge around the horse's muzzle, mouth and nostrils, rinsing the sponge as required. Remove any discharge from around the nostrils.

Washing the dock

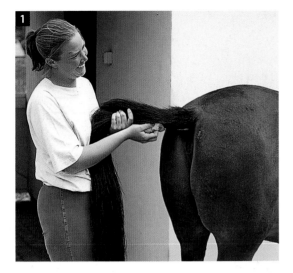

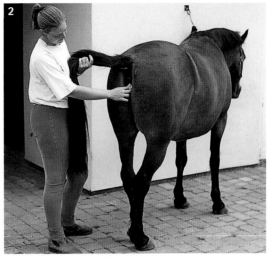

1 With another damp sponge kept for this purpose, gently sponge the dock (the skin at the top of the tail and above the anus). Stand to one side of the horse while you do this.

2 Lift the tail while you clean around and sponge the area underneath. It is best to keep a second sponge specially for this task. Take care not to muddle up your sponges.

Laying the mane

Using a damp water brush from which you have shaken out any excess water, brush the mane downwards from the roots to the ends of the hairs, stroking the hair into place. This makes the mane look neat and tidy with the hairs lying flat against the horse's head and neck.

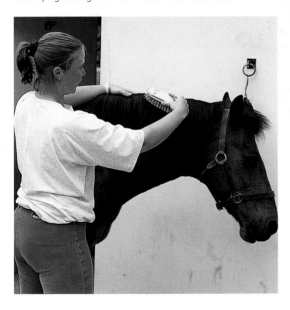

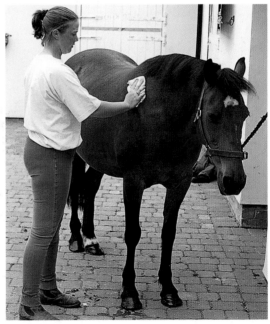

Polishing

Finally, use the stable rubber all over the body to 'polish' the coat and give it a healthy, glossy finish. Always wipe the horse's body in the direction in which the coat lies.

6.3 Sponging and washing

A very sweaty horse, such as one finishing a cross-country course on a summer's day, may be sponged over once his breathing has returned to normal (he will need to be walked about until he has recovered from his exertions).

If the weather is hot, use cold water or a hose pipe, which will clean and cool the horse off. In cold weather, use tepid water. Never use hot water: the horse may get a chill. Use a sweat scraper to remove the surplus water. If it is warm, walk him about uncovered until he is dry. In colder conditions, cover him with a cooler rug, kept in place by a roller and breastplate, or use thatching (see page 85).

BELOW: *You can gently wash off any dirt, mud and stains on the horse's legs with a water brush.*

All-over washing

All-over washing or bathing with an equine shampoo will certainly get a horse clean (greys are often difficult to keep clean and may need regular bathing) but it is no substitute for thorough grooming, since it tends to remove the natural oils from the horse's skin. If you really do need to shampoo your horse, never do so on a cold day as it is important to dry him quickly afterwards. You will need several buckets of warm water, some horse shampoo, a large sponge, a sweat scraper and some towels.

Washing manes

1 To wash your horse's mane, wet it well (including the forelock) with your sponge and warm water, and then work in the shampoo before rinsing well, especially the roots.
2 Remove excess water from the horse's neck with a sweat scraper and dry his ears with a towel. A towel is also useful for soaking up any excess water from a thick mane.
3 Finish by brushing the mane out gently, a section at a time, with a clean body brush.

Washing tails

1 To wash your horse's tail, use a wet sponge to clean the dock (the top, bony section) and then immerse the long hair in a bucket of warm water. You may need an assistant to stand at the horse's head and to steady him for you. If he is restive, they can hold up one of his forelegs to keep him still. Rub shampoo into the tail hairs and dock area.
2 Rinse the whole tail thoroughly in several buckets of clean water. The best way to remove the excess water from the long hair and to dry the tail is to stand beside the horse, with your back towards his head, and then grasp the long hair just below the end of the dock and swish it swiftly round and round.
3 Finally, you should brush the tail hair out carefully with a clean body brush or, if the tail is quite thin, with your fingers.

RIGHT: *You should only give your horse an all-over wash on a warm day so that he can dry off quickly. After rinsing and removing surplus water, walk him about uncovered.*

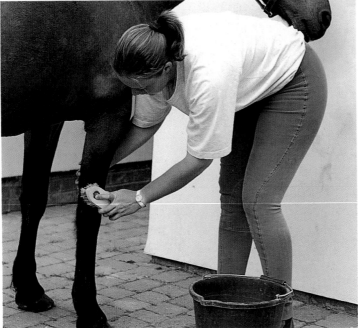

Bathing a horse

Most horses do not need frequent washing, although grey horses may have to be bathed regularly to keep them clean. Nor should washing ever be a substitute for good grooming. Always dry the horse off quickly afterwards by lungeing him with a cavesson and boots on, or walking him in hand with a clean cooler rug to keep him warm.

1 Start at the neck and work your way down the front and sides of the body, using a large sponge and some gentle non-irritant shampoo.

2 Wash the front legs and feet, sponging them gently with plenty of cold or lukewarm, soapy water.

3 Work your way along the horse's back, paying extra attention to any very sweaty areas.

4 Wash the hind legs and feet, taking care to position yourself to the side rather than behind the horse.

5 Next wash the mane, making sure that you rub in the shampoo thoroughly.

6 Soak the tail in a bucket of water and, using a different sponge which is kept for this purpose, shampoo the tail.

7 Sponge the head, taking great care not to let any of the shampoo get into the horse's eyes.

8 Now rinse out the shampoo with plenty of fresh water poured all over the horse's body.

9 Rinse out the sponge thoroughly and keep rubbing the coat to rinse out any remaining traces of shampoo.

10 Stand to the side of the horse and, holding the tail at the end of the dock, swish it round in a circle to dry it.

11 Use a sweat scraper to remove any surplus water from the coat, working back from the neck over the body.

6.4 Neat and tidy

In addition to grooming and washing your horse, you may need to trim and pull his tail and mane occasionally, especially if you are planning on showing him or competing.

Pulling manes

A horse's mane can be kept neat and manageable by means of 'pulling', which involves plucking out a few strands of hair at a time until the mane is the desired length and thickness. Like humans, some horses are more sensitive than others, so you should be prepared to work on only a small section of mane at a time, taking several days to complete the job. It will be easier and more comfortable for the horse if you do it when he is warm – after exercise while the pores are open. However, if he will not tolerate having his mane pulled, tidy it with a thinning comb, not scissors.

Hogging manes

You can improve the appearance of a really thick and unmanageable mane by removing it altogether with the clippers. This is caused hogging and is done by running the clippers up either side of the neck, starting from the withers. It looks best on a heavily built horse such as a cob. To stay neat, it will need hogging every few weeks.

Pulling tails

Pulling is also used to neaten the top of the horse's tail (the dock) if it is bushy and untidy. As with the mane, pulling the tail should always take place when the horse is warm and should never be rushed, otherwise

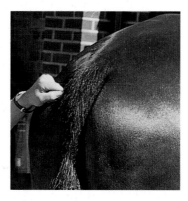

ABOVE: *Pulling the tail will neaten the top and keep it looking tidy.*

the dock may become very sore. Small amounts of hair are removed, mainly from the sides. After pulling, apply a tail bandage for a few hours to encourage the hair to lie flat.

To avoid being kicked if the horse objects to having his tail pulled, hold the tail over the stable door (with an assistant holding the horse's head). With a very sensitive-skinned horse, it is kinder and safer to leave the tail as nature intended and for smart occasions simply to plait it.

If your horse lives at grass it is best to leave his tail unpulled, since the hair helps protect the dock. It is customary with finely bred horses, like Thoroughbreds, and some breeds, such as Arabs, to leave the top of the tail in its natural state. Damping down the hair will be sufficient to keep it looking neat and tidy.

Shortening tails

To shorten the length of a horse's tail, raise his dock to the position where he normally carries the tail when he is on the move. Hold the hair at the end of the tail with your other hand and then cut to the required length. The end of the tail should be parallel to the ground when the horse is moving. For safety reasons, always use blunt-ended scissors for this.

Ears and legs

If you are to keep a stabled horse looking smart, the long hair that grows round the front edge of the ears and around the heels and the fetlocks may be trimmed off.

To trim an ear, hold it closed with one hand and use the scissors from the base of the ear to the tip. The internal hairs provide protection from dirt and insects and thus they should never be removed.

Heels and fetlocks can be trimmed using a comb and a pair of blunt-ended scissors. It takes practice not to leave unsightly 'steps', so make sure that you take your time. If your horse has large quantities of feather (leg hair) then you may need to use the clipping machine fitted with a special leg blade, which is designed not to crop the hair too short. Again, do remember that with some breeds (such as native ponies) it is traditional not to remove feather. If your horse lives out, he should always be left untrimmed in winter as the hair will give protection from the weather.

RIGHT: *Many people trim off the whiskers around the muzzle but it is preferable and much kinder to leave them alone. They act as sensors.*

6.5 Clipping

The thick coat which a horse grows in order to protect him from the winter elements can cause problems if you expect him to do anything other than very light work. He will sweat excessively, lose condition, become very uncomfortable and could even end up with a chill if he is not always dried off thoroughly after exercise. Clipping will solve this problem.

Try to imagine running several miles wearing a heavy overcoat and you will appreciate the problems of a horse with a thick coat. The solution is to clip off some or all of the coat and then to make up for the loss of his natural protection by covering him with blankets and rugs to keep him warm when he is not working. A horse that is clipped, or partly clipped, and spends some of his time out at grass will need a waterproof and windproof rug which is specially designed for outdoor use. A New Zealand turn-out rug is ideal.

The best way to learn how to clip is to employ a professional and learn the techniques by watching them at work. You should never attempt it on your own. However skilful you may become, it is wise, sometimes essential, to have an assistant present.

Types of clip

The amount of hair that you remove will depend on the type of coat your horse grows and the amount of work that he is doing.

A full clip will involve removing the coat from his whole body and legs. It is often a good idea to give a thick-coated horse a full clip the first time and then to leave the hair on his legs at subsequent clippings in order to afford him some protection against any knocks.

The frequency of clipping will depend on how quickly the horse's coat grows. Some horses will need clipping every two to three weeks; other more finely coated ones might go for four weeks. The first clip is usually done in October when the horse's winter coat is through.

Hunter clip

The usual type of clip used for horses in hard work is known as a hunter clip. It involves removing all the coat except for the legs and saddle patch (the latter helps prevent sore backs).

Blanket clip

For horses doing medium to hard work, a blanket clip may be suitable. This leaves an area of the back, loins and quarters unclipped, plus the legs.

Trace clipping

Horses that are kept stabled but not in hard work, or those living outside, can be trace clipped. This consists of removing the hair from the underside of the neck, between the forelegs, the belly and upper part of the hindlegs.

Clipping variations

■ The chaser clip (so named because it is often seen on racehorses), where the hair is clipped from the horse's poll, lower part of the neck, the chest and the belly.

■ The bib clip, where the hair is removed from the jowl, the underside of the neck and front of the chest.

Take care

Be especially careful when clipping your horse's delicate places, such as round a gelding's sheath or those awkward spots between the forelegs and round the stifle. Straighten out the folds of skin in these areas with your spare hand. To clip behind the elbow and between the front legs, get your assistant to pull each front leg as far forward as it will go and keep it stretched out by clasping their hands round the fetlock. Providing the horse with a haynet will help to distract him while you clip.

If your horse is really nervous, he may be less worried if you use a battery-operated clipper, which will be quieter and vibrate less than an electric clipping machine. However, clipping an entire horse in this way is very time-consuming as the clipper will over-heat more quickly and you will have to keep stopping.

If a horse is dangerous to clip, perhaps because of a previous bad experience, you may have to resort to sedation (your veterinary surgeon will advise you on what is best).

How to clip

1 Once you have decided on which type of clip you want to use, you can mark out the lines – for example, the saddle patch and the tops of the horse's legs – with some chalk or a damp piece of saddle soap.

2 If you are using a mains hand clipper, assemble the machine, and check the cable and plug. Make sure you have machine oil, blade wash, a soft brush and spare blades. Then plug in the machine to check that it is working properly. Switch it off and put it in a safe place out of the horse's reach.

3 Start clipping on the horse's neck or shoulder and then work your way back over his body and hindquarters, section by section.

4 You must always use the clippers against the lie of the horse's coat and keep each stroke parallel to the one that is above or below it and slightly overlapping the previous one.

5 You must always take great care when you are clipping the top line of the neck as you do not want to clip into the horse's mane.

6 Finish clipping the top of the tail with an inverted 'V'.

Clipping the head

A horse that is disturbed by the noise or vibration of the clippers should have his head left unclipped. Remove untidy long hairs around the jaw with scissors and a comb and leave the edge of the ears. When clipping the head, use the clippers lightly to reduce vibration. Be especially careful when working round the eyes and never clip the eyelashes. Many people just clip half the head as far forward as the protruding cheek bone.

Clipping tips

■ Always make sure that the horse is both clean and dry before you start clipping. Never try to clip a dirty or sweaty horse.

■ You should clip your horse only in good light. Start in the morning rather than the afternoon or evening.

■ To achieve the correct position and angle of leg-lines on the forelegs, while your assistant has the leg pulled well forward, go from the point of the elbow following the line of the muscle to the top of the front of the foreleg. For the hind legs, follow an oblique line which is approximately one or two stretched hands' width above the point of the hock to the stifle.

■ To mark the saddle patch, put the horse's usual numnah on his back exactly where it lies when he is being ridden. Draw round it with tailor's chalk, making the patch a little larger than required (it is easy to clip off a little surplus hair but you can't put it back once you have made a mistake).

■ Check the underside of the clipper blades every few minutes on the back of your hand. If they begin to feel hot, switch off the motor until they cool down.

■ Keep the horse warm during clipping by covering the clipped areas with a rug. A cold horse will fidget more than a warm one.

■ Clean and oil the blades of the clippers frequently in order to keep them running smoothly.

■ For the best results, you should let the horse's coat 'set', i.e. grow completely, before you attempt the first clip of autumn/winter.

■ You can accustom a nervous horse, or one that has never been clipped before, to the feel of the clippers by running some hand clippers (without a motor) over him a number of times during the days leading up to his first clip.

■ It is always a good idea to let the horse get accustomed to the sound of the clippers before you begin.

■ Music sometimes has a calming effect on restless or nervous horses, whereas some will relax if they are within sight of another horse.

■ Never become impatient with a nervous horse. It will simply confirm his opinion that being clipped is a frightening experience.

■ Have your clippers serviced, and the blades reground, regularly.

■ The first clip should be in the late autumn when the winter coat is completely through.

■ Clip as often as is necessary throughout the winter months until the end of January. After this, the summer coat is starting to come through and, if you clip it, its quality may be damaged.

■ Always try to be as quick and as efficient as possible or your horse may start to fidget.

■ Do remember to switch the clippers off every time you check your handiwork.

6.6 Plaiting

A mane and tail may be plaited to make the horse look smart for showing, competing and special occasions. An untidy mane on a stabled horse can be tamed by putting it into long plaits.

How to plait a mane

To plait your horse's mane for, say, going to a show, you will need a comb and water brush, a small bucket of water, some rubber bands or a needle and thread (choose a colour that tones in with the mane) and a pair of scissors. If necessary, you should find something solid on which you can stand, such as an upended box, so that you can reach the horse's mane comfortably.

BELOW: *A well-plaited mane makes a horse look smart for shows and special occasions. It does not take long and is well worth the effort.*

Number of plaits

It is customary to have an uneven number of plaits along the horse's neck but the total number can be varied. Note that a short neck will look longer if you use lots of small plaits, whereas a long neck will look shorter if you use fewer plaits. You can help to disguise a ewe-neck on a horse by making the plaits in the dip of the neck a little larger than the rest.

Sewn plaits or rubber bands?

Sewn plaits are the most secure and should be used for lengthy periods of work, such as hunting. They will look better if the thread does not show. If the mane does not have to stay plaited for long – for example if you are going show jumping – rubber bands will suffice. Again, use a colour that matches the horse's mane.

The plaits need to be fairly tight if they are to stay in place, but beware

Plaiting tip

To make an unruly mane lie flat, divide it up, then make loose plaits and secure the ends with rubber bands. There is no need to roll them up. Re-plait the mane on a daily basis.

of making them so tight that they cause the horse discomfort; he has to stretch his neck when he is working.

Plaiting a mane

1 Start off by gently brushing or combing the horse's mane to tease out and get rid of any tangles.

2 Divide the mane into as many bunches as are required, and separate each bunch into three equal strands.

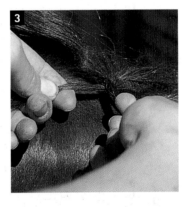

3 Taking the three strands in one bunch securely in your fingers, plait down as far as possible

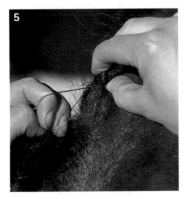

4 Use a rubber band in a matching colour to secure the end, or take a needle and thread and sew firmly.

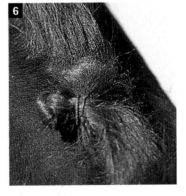

5 Turn the plait under and secure with a rubber band or stitch each turn so it is firm without any loose ends.

6 The rubber band or thread should be neatly visible only at the top end of the plait. Proceed down the neck.

How to plait a tail

If you plan to plait your horse's tail for a show, you will need to have some long hair at the top of the dock, so always make sure that you leave it unpulled. It is much easier to plait a tail that has first been washed and then well brushed through.

There are two methods of plaiting a tail: you can use a simple flat plait, as shown here, or a more complicated ridge plait which will require more skill, patience and plenty of practice.

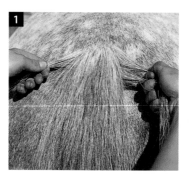

1 Start the plait by taking a few hairs from either side of the top of the dock and some from the centre.

2 These are the three locks of hair that make the plait. Now plait them together and work down the tail.

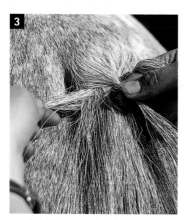

3 As you work your way downwards, each time take a few more hairs from the sides.

4 Continue plaiting in this way, gradually taking a few more hairs from each side as you go down.

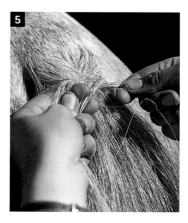

5 As you can see here, no more hair is taken from the centre of the tail, just a few at a time from the sides.

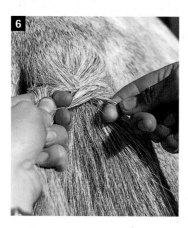

6 This process may seem fussy and take a little time but the plait will soon become evident and look tidy.

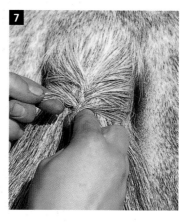

7 When you are two-thirds of the way down the dock, continue without taking any more hair from the sides.

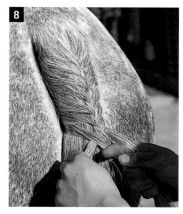

8 Keep plaiting until the end of the plait is reached, then stitch the end, double it underneath and stitch again.

6.7 Shoeing

Like the human fingernail, the outer horn of a horse's foot is constantly growing. The average monthly growth for our horses is about 5–9 cm (2–4 in). However, in the wild, excess growth would be kept in check by natural wear and tear.

The hooves of a domesticated horse, which is required to work, either by carrying or pulling heavy weights, would soon become damaged by this unnatural wear. The hooves need to be protected if the horse is not to become lame, which is why man has been shoeing horses with metal shoes for more than 2,000 years.

The hooves of an unshod, resting horse turned out to grass will also need regular attention. They will not wear down in the same way as they would in the wild and will have to be trimmed to prevent them growing too long and becoming misshapen.

Most horses need to have their feet trimmed once every four to six weeks. The farrier removes the shoes, trims away excess horn and, if the shoes are worn, replaces them with new ones. If the old ones are not very worn, they may be refitted. These are known as 'refits'.

Fitting the shoes

Shoes can be fitted either hot or cold. The benefit of hot shoeing is that the shoe (which is bendable when hot) can be finely adjusted to the shape of the horse's foot, thus ensuring a better

fit. The shoe is heated and placed in contact with the insensitive underside of the hoof for a short time. The imprint it leaves will show the farrier whether any further adjustments are required and if the sole is flat. Once the farrier is happy with the fit, he will plunge the shoe into cold water before nailing it into place.

The nails are driven up into the insensitive wall of the hoof, the points protruding through the wall. These are twisted off to form clenches, which prevent the nails from being pulled back through the hoof.

The role of the farrier is a crucial one, as there is little room for error when shoeing horses since the inner structures of the foot are highly sensitive. One little slip and you will have a lame horse on your hands.

Studs

For competing, there is a variety of designs of studs. Screw-in studs come in various shapes and sizes. They can be quickly removed and replaced with cotton wool when they are not needed. If you do start competing and feel that you need studs, you should ask your farrier and your instructor for guidance.

RIGHT: *The modern farrier is a highly skilled craftsman and you should make regular appointments with him.*

The process of shoeing

Before shoeing the horse, the farrier will often ask you to stand him square and will then observe him being walked and trotted up. This is to look out for any abnormalities in the horse's action which it might be possible to correct by shoeing the horse appropriately.

He will also check the old shoes for any tell-tale signs of uneven wear. These may be caused by a number of factors: faulty conformation, unsoundness or from faults in the fitting of the shoe. After removing the old shoes, the farrier may observe the horse unshod and walking.

1 The horse should always be tied up securely or held by an assitant when it is ready for shoeing. The farrier will approach the horse from the side, running his hand along the horse's body and talking to him reassuringly.

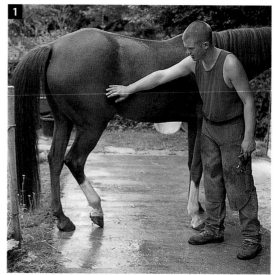

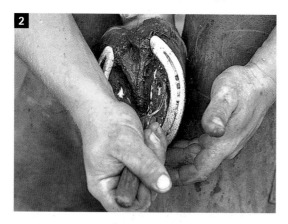

2 The foot must be cleaned out thoroughly before the farrier can start work on shoeing the horse.

3 The farrier knocks up or cuts the clenches (nails) in the horse's shoe with a hamme

4 The shoe is carefully removed from the horse's foot with a pair of pincers.

5 The farrier now sets to work on the horse's foot, first removing any excess sole with a knife.

6 Next, he trims any untidy pieces of the V-shaped frog with a loop knife. He will not do this if it is healthy.

7 The horse's foot is trimmed next with some hoof cutters to keep it neat and tidy.

8 A rasp is used to reduce and level the foot. – the sides and toes first, then the heel if it is necessary.

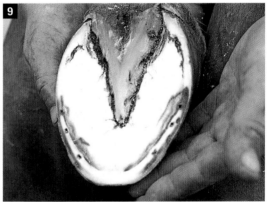

9 This foot has been prepared and is ready for shoeing. The horse is observed standing unshod to check balance.

10 The prepared new shoe is heated in the furnace and its shape can then be adjusted by hammering on an anvil.

11 At a dull heat, the shoe is burnt on to the foot to check for fit. It should not be left against the foot too long.

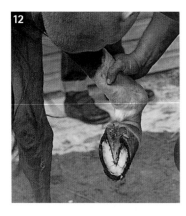

12 The farrier checks that the shoe is burnt on level all the way round before removing it from the foot.

13 The farrier boxes off the shoe to take off all the sharp edges before checking it again for fit.

14 The hot shoe is quenched in a bucket of cold water to cool it down before applying to the horse's foot.

15 The shoe is nailed into place. The nails must be of a suitable size and fit into the fullering.

16 The excess nail emerges about one-third of the way up the hoof wall and the point twisted over.

17 The clenches (nails) are rasped down so that they are ready to be bent over into the horse's foot.

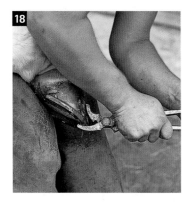

18 The clenches are now bent over with clenching tongs ready to be hammered flat against the foot wall.

19 The rasp is used to smooth off the clenches and the edge of the wall to make the foot and shoe tidy.

20 The newly shod hind foot viewed fom below, showing the shoe and nails in position.

6.8 Checking the feet

Check your horse's feet every day and, if he is shod, make sure that his shoes are not becoming loose or the clenches raised, i.e. sticking up above the level of the hoof. A raised clench can cause injury to one of his other legs if he strikes himself. If you are in doubt, call the farrier.

A horse that is kept out at grass and not working should not require any shoeing, provided that he has good, strong hooves, but they will still need to be checked and regularly trimmed. For a horse that has less good horn growth, it is usually best to keep his front feet shod. If you are unsure,

BELOW: *A liberal application of grease to the sole of the horse's hoof is wise on snowy winter days.*

take advice from your farrier. If your horse or pony has unshod feet, it is important to inspect them regularly, removing any small flints or debris that could cause lameness.

Care of the feet

A stabled horse on a balanced diet or a horse that is turned out on good pasture should be getting all the essential vitamins and minerals that are required for the production of

Unshod horses

An unshod horse will still need regular attention from the blacksmith. The hoof is a living tissue which is constantly growing. As the hoof wall grows longer, it has a tendency to crack, with potentially serious results. Skilled trimming is necessary in these cases. Wild horses, of course, never see a blacksmith, but they keep their hooves naturally trimmed as they constantly move over rough or rocky ground.

strong horn growth without any help from man. However, just as some people have brittle fingernails, some horses on a good diet will still have weak and brittle hooves. Your farrier or veterinary surgeon will be able to advise you on a suitable additive or ointment, if it is required.

Even if your horse's or pony's feet are unshod, they should be dressed by the farrier every four to six weeks to maintain their balance. Some horses wear the toe or the heel area, while others wear more on one side.

Oiling the feet

Special hoof oil can prevent the feet from becoming too dry (oiled hooves also look smart for special occasions). Oiling of the wall will help to prevent undue evaporation, but care must always be taken not to over-use it, particularly around the coronary band and on the sole.

However, too much oiling can be counterproductive and can actually cause brittle feet as it will prevent the natural absorption of moisture.

Special care

■ In winter, if the horse is going out onto snow, you can apply a thick layer of grease to the soles of the hooves in order to prevent any snow compacting there.

■ If your horse has hooves whose walls seem to be prone to dryness and splitting, then supplementing his food with some biotin, a member of the vitamin B group, can be helpful. Biotin powder can be obtained from most feed merchants, veterinary pharmacists and horse tack shops. Other useful dietary additions are methionine, zinc or glycerine. Ask your vet for advice.

Chapter 7

Feeding and diet

• •

Horses are continuous 'trickle' feeders and have a comparatively small stomach capacity. Over the years, the horse has adapted to compound feeds, but with so many feeds on the market and so much controversial information available, feeding horses can become a headache for many owners and carers. This chapter will give you an insight into the digestive system of the horse, the various feed types available, and the role they can play in his diet. Even experienced owners may struggle to devise feeding regimes that are suitable for each individual horse on their yard. If there is any doubt about what you should be feeding, seek advice from a qualified nutritionist or vet.

7.1 The rules of feeding

All owners should adhere to the following rules when feeding a horse. They should be used not only as guidelines when you are devising regimes but also as daily good hygiene practice. The rules are in no order of priority, but are equally important.

Always feed good quality feeds

All feedstuffs and forage that are fed to horses should be of good quality. It is a false economy to purchase cheaper, inferior quality feeds. Feeding inferior quality feedstuffs, such as dusty hay or badly harvested feedstuffs, could result in health problems, including COPD (Chronic Obstructive Pulmonary Disorder) or colic.

Always feed according to your horse's individual requirements

Horses are individuals and they need to be fed according to their own requirements. Two horses of the same height, age and breed may require totally different diets. Factors that need to be considered when devising a diet include: height, age, condition, breed, exercise regime, temperament, fitness and time of year..

Always feed plenty of roughage

Roughage plays a major part in the horse's digestive system; not only is it a good source of fibre but it also bulks out the diet. Sources of roughage include hay, haylage and chaffs.

Always feed little and often

Horses are 'trickle feeders', which means that their digestive tract is designed to cope with small amounts of food at regular intervals. Feeding large meals twice daily can cause a horse to bolt its feed and could even lead to colic or choke. This will also overload the stomach, which would result in the undigested food being passed out in faeces.

Never make sudden changes to your horse's diet

The gut of a horse contains bacteria that adapt according to the foods passed through it; this adaptation needs to happen slowly over a period of time. When introducing a new feed to the diet, it should be done gradually, introducing a small handful to start with, and then increasing it over a period of time. This rule also applies to a new batch of hay or forage, especially batches obtained from a different supplier.

Always stick to a feeding routine

Horses thrive on routine and expect their food to arrive at the same time every day. It is this anticipation of food that may cause problems. Horses may become agitated and bang on the doors if stabled, or, if turned out with other horses, fights may occur due to them gathering at the gate, waiting for feed times.

Altering their feeding regimes may also cause digestive upsets, so it is vital to try to manage your time effectively to establish and maintain a feeding routine for your horse.

Always feed succulents

Ideally, horses should have access to grass every day, although this is not always possible. Succulents provide an additional source of vitamins and minerals and can help to stimulate appetites. Favourite succulents include carrots, apples, swedes and turnips. These can be added to a horse's diet on a daily basis.

Never exercise your horse immediately after feeding

On average it takes a horse one-and-a-half hours to process food through the stomach into the small intestine. Digestion can be interrupted if the horse is asked to exercise. A horse should either be fed well in advance of being exercised, or after exercise, when he has cooled down if he has worked strenuously.

Always provide a constant fresh water supply

Water is an essential part of every horse's daily requirements. It is required to aid the digestion process; it helps in the production of saliva and the swallowing of foods; and acts as a lubricant when food is passing through the digestive tract. Horses should have constant access to fresh, clean water; the only exceptions are prior to fast work, and after fast exercise when water should be restricted.

RIGHT: *If your horse is living out, he may only need extra food when the quality of the grass is poor. Keep an eye on him and check the grazing.*

Always practise good hygiene

Good hygiene is essential for every horse owner in helping to prevent the spread of diseases and viruses and keeping your horse happy.

■ Feed and water buckets, scoops and spoons should be scrubbed clean after each use.

■ Feed room floors should be kept scrupulously clean.

■ Feed should always be kept in rodent-free bins.

■ After the contents of a feed bin have been used it should be washed out and throroughly dried before it is filled with new feed.

■ Forage should be kept in a clean, dry, well-ventilated store.

Always measure out quantities of hay/feed

Weighing food is essential to ensure that you are not over- or under-feeding your horse. The easiest way to measure food is by weighing an empty scoop, then adding each different food that you feed to your horse, and weighing the scoop again. When you have done this, you should subtract the weight of the empty scoop from the total weight when the feed is added.

Hay/forage can be measured by using a weigh hook. You simply fill a haynet and place this on the hook, which, ideally, will be suspended, and then read the weight.

BELOW: *It is very important that you always ensure that you know the exact weight of the food you are feeding to your horse.*

7.2 Feed compositions

Horse feed can be divided up into five main groups. These are protein, carbohydrates, fibre, vitamins and minerals, and lipids – fats and oils. They all have a function in a horse's diet.

Protein

This is essential for growth and repair. It is formed from chains of amino acids; the horse produces some amino acids, while others are produced in the gut by micro-organisms. However, not all essential amino acids are produced naturally by the horse and therefore these need to be included in its diet.

Carbohydrates

The carbohydrate group includes cellulose, sugars and starch. They are a horse's main source of energy.
■ Cellulose: this is insoluble carbohydrate, and it is also known as fibre.
■ Sugars: these are carbohydrates in their simplest form.
■ Starch: this is the plant's major energy store.

Fibre

Fibre is a vital nutrient in a horse's diet; without it, your horse would find it difficult to digest his food. Fibre stimulates the gut to contract, which allows for the passage of food. The majority of a horse's diet should contain fibre. Fibre can be found in forage, including hay, straw and grass.

RIGHT: *Some people feed hay and haylage to their horses in a net to prevent any wastage.*

Vitamins and minerals

Vitamins can be divided into two groups: water soluble and fat soluble. Water-soluble vitamins cannot be stored in the body unlike fat-soluble vitamins. If a horse is being fed a correctly balanced diet and has a normal work regime, it will probably not need supplemented vitamins. The main vitamins are A, B (complex), C, D, E and K. Each vitamin has its own role to play in maintaining equine health.

Minerals, like vitamins, are only required in small quantities, and supplements are rarely needed if a horse is fed a good, nutritious diet.

When adding any vitamins or minerals to a horse's diet, you must take care: exceeding a recommended dose could be more harmful to the horse than not supplying any at all.

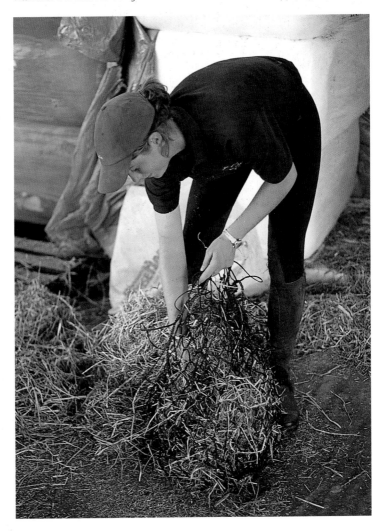

7.3 Feed types

There are various food types that are available to horses, and these can be categorized into the following groups: roughage, including grass, hay, silage, haylage, processed feeds, straw and chaffs; concentrates, including compounds and cereals; supplements, including vitamins and minerals; and, lastly, succulents, including carrots, apples and swedes.

Roughage

This important food group for horses includes the following items.

Grass

Horses have evolved to survive on grass. Grass quality (i.e. its nutritional value) and quantity will vary greatly between pastures. The majority of horses' and ponies' diets will consist purely of grass from spring through to autumn, with many having to be on restricted grazing in order to prevent problems, such as laminitis and obesity. It is essential that you monitor your horse's body condition on a daily basis if he lives out at grass. In the winter months, when grass may be sparse, supplemented hay or feed may be required to maintain a good body condition.

Hay

When producing hay, ensure that cutting is performed in the right weather conditions and at the correct time of year, so that the best quality hay is produced. A number of different grasses is used in haymaking, each having its own nutritional values.

When produced, hay should be stored in a suitable cool, dry, well-ventilated store. Good quality hay will be dust free, pleasant smelling, and should be free from mould, damp, thistles and weeds. Note that ragwort in hay is poisonous and should never be fed to horses (see page 86).

Feeding freshly cut and baled hay can be harmful because it is still developing; ingestion of this hay can cause digestive upsets, such as colic, laminitis and metabolic disorders. It is not advisable to feed new hay until approximately three months post baling, and, like any new food, it should be introduced gradually.

Silage

Silage is rarely fed to horses. It is a less matured crop of grass, with a much higher nutritional value than haylage and hay, and a high level of additives. Care must be taken if it is given to horses, because if it is not fed correctly, it can predispose a horse to botulism, resulting in colic, obesity, laminitis and other metabolic and digestive upsets, possibly even death.

Haylage

This comes in a vacuum-packed, sealed plastic wrapping. Good quality haylage has a high nutritional value and is free from dust. It should not be fed within the first two months post cutting. Haylage is similar to silage, except that it is wilted for longer, allowing the extraction of air. It is essential that haylage is stored carefully and that the bags are not punctured. Any air that gets into the haylage will result in it turning bad. If haylage is home produced, it is advisable to have its nutritional value analyzed before it is fed, so that this can be accounted for when devising your feeding rations and regimes.

Pelleted or dried grasses

These are cut at different intervals in the season. Concentrated grass products are high in carbohydrates and protein. They are normally classed as part of the concentrate ration, not the roughage ration.

Straw

Oat or barley straw can be fed as a bulk food and is of comparative nutritional value to poor quality hay. Straw is usually fed to horses on a controlled diet in order to add bulk to their daily ration.

Chaff/chop

Chaff or chop is made up of chopped straw and hay and sold in feed sacks. It can be bought mixed with molasses, honey and/or flavoured with apple, etc. It is useful to feed to stabled horses, those on restricted diets, and horses that rush their food. These products are high in fibre and are usually fed to provide bulk in the diet.

RIGHT: *When feeding hay or haylage from a net, always ensure you know the weight. Giving a smaller net three times a day can help keep a stabled horse occupied.*

Concentrates

Concentrates are divided into straight feeds (not mixed) and compound feeds. Cereals are straight feeds and include oats, barley, wheat, rice and maize. A good source of carbohydrates, they contain a sufficient level of protein, but lack calcium. Cereal grains can increase horses' excitability and/or energy levels; it is thought that this is because of the fermentation of the micro-organisms in the gut, which causes an increase in sugars and lactic acids. Cereals are processed using the following methods:

- Bruising
- Steam pelleting
- Steam flaking
- Extruding
- Micronizing

Oats

These have been a very popular feed amongst horse owners for many years, providing a good source of carbohydrates and rations of starch, protein and fibre. Oats are now more commonly fed by racehorse trainers and those owners who regularly do fast work with their horses.

It is essential that the oats used are of top quality in order to ensure maximum utilization by the horse. Oats do not have a high calcium to phosphorus ratio, and therefore supplements are required to balance this out, especially for young and growing horses. Oats are not an advisable food for horses that are worked lightly or irregularly.

LEFT: *Stabled horses should be turned out every day for a few hours to graze. In the wild, the horse's diet consists mainly of grasses.*

Barley

This should never be fed unless it has been suitably processed for ingestion by horses. Its energy content is higher than that of oats, but the fibre content is significantly lower. As with most cereals, barley has a low calcium to phosphorus ratio and supplementation may be required. Flaked barley has been processed so that it is easier for horses to digest, although this is a more expensive product.

Maize

Maize is usually fed cooked or flaked. The digestible energy is higher than in oats, but the fibre content is lower. Maize is high in starch and can cause digestive problems if fed in excess.

Wheat

Wheat should never be fed as a whole due to the digestive problems that it can cause. It is not commonly used as a feed for horses.

Bran

A by-product of wheat, bran has been a traditional foodstuff for many years, but consider the following before feeding it to your horse:
- It is a by-product, and thus has poor nutritional value.
- If it is fed in large quantities it can act as a laxative.
- It has a high fibre content.
- It has a low protein content.
- It is difficult for the horse to digest.
- It has a bad calcium to phosphorus ratio. If fed in excess, it may cause bone defects as it is low in calcium and high in phosphorus. Therefore, should you choose to feed bran, you must balance the calcium/phosphorus ratio in the feed ration as a whole.

Linseed

Another food that has traditionally been fed to horses, linseed must always be cooked beforehand to inactivate the poisonous hydrocyanic acid, which is present in the seeds. Cooking will also ensure that the incredibly hard seeds are softened before feeding.

Linseed should always be weighed before cooking as no more than 100 g (3$^{1}/_2$ oz) should be fed to an individual horse in its daily ration. Linseed is usually fed because it is a good energy source and improves the coat condition of the horse. Although it is high in both protein and oil, the protein is of very poor quality.

Sugar beet

This is a popular food to feed to horses. Sugar beet is a root vegetable which is processed to remove the sugar, thereby enabling what is left to be developed into sugar beet shredded pulp or cubes.

It is very important to ensure that the sugar beet has been adequately soaked before feeding. It is a good energy provider, easily digestible, with a good source of digestible fibre, and it has the additional benefit of not 'hotting' horses up due to its slow energy release of glucose.

Sugar beet is rich in calcium, salt and potassium, which means that it can be used as a balancer to add to cereal feeds which are lacking in these particular nutrients. It is also useful for adding to dried food and for 'bulking' up a horse's rations. It encourages the horse to eat more slowly, masticate the hard feed more effectively, and can sometimes act as an appetizer.

Compounds

Compound foods are a mixture of foods that have been manufactured. They may be cubes or coarse mixes.

Cubes

These are ground up, steamed and then pelleted. They are only produced from selected foods. They come in a range of types for different horses.

Coarse mixes

These may range from high-protein mixes to a basic plain cereal mix. The contents may be flaked, micronized or rolled. In order to make them more palatable to the horse, syrup or molasses are sometimes added.

Always look on the manufacturer's label to see what ingredients have been included in a compound food. Vitamins and minerals are usually included, which reduces the need for additional supplements.

Compound foods include:

■ A complete mix, which can be in the form of a cube.
■ A balancer, to be fed with cereals.
■ A concentrate mixture, such as a coarse mix.
■ A fibre mixture, which is mixed with other foods and provides an alternative to bran, chaff or sugar beet.

To encourage your horse to eat more slowly and chew food properly, it is advisable to add some form of bulk to his compound feed or grain. Sugar beet or a form of chaff is often favoured for this.

Succulents

These foods for horses include cut grass, some fresh vegetables, herbs, plants and fruit, and seaweed.

Cut grass

This is safe for horses, provided it is long, fed immediately after being cut, and has been scythed. However, lawn mowings should *never* be fed to horses. They heat up and ferment very easily and, if eaten, may cause severe colic.

Carrots, apples, cabbage leaves and pea pods

These do no harm if they are fed in small quantities. Carrots are rich in carotene and are a useful addition to a horse's diet. However, to avoid the danger of choking, you should always cut them lengthways before giving them to your horse.

Fresh herbs

Horses often select herbs from their grazing; these are usually high in essential minerals and trace elements. Dried herbs can also be added to a horse's daily feed rations, but you should only feed them according to the guidelines on the packaging.

Garlic

This is often fed as a powder or as granules. It is helpful for those horses with respiratory problems and can be used to disguise the unpleasant taste of some medicines. However, the most usual use of garlic is as an effective fly repellent.

Comfrey

Know as the 'healing plant', comfrey contains a high content of easily absorbed calcium.

Dandelions

The leaves are high in vitamins and minerals, and they are often very much enjoyed by the horse.

Nettles

A very good source of iron and other minerals, nettles need to be cut and wilted before feeding.

Seaweed

This is organic and high in iodine, and hence the amount you feed to your horse needs to be carefully monitored. Seaweed is thought to improve the condition of bad doers.

Supplements

It is all too easy to be taken in by all the supplements that are available on the market. If you are feeding a compound food to your horse, make sure that you check which supplements the manufacturer has added: you will find that more often than not, additional supplements are not needed. It is important to note that supplements can be detrimental if they are fed in excess.

If the horse is fed a mixture of straight feeds, then the rations and nutritional values must be checked, as they may be low in calcium, salt, lysine and methionine. It is very important not to consider vitamins and minerals individually, as they can interact with each other. It is still not clear exactly how or why specific vitamins and minerals interact; hence expert advice and guidance should be sought when adding these to a horse's diet.

Supplements include:

■ Salt
■ Dried herbs
■ Vitamins
■ Minerals (including trace elements)
■ Feed balancers
■ Bacterial cultures

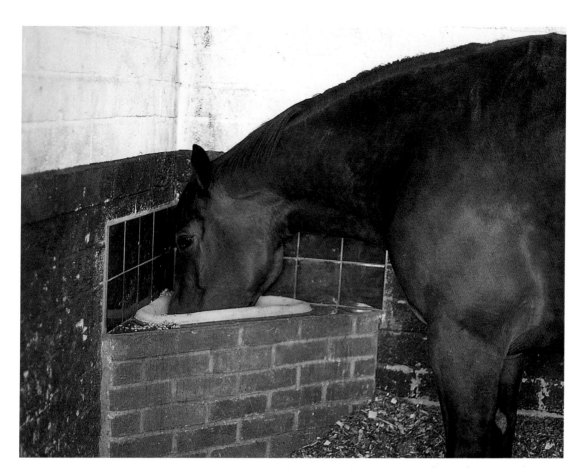

Common salt

There are a number of ways in which salt can be added to the horse's diet. These include the following methods:

■ Adding the salt directly to the horse's daily feed. This enables close monitoring and control of exactly how much salt intake the horse is having.

■ Placing a rock of salt in the horse's manger. This is very cheap to buy and can help to prevent the horse bolting his food. However, the he may not choose to chew on the rock each time he is fed, and thus will not get the desired intake of salt.

■ Providing the horse with a salt lick in the stable. This has the advantage of making the salt supply readily available to him at all times. However, some horses may choose not to use it, and it can even pose a danger of infection should horses with colds or other health problems be moved from stable to stable.

■ Placing a salt block in the horse's field. Again, this has the benefit of being available to the horse at all times. However, it must be placed in a container as it will dissolve on the ground, and the horse may ignore it.

Feed balancers

These come in small cubes, which are a good source of vitamins, minerals,

some probotics and good quality protein. Feed balancers are specially designed to be added to a horse's daily ration of food.

Probiotics

These are designed to create and enhance the performance of existing digestive micro-organisms. However, exactly how useful they are, and the potential nature of their risks, have not been fully assessed yet. Discuss them with an expert before deciding to use them as a supplement.

Antibiotics

These are sometimes added in feeds for medicinal purposes. This should be done only on your vet's direction.

7.4 Preparing food

The way in which food is fed to the horse is an important factor which is often not taken into consideration when feeding regimes are being devised. Horse feeds are expensive and they should be stored and prepared correctly to prevent wastage and to allow maximum utilization.

Feeding hay

There are a number of ways in which hay can be fed. These include:

Hay mangers

These have the same benefits as feeding hay loose on the ground, except they are less wasteful. However, they are not a good idea as they can be difficult to clean out, and it is easy for a horse to pull the contents out on to the floor. Also, the hay spores are trapped and horses can breathe them in easily.

Loose on the ground

This is a natural way for the horse to eat as it imitates how it would eat in the wild. It also saves you time, is less labour intensive than filling a haynet (see opposite), and is safer for the horse as no haynets or racks are used.

However, this method does have some disadvantages. It can become untidy and wasteful as hay could be trampled into bedding or the ground. The horse may urinate and/or defecate on it. It may be difficult and awkward to present soaked hay to the horse in this manner, and it is harder to weigh.

The hay should be shaken before feeding and weighed by placing the loose hay in a sack. This also makes transporting the hay across the yard less wasteful and keeps the yard tidy.

In a haynet

Haynets are economical as they help prevent wastage and make it easier for hay to be weighed and soaked. They have the benefit of encouraging a horse to eat more slowly, especially if the hay is presented in a small-holed net, thus helping to prevent boredom. The nets can be prepared in advance, ready to give to a horse at a later time.

However, this does make feeding hay more labour intensive, and it is important to ensure the net is tied up correctly to prevent a horse trapping a leg or it falling down when tugged. Tying the net in this manner (as shown opposite) creates an unnatural eating position for the horse, with the danger of dust and particles getting into the eyes.

Hay should be shaken, placed in a haynet and weighed. Haynets make carrying the hay easier; they should always be tied up high enough to prevent the horse trapping a leg. Bear in mind that once the hay has been eaten, the net will hang lower to the ground than it did when full. Hence it should be tied as high as possible and secured with a quick-release knot.

In a hayrack

Hayracks tend to be attached high up on the wall. There is a possibility of hayseeds entering the horse's eyes; therefore they should be placed at an appropriate height. A hayrack can also be a potential hazard in a box.

Soaking hay

Soaked hay is fed to horses that have an allergic cough, but it should always be weighed before soaking. The hay should be put into a haynet and then soaked in water for up to ten minutes. It should then be hung up to drip dry, but not dried out

Mould spores

Some horses are allergic to the mould spores that are present in chaffs, hay and straw. These are a danger to particular horses, not because they are eaten but because they are inhaled. Horses and ponies bedded on mouldy material are at risk of inhaling more spores than their respiratory system can manage. If a horse is continually bedded on mouldy material, the spores will eventually reach the bottom of the airways, and although a healthy animal should be able to recover, in an allergy-prone horse a disease state is stimulated.

It is advised that allergic horses should be fed soaked hay, as this prevents the spores entering their airways. Instead, the spores are chewed with the hay and swallowed rather than entering the lungs. Veterinary advice should be sought for a horse that has an allergy to the spores in hay and straw.

completely, before being fed to the horse. Hay should never be soaked for longer than a maximum of 30 minutes, as valuable soluble nutrients will be lost to the water.

Soaking sugar beet

Sugar beet must *always* be soaked in cold water before feeding.

Whereas the cubes require 24 hours of soaking before they are fed, shredded pulp needs 12 hours of soaking. Sufficient water should be used to make the sugar beet soft but not too watery.

If they are not adequately soaked, the cubes or shreds could swell in the horse's stomach and

even cause an impaction and/or colic and choking.

In hot weather, sugar beet should be kept in a cool place, as heat will cause it to ferment. Fermentation will also occur if the sugar beet is left soaked for too long: hence a new supply should be soaked each day.

Tying up a haynet

1 Start off by putting the string through the haynet ring.

2 Next, pull the haynet up as high as possible to touch the ring.

3 Put the string through the bottom of the net. Pull it as tight as possible.

4 Use a quick-release knot round the string to make the net firm.

5 Put the end of the string through the quick-release knot.

6 Lastly, turn the knot towards the wall of the box.

■ Barley mash is prepared in the same manner as a bran mash, except the boiling water is poured on to the flaked barley or, as an alternative, cooked barley can be fed when cooled.

Cooking barley or oats

Barley or oats can be boiled in a large pan. Careful monitoring of the water needs to be taken into consideration as not enough can lead to evaporation, a burnt pan and spoilt feed, while too much can cause loss of goodness.

Whole barley will need between three and four hours of steady simmering, whereas oats will take approximately one-and-a-half to two hours, as their husks are softer, reducing the cooking time. Check they are cooked properly by pressing the grain between finger and thumb: they should feel soft and most of the water should have been absorbed.

Making oatmeal gruel

Approximately two handfuls of oatmeal should be placed in a bucket. Add boiling water while stirring, then leave to cool before feeding.

Cooking linseed

It is important to destroy the enzyme linase before the linseed has time to release hydrocyanic acid. You can achieve this by placing the linseed in boiling water. Always ensure enough water is used, as, when cooled, the linseed will turn to jelly.

Once the water has come to a boil, reduce the heat and then simmer the seeds for four to six hours. The cooked seeds and jelly are added to the feed when they have cooled down, or they can be added warm as a liquid to make a linseed mash.

Mashes

The most traditional form of mash is a bran mash, but barley, linseed, dried grass cubes or sugar beet can also be used. Contrary to previous thinking, bran mashes appear to have few benefits for the horse. They were once fed to horses that had completed a strenuous day's exercise or had a rest day, but they are now considered somewhat problematic, as they are not a balanced food. Occasionally feeding bran mashes means that sudden changes are made to a horse's diet, and thus the food is not utilized and digested properly and therefore will be wasted.

ABOVE: When you are feeding your horse a carrot, you should always cut it in half lengthways in order to avoid the hazard of choking.

■ A bran mash usually takes about 20 minutes to prepare. Boiling water is poured onto the bran until the texture is of a crumbly consistency, but not wet. The mash should then be covered and left until it is cool enough to feed to the horse.
■ A linseed mash is prepared in exactly the same way, except that the water from cooked linseed is used instead of boiling water.

7.5 Storing and equipment

It is vitally important to ensure that you are scrupulous at all times about cleanliness and stable hygiene. Many horses are very fussy about their food and they can be put off easily, so don't give them an excuse with poor hygiene.

Storage

When you are in the process of planning and organizing your feed room, you need to think about how you will store the feed as well as some basic hygiene considerations. All types of feed can deteriorate if they are stored in poor conditions. Ideally, feed should be stored:

- At a low temperature.
- Where there is minimal or no temperature variation.
- Where there is low humidity.
- Where there is good ventilation.
- In a closed container where direct sunlight cannot reach it.
- It should be adequately protected from infestation by rats, mice, birds, insects and mites.

A good quality container will prove cost-effective in the long run by reducing the amount of food that is wasted from being kept in poor conditions. Metal bins and plastic dustbins make good food containers.

Storing vacuum-packed forage

It is important that vacuum-packed bags are not punctured, as they must stay airtight until they are to be used. Vacuum-packed forage must be kept safely away from rodents, which may chew the plastic, as well as sunlight, and any sharp edges that may puncture the bags.

Storing hay

All hay will deteriorate over time, but the provision of good storage conditions will keep it edible for a longer period. It is important to protect hay from the weather, especially damp, to provide good ventilation, and keep it vermin-proof.

Storing salt

Salt should always be kept in airtight containers as it will absorb moisture from the atmosphere. Salt corrodes metal, and hence it should never be placed in contact with air.

Feed containers

These can be feed pans that are given straight to the horse and used when there is no manger. Alternatively, you can use buckets for transporting the food from the feed room into the manger in your horse's stable.

Buckets

These have the advantages of being cheap, easy to wash out and keep clean, and simple to store. However, it is more difficult to mix the feed in a bucket, and the bottom may be dirty which will, in turn, make the other buckets dirty if they are stacked.

A number of different types of bucket are available, and these include: the standard water bucket; the feed bucket that can be left hooked over the stable door; and the flat-backed bucket that can be attached to a ring in the stable.

Feed pans

These are often easier to use than a bucket when mixing a horse's food. The advantage is that all the food goes direct to the horse. However, they can become difficult to keep clean and will need to be removed from the stable, especially if the pan is made of metal or plastic.

Equipment

If you have the opportunity to design your own feed room or redesign an existing one, then you may wish to consider installing the following:

Water supply

It is very useful, where possible, to have a tap and drain both inside and outside the feed room, ideally with hot and cold water.

An electricity point

This should always have a circuit breaker and, for obvious reasons, it should be kept well away from the water supply.

Cupboards

These are ideal for keeping things out of reach of small children, and for locking away medicines and any dangerous items.

Scales

These are essential for weighing your horse's rations. They need to be large enough to hold a scoop of horse feed, so general household scales are usually not adequate for this job.

7.6 Planning a special diet

Like humans, horses come in differing shapes and sizes, and their energy expenditure and workloads will vary. In order to maintain good condition and a fit and healthy lifestyle, each individual horse's needs must be taken into consideration.

Devising a feeding regime

Feeding a horse can be extremely complicated. Your first objective when devising any feeding regime is to work out a maintenance ration depending on the horse's size, age, type and the time of year. The maintenance ration is how much food is needed to keep a horse that is not in work in good condition. You then need to work out how much energy ration the horse will need, whether it's for work or growth. Next, decide what concentrates to feed the horse, taking into account their energy and protein value.

Factors to consider

There are a number of factors that must be taken into consideration when feeding a horse. These include:

Size and type

Native type horses and ponies will generally tend to require less hard food than warmblooded types.

Age

Young, growing horses that are in work may need hard food to provide extra carbohydrates and protein which are utilized during exercise. Old horses may require extra rations in order to help them deal with the effects that cold weather conditions may have on them. Food that is easily digestible and masticated should be available for older horses.

Condition and health

Condition scoring (see page 250) is essential for assessing the overall condition of the horse and to assist in devising a suitable diet.

Height and weight

The height and weight of your horse can provide a guide to feeding him, although this is not an accurate method of determining the correct regime. The easiest way of estimating a horse's weight is to use a specially calculated equine weigh tape, which is available from most feed stores and tack shops. Weigh bridges are the most accurate method for weighing horses. However, these are only available at some veterinary practices and yards.

Weather

As food is used to maintain the horse's body temperature, weather conditions must be taken into consideration when you are deciding upon a feed ration. If the weather is cold, horses will need more food to help maintain the extra heat. (This is something you may wish to bear in mind, especially if you are having your horse clipped.) It is the risk of losing body fat in cold weather that makes winter feeding very important for most horses.

Economy

The cost of buying food should be taken in to consideration. Do not fall into the trap of persuading yourself that cheaper food is the better option; feeding poor quality food is a false economy as it will be harder to keep the horse in good condition.

Availability of foodstuffs

Where and when possible, enough forage, such as hay, should be bought and stored. Forage can often prove to be in short supply towards the end of the winter.

Temperament

It is often difficult to feed excitable horses enough hard food for the work they carry out without increasing their excitability. These horses often tend to be better on plenty of roughage and a feed that does not contain too much cereal.

Work and circumstances

■ Provided that the grass is of good quality and quantity, horses and ponies living out without doing any work should need no additional feed. In the spring and summer months, grass is usually of high nutritional value, but while horses may not require extra food, they may need restricted grazing.

■ During the winter months, the grass is of lower nutritional value, and therefore horses living out, without doing any work, may need supplementary food to keep their condition. You must always monitor their weight very carefully: long winter coats and rugs often hide sticking-out ribs.

■ If the horse is regularly exercised strenuously, do not be tempted to over-feed him in an attempt to create fitness, as this will not work.

■ For a one-horse owner whose horse is not going to do anything too strenuous, it is recommended that you choose to feed your horse a reputable manufacturer's compound feed, either in the form of a mix or cubes. This will ensure that all the required vitamins and minerals your horse needs are included in the one feed. The majority of the horse's diet should consist of roughage.

BELOW: *If your horse lives out and the grass is of good quality, he may not need any additional feed in the spring and summer months.*

7.7 Water

Water is a crucial factor in horses' lives. It plays an essential role in all the horse's bodily functions; every cellular activity and all the bodily fluids require water. It is thought that although a horse could survive for weeks without food, it would probably die after about six days of having no water. So it is essential that your horse has constant access to water.

Water purity

It is extremely important to ensure that the water provided for horses is always clean and fresh. If the water is contaminated in any way the horse may reject it. Soiled stables, droppings, feed, roughage and simply having the water standing around for too long can all cause contamination.

The water-storage tank for the yard should be covered to protect

LEFT: *Horses living out at grass should always have access to a clean, fresh supply of water.*

it from dust particles and vermin. It should be regularly checked to ensure there is a fresh, clean supply of water readily available for daily use. If your horse is particularly choosy about what he drinks or if he plays with the water, it may be a sign that it is contaminated.

Systems for stables

Automatic water bowls

These provide a good constant supply of water and save time and labour, as, unlike buckets, they do not need filling. However, it can be difficult to

monitor how much water the horse is drinking. They can be hard to clean; may freeze in cold weather; and have the potential to cause physical injury to the horse. Automatic water bowls should always be large enough for horses to place their muzzles in them. They should be cleaned out frequently.

Buckets

Buckets enable easy monitoring of how much water the horse has drunk. However, they do not provide a constant supply, so the horse may be without water at times. They can be easily knocked over; are labour intensive; and are a potential hazard to the horse, i.e. its foot may become trapped in the bucket or the handle.

Buckets should be sited in a corner of the stable well away from the door. They can be placed in a rubber tyre to prevent them being knocked over. They should be made of a heavy-duty material, cleaned out twice a day and regularly topped up with fresh, clean water.

Dehydration

Dehydration is when a horse does not have enough fluid in its body to sustain normal physiological conditions. This occurs when more salts and water are lost from the horse's body than are taken in.

Causes of dehydration

- Fast, energetic work
- Sweating
- Heat exhaustion
- Urinating excessively
- Diarrhoea
- Haemorrhage
- Lack of available water

Dehydration can cause death in the most severe cases. However, it can also lead to a number of other very serious problems including: azoturia, colic, laminitis, muscle damage, reduction in kidney function, reduced performance and coma.

Signs of dehydration

Keep a watchful eye out for the tell-tale signs of dehydration, which are listed below.

- Skin losing pliability: this can be tested for with the 'pinch test'. Hold a pinch of skin between the thumb and finger. The horse is dehydrated to

some extent if the skin does not return to normal within five seconds.

- Thumps: this happens when the diaphragm and heart beat rhythm synchronize. The flanks of the horse can be seen or even heard to be in the same rhythm as the heart beat. You should seek veterinary advice immediately.
- Other signs include the following:
- Muscles quivering
- Listlessness
- Thick, patchy sweat
- Loss of normal colour from the membranes of gums and eyes
- Small pulse

Chapter 8

Exercising your horse

••••••••••••••••••••••••••••••

Horses and ponies are complex animals. To keep them healthy is never going to be easy but, like humans, if they are well-cared for, fed correctly and they receive regular, appropriate exercise, they will stand a good chance of living a long and healthy life. Horses are individuals and, as such, they require tailored feeding, care and exercise regimes. It is only by getting to know your horse that you will be able to design a custom-made programme for him that will suit his lifestyle and needs – this takes time and patience.

8.1 Keeping your horse fit

Like humans, horses and ponies sometimes suffer from a health complaint – a cold, an allergy, a sore foot or aches and pains. One of the best ways to keep your horse healthy is by giving him the right type and amount of food (see page 168). If he is healthy from the inside, then he stands a very good chance of being healthy on the outside as well.

Water and diet

Water is essential for horses and ponies – they must have access to clean, fresh water 24 hours a day, whether they are stabled or kept out at grass. They become dehydrated more easily than you think so if your horse is working hard, sweating a lot or the weather is hot, you must ensure a constant supply of fresh water.

One of the best ways to make sure that your horse will stay healthy is to give him succulents, such as apples, carrots or grass. 'Doctor Green' or, quite simply, grass is the optimum way of keeping your horse's digestive system working well, but he can have too much of a good thing!

If the grass is too rich or too lush or the horse is kept out on the paddock for too long when he is not used to it, he could become ill and contract health problems such as laminitis or colic (see pages 274 and 276).

Avoiding lameness

Depending on whether your horse or pony is living out in a paddock, either by himself or in the company of other horses, or whether he is kept in a stable, he can still become ill or lame.

For example, if your horse is living outside in a paddock with a number of other horses or ponies, he could be kicked and lamed by another horse. Segregating the mares and geldings into separate fields is a way of reducing the possibility of them injuring one another.

RIGHT: *Your horse will enjoy being turned out in a field or paddock for a few hours every day if he is usually stabled at night.*

BELOW: *In cold weather, or rainy or windy conditions, horses that are turned out should wear waterproof rugs to keep them warm.*

A safe environment

If you keep your horse at grass, he must be visited and checked ideally twice a day to ensure he is fit and well and that no debris, such as cans, wire, bottles or plastic, has been thrown into the paddock. Poisonous plants, like deadly nightshade and ragwort, (see page 86), *must* be destroyed correctly and safely. All fencing and gates must also be checked for security and safety (see page 78).

ABOVE: *Regular visits from the farrier are critical if you want to keep your horse sound and healthy. Ideally, a horse should be shod once every four to six weeks, especially if he is doing a lot of road work or competing.*

Providing shelter

Adequate shelter from the elements is very important for your horse, both in the winter (for protection against wind, rain and snow) and summer (for protection against sun and flies). If you do not have a man-made field shelter, then a stout hedge, bank or tree will be adequate.

Grass management

Caring for the grass in your horse's field or paddock is very important for his continued wellbeing, and you should check whether your soil and grass are of good quality and what action may be required to improve them (see page 72).

Try to pick up any droppings in the paddock daily; if you have a number of horses in the paddock and there are too many droppings to pick up manually, you can either chain harrow the land or you can use a paddock sweeper pulled by a tractor. If you diligently keep the paddock clear of droppings, you will minimize the risk of worm damage to your horses and ponies. They should be wormed regularly, whether they are grass or stable-kept (see page 252).

Stable safety

Even if your horse is stable-kept, he can still get into trouble. You must check on a daily basis that there are no sharp projections in or around the stable, such as splinters or nails.

Make sure that the stable door is safe and secure – loose bolts are extremely attractive to some horses which will play with them and learn very quickly how to escape. You must also ensure that the windows, electric light fittings and wires are covered and that they are well out of reach and inaccessible to horses.

Horses do enjoy something to play with – apart from us – and a plastic football or a whole swede or turnip which is left on the stable floor will occupy them for ages.

Ensure your water supply is safe and secure so your horse cannot play with that as well. Any fittings, such as tie rings and feed bowls, must also be checked regularly. If they are loose, your horse will tamper with them.

Tack and equipment

These need to be regularly inspected both for safety reasons and general wear and tear. Whether it is a halter, a headcollar or a saddle and bridle, it must fit your horse or pony properly (see page 95). A horse that is in pain will never work efficiently, and can lose weight and become ill very quickly.

If you notice any new rub marks appearing on your horse's head, back, withers or girth area, immediately stop using that piece of equipment and ask for advice regarding its fit (see page 95).

The bit you choose for your horse must also fit correctly – if his mouth is uncomfortable, he might not like being tacked up, let alone ridden. If you use tack and equipment that is ill-fitting, you run the risk of causing injuries to your horse, which might have long-lasting physical effects.

Horses and ponies do change their shape, depending on their level of fitness, general condition, age and the amount of work that they do. There are many expert saddlers and riding trainers who will be able to give you sound advice on the correct fitting of tack (see page 95).

Healthy hooves

'No foot, no horse' is a very sensible and true saying, and the farrier is essential in ensuring that your horse remains as healthy as possible. Whether he is working on the roads or competing, he will need to wear shoes and must be regularly shod (possibly every four to six weeks).

However, if he is in light work, his feet are in good condition and the farrier trims and cares for them correctly and regularly, he may not need to wear shoes at all. Some horses only wear shoes in front.

Ask your farrier

If you are unsure as to the sort of treatment your horse needs, why not ask your farrier for advice? The care of your horse's feet, whether they are shod or unshod, is critical to his wellbeing and it is not worth taking any short-cuts. You may also have to look at your horse's diet as this can influence the condition of the feet.

Vaccinations and teeth

Injections and care of the teeth also require attention and thought. Horses will need flu and tetanus injections and your vet will help you devise a programme (see page 257). If you are competing or visiting different riding centres, you may have to show proof that your horse is up to date with his injections. The vet will also check your horse's teeth to make sure there are no irregularities, such as sharp edges, which will prevent him from chewing his food properly or accepting the bit happily.

8.2 Fitness counts

Riding will exercise you as well as your horse. In order for you to ride effectively and ensure you do not injure yourself, it is advisable to get fit. Simple exercises, such as some brisk walking, stretches and arm circling, will help riders to use the necessary riding muscles.

A fit rider

To be fair to your horse or pony, you should endeavour to be fit enough to carry out the riding tasks you have set yourself without either becoming stressed physically or stressing the horse. If you are a recreational rider who likes to hack out once a week from a local riding school, your level of fitness will not need to be as high as someone who is riding their own horse in competition. Before you mount, it is advisable to embark upon a few simple stretching exercises. During lessons, your riding instructor will explain how important it is to make the horse supple and relaxed before asking more from him, so it is equally important for you to be supple.

Whatever riding you do, you must be sensible! Depending upon your age, expertise and fitness level, you should be careful not to overdo the exercise – check with your doctor if you are unsure as to whether you should start exercising. Riding is a unique sport, in so far as you use riding-specific muscles that can only be exercised through the act of riding itself. Wind-fitness can be improved by cycling or jogging or work on the treadmill but make sure you seek medical advice before embarking upon any fitness programme!

A fit horse

Your horse is an athlete and he needs to be conditioned to enable him to undertake the required work. Several methods are available to you when you are getting your horse fit. However, whichever your chosen method, there are some basic questions that you need to consider:

- What is the job or discipline that your horse is being prepared for?
- How fit does your horse have to be in order to carry out the work that is required of him?
- How experienced and how fit are you, the rider?
- What food is the horse receiving?
- How long has the horse been off work (if applicable)?
- How long does the procedure of getting the horse fit need to take?

Getting fit

To get a horse fit can take up to three to four months if he is an eventer that has been off work for, say, six months and is being brought back to competition fitness. Conversely, if your horse is only being hacked out once or twice a week and you are not very fit yourself, then it would be foolhardy to get the horse so fit he might buck you off as soon as you put your foot in the stirrup.

Like humans, horses will need a progressive fittening programme that suits them and their rider. You must take care as you can cause long-lasting damage to a horse's wind and limbs if the fitness programme you adopt is too intense, too quick and poorly planned. The programme must be progressive and purposeful.

Work versus exercise

Horses and riders can both manage the work that is asked of them if they undertake regular exercise. First, let us examine the important question of work versus exercise.

Work

This is where the horse is being asked to use himself both physically and mentally (ridden or lunged) so that all parts of his body are being tested and utilized. If he is allowed to perform above the bit, with a hollow back, hocks out behind him and not going forward, then he is not working, but if he is asked to use his whole body and mind, he is working.

Exercise

This is when the horse is ridden or lunged to the extent that he is using sufficient muscles to carry out the task that is asked of him. For example, if you are ill and cannot get to the yard to ride your horse, then a yard employee or friend could ride him out for 45 minutes or lunge him for half an hour so that he is not just standing in his stable all day.

Stabled horses and ponies should not be allowed to stand in the stable for 24 hours a day without going out for some exercise, particularly if they are receiving full feed. Much physical

and psychological damage can be caused to horses if they are fed and not adequately exercised.

Even if they are turned out for a few hours, they can at least stretch their legs, but if they are not being ridden or lunged then their feed ration should be reduced accordingly.

'Being ridden' can range from the horse being hacked out on a long rein at walk for 30 minutes to being worked on the bit in preparation for a dressage competition. The amount of muscle and mental usage for horse and rider would, of course, be more in the latter example.

Horses are essentially domesticated animals and they rely entirely on us, their human owners and carers, so even if they live outside in a paddock,

ABOVE: *You should make the time to exercise your horse every day if possible. You will both enjoy it and your fitness levels will improve.*

they will still require attention from their human owner at some point. Thus exercise is an essential element in the continued wellbeing and health of the horse or pony.

8.3 Warming up

Warming up, like cooling down (opposite) is often neglected by riders, usually from a lack of knowledge rather than choice. Rider and horse fitness and suppleness are important to enable the partnership to carry out the required work, but you also need to know how to warm up and cool down.

The 'warming-up' process for the horse need not be complicated; just imagine if you had got out of bed in the morning and immediately had to go for a fast run on the local roads. You were not given the opportunity to wake up or warm up sufficiently and your muscles felt stiff and tight.

This is how a horse feels if he is tacked up and immediately mounted and asked to perform some dressage movements or to start jumping without any warming up.

The horse can be muscle-damaged if he is insufficiently warmed up and prepared for the work that you are asking him to perform. Warming up a horse in preparation for work could range from the rider walking him on a long rein for about 10 minutes before taking a contact and 'connecting' the horse, to walking for 15 minutes and then trotting and cantering in a round, deep outline for another 15 minutes in order to ensure that the horse is supple and using his back and hindlegs correctly before 'connecting' him.

RIGHT: *If you have easy access to an outdoor arena, you can warm up your horse by walking him, then trotting and cantering, in preparation for working him. Alternatively, do this in his paddock or near the stable.*

How to warm up

You might take a light seat or at least rise to the trot more softly until you can feel the horse's back 'swinging' underneath you. Once the horse feels ready to work, he will be swinging through his back and more supple.

Every horse is different and needs individual attention and work. What might suit one horse will upset and worry another. Depending on his age, temperament, physique, the work he is about to undertake and the standard of his rider, he will need more or less warming up, so always take these factors into account.

If you are preparing to enter the show jumping phase of a one-day horse trial, for example, you should know your horse's temperament and ability. He may need 30 minutes' preparation time, including some working on the flat to loosen him up, followed by a spell of trotting into and over some low fences. This could be followed by cantering into a few fences of varying heights so that you and your horse 'get your eye in'.

However, if you are preparing for a local, unaffiliated dressage competition and your horse has a 'laid-back' character, he might only need 20 minutes' warming up before entering the arena.

There are no set rules for warming up a horse, but if your horse is new to you, you must explore different regimes before settling on the most suitable one for you both. Whatever you choose, you should continue with it as a horse likes a routine and he will feel comfortable knowing what is expected of him.

8.4 Cooling down

Cooling down, or warming down as it is sometimes referred to, is another important aspect of training horses and riders. Cooling down a horse constructively helps to prolong his life.

After a session of hard work, such as fast cantering, the horse may be 'blowing' – breathing very hard and trying to pull as much oxygen into his lungs as possible. It would be irresponsible not to cool the horse down correctly – not doing so could damage his health. A horse needs time to 'unwind' and calm down.

How to cool down

The best method is just to walk your horse round quietly until his breathing starts to return to normal. Similarly, if a dressage horse has just finished a training session, then it would be inadvisable to stop work, dismount and put him in the stable. If he has been working hard, using his muscles efficiently, he needs to be encouraged to stretch his head and neck down at a steady trot and finally walk, so his top-line muscles relax. This process might take 10–15 minutes in total. You might take a lighter seat to allow the back of the horse more freedom whilst stretching.

After hunting, when hacking home, you are told to loosen the girth a hole to allow air to circulate between it and the horse; this is a nice idea but do not loosen the girth too much or the saddle could become loose and might slip, causing a nasty fall. After a hard day's hunting, allow the horse to walk home on a long rein and do not sit heavily on his back – stay upright and light in the saddle. When you get near to home and you know your horse, perhaps dismount and lead him the last few hundred yards.

After you have jumped a round in a competition, never jump the last fence and leave the ring; this teaches your horse a very bad habit and could be dangerous. Once the last fence is cleared, land in canter and turn away past the exit, come back to walk and quietly leave the ring. Allow the horse a long rein and let him stretch.

Take your time

Rushing the horse during all these processes is a mistake. He will benefit if you take your time and allow him to warm up and cool down correctly. Make the warming-up and cooling-down processes the same whether you are at home or at a competition; horses like routine and repetition.

BELOW: *To cool your horse down after vigorous exercise, walk him quietly until his breathing returns to normal.*

8.5 Schooling areas

We have created a variety of ways whereby horses can be worked or exercised, such as horse walkers, treadmills, playpens and gallops. Sometimes, there might be a valid reason why a horse cannot be ridden or lunged so he needs to be exercised in an alternative way.

Horse walkers

These are an effective way of warming up and cooling down horses and there are many good ones currently on the market. Criticisms, such as they are 'monotonous', 'boring' and 'unrealistic', have been levelled at them, but they do fulfil a need and horses can be walked in both directions, at a variety of speeds, for however long you require.

Walkers are safe but you should always keep an eye on the machine when horses are loaded in case a problem arises. The footing must be secure, not slippery when it is wet, non-abrasive and easily cleaned. Sometimes sand, rubber matting, vaseline-covered materials, concrete and wood chips are used, or even a mixture of these. That said, walkers are very expensive and are not a viable option for the ordinary horse owner. Treadmills should never be used as the sole means of a horse's daily exercise.

Treadmills

High-speed treadmills can be very useful for working, as well as for exercising, horses. Usually they are employed for a specific purpose, such as to test a horse's gait or wind, for rehabilitation or improving fitness.

However, they are specialist items of equipment and can be expensive.

Water treadmills are also very useful for fittening horses as well as helping them to recover from limb or back injuries.

Playpens

These are useful when turn out is restricted due to poor soil. Horses can be left in the pen for a period of time to 'let off steam' if they have not been able to go out in the paddock or have been unwell and need a restricted area to move around in. The footing needs to be secure, yet giving. Sand, wood chips, vaseline-covered sand and rubber strips can be used as surfaces. It is advisable to watch the horse whilst he is turned out in the pen.

Paddocks and arenas

Many riders work their horses in a riding arena or paddock. Some riders have access to an all-weather, outdoor riding surface nowadays. This can vary in size and surface depending on your finances. Some riders are lucky enough to have access to an indoor school as well. With the competition season running all year, riders require an area to work their horses all the time.

Exercising in a paddock

The paddock or field is still a good place to ride but you are limited by the weather and ground conditions. In the UK, from the end of October to mid-April, a paddock is often too wet and muddy, and from the beginning of May until the start of October, the ground is often too hard.

Exercising in an arena

An all-weather, outdoor or indoor riding arena is the ideal solution for those riders who need to work their horses all the year round. There are many reputable arena construction companies that advertise in national horse magazines or on the internet. The best way for you to check as to whether a particular arena will suit your purposes is to go and visit one that has been constructed by a specific company. By doing this you will be able to discuss the efficiency, drainage, surfaces and durability of the arena with the owner.

Choosing an arena

The factors you need take to take into consideration when you are deciding upon an arena are as follows:
- Your budget
- The siting of the arena
- The size of the arena
- The drainage
- The surface material
- Maintenance.

Drainage and maintenance

These are important because if the arena drains well during heavy rain, the surface should remain in good condition; if the surface is not looked after correctly – if droppings are not

ABOVE: *An outdoor arena is a great way to exercise and school your horse and keep him fit, especially if you compete. It can be used all the year round.*

picked up and it is rarely levelled – it will rapidly deteriorate.

During the cold winter months, depending upon the surface, freezing can be a problem. A sand surface tends to freeze and will need attention. Salt can be added to lower the freezing point so that the sand will not freeze

so readily. Also, particles of rubber or plastic can be mixed with the sand, which will help it to break up more easily when it is ridden on.

During very dry spells, surfaces can become dusty, which can be a health hazard for both horses and humans. An efficient sprinkler system is a welcome addition to any arena but it can be quite expensive and, like the surface, it will need attention and maintenance.

It is worth visiting different arenas and looking at their systems before

making a decision. All-weather outdoor arenas are expensive to install and it is essential that they are well cared for and are not entered into lightly.

Indoor schools

If you want to improve your riding and school your horse, you could hire your local riding school's indoor arena once a week or book a lesson with an instructor there. An indoor school at home is an expensive venture and not very practical.

8.6 Working your horse

Whether your horse is kept at grass or in a stable, it is essential that he undertakes some form of regular exercise. Achieving the correct balance between feeding, exercise and work will determine whether he is healthy and successful.

Grass-kept horses

A grass-kept horse, walking round his paddock all day searching for the best grazing, will be exercising himself on a daily basis – particularly if his paddock is hilly. Horses are very selective feeders and they will wander the paddock looking for the best tasting grass. Walking is an excellent form of exercise, and if the paddock is large, has sparse grass and is shared with a number of horses, then the exercise your horse will be getting may be considerable.

If you are planning on working your horse off grass, you will have to be careful how you plan his regime. If he is permanently out at grass, it would be more difficult to keep him competition fit. However, if you 'mix and match' his grazing, feed and exercise regimes, i.e. he is out at night and in during the day, it is easier to keep him competition fit.

You can use a horse or pony kept at grass for light to medium work and hacking, but if you want him to perform hard work then you must give him regular exercise and also increased concentrates. In winter, he needs to be stabled at night and turned out by day (ground permitting).

Stabled horses

A stabled horse, which is competing regularly at one-day events and receiving feed and hay rations that are applicable to his height, weight, temperament, breed and work, will need to be kept much fitter than one that is unaffiliated show jumping every other weekend. It could be physically and mentally damaging to your horse if his work/exercise/feed regime is not kept well-balanced.

If he is worked hard whilst he is unfit or is being over-fed and under-worked, not only could he be injured but you could be in danger, too. If you are unsure as how to much work and feed your horse requires, ask your vet or riding instuctor for advice.

RIGHT: *If you compete with your horse, you must ensure that you balance his work, exercise and dietary regimes.*

BELOW: *If you want your horse to work hard, exercise him regularly.*

8.7 Improve your riding

One of the first questions you must ask yourself is: 'What type of riding do I want to do?' The answer to this question will determine the training you undertake, the fitness you require, the tack your horse wears, your riding clothing, the type of horse you select and the yard you go to for training.

If you are planning on hacking-out once a week, at a walk interspersed by several trot sessions, your level of fitness and that of your horse will be significantly less than if you were one-day horse trialling once a week.

Whatever facet of riding you pursue, you will need to be relatively fit so as not to incur physical injuries, and your horse must be suitable for the chosen activity. Rider fitness is very important, as we have seen, and must never be understated or overlooked.

Improving your ability

There are several options available to riders who wish to improve their ability. Some attend regular lessons at a local riding school. The best way to ensure that you select the most suitable school for you is to go and visit the centre, talk to the staff, watch some lessons and look at the facilities, including the horses and the way they are cared for. If you own a horse, you might wish to take him to a riding centre for lessons as opposed to riding their horses.

Finding an instructor

Word of mouth is an excellent way for you to find the right instructor or teacher. The instructor might be freelance whereby they can visit your yard and teach you at home. Discuss with your instructor exactly what your aims and objectives are for having lessons. Make sure you listen to him or her – let them assess your riding ability and discuss a training plan with you, which will give you an idea of where you will be going in future lessons. You might arrive for a lesson wanting to show jump but if your instructor is competent and assesses you accordingly, then decides to work on the flat, accept this decision and discuss the reasons for it.

There are many excellent qualified and unqualified instructors available. It is essential to check that your instructor does hold the qualification they claim, is covered by public liability insurance, is first-aid qualified and, if teaching children, has attended a child protection course.

Your horse is the best teacher

Many novice or less experienced riders frighten themselves by buying or riding young, inexperienced and often nervous horses, so it is strongly recommended that an older, more experienced horse is sought. When you have acquired more experience and competence, then with the advice and support of the instructor, you can start looking for a more challenging horse to ride or purchase.

Summary

There are many ways in which your riding can be improved – with an instructor giving you their individual attention, by being lunged, in private lessons, class lessons or lead-rein lessons. The key to success is to find a horse that suits your needs and to be trained by an instructor who will fulfil your personal requirements.

OPPOSITE: *You can improve your riding by taking lessons from a qualified instructor and then by putting into practice what you have learnt.*

Praising your horse

One aspect of riding that is often forgotten is praising the horse; riders are quick to reprimand their horse for being disobedient but they should be just as quick to praise him when he is good. A quiet word or a pat on the neck makes a big difference to all horses – you can feel the horse relax if he is tense. If you complete a cross-country round or finish an exhilarating ride through the woods and the horse has behaved well, do not forget to pat him as a reward – he will appreciate it.

Praising your horse when he has behaved in the way you wanted him to is vital if he is to understand what is required of him. It helps to strengthen the bond between the two of you and will also increase your trust in one another so that you work well together.

Chapter 9

Transporting your horse

....

Having your own horse transport means you can go where you want when you want and have the means to move your horse in an emergency, like getting him to a vet. However, the decision to buy and run your own transport is not one to be taken lightly. It will involve owning a heavy vehicle which, in an accident, has the potential to do considerable damage, putting your life at risk and the lives of your horse and other road users. Therefore it is essential that you take advice and consider carefully how you are going to transport your horse.

9.1 Licences

• •

The licence categories are mainly based on the maximum authorized mass (MAM) of the vehicles, which is the maximum laden weight laid down by the manufacturer so this is the weight of the trailer, lorry or car and what it is built to carry safely. It is also known as gross vehicle weight and is shown on chassis plates of vehicles, although some very old trailers may not have a chassis plate. Weights referred to here are MAM unless otherwise stated.

What can you drive?

In the UK, if you passed your driving test before 1 January 1997 you are entitled to drive a vehicle weighing up to 7.5 tonnes, with a trailer weighing up to 750 kg, giving a total weight of 8.25 tonnes. The towing vehicle must be capable of towing the MAM weight of the trailer.

However, if you passed your test after that date you may only drive vehicles up to 3.5 tonnes, having no more than eight passenger seats, with a trailer not exceeding 750 kg, giving a maximum weight of 4.25 tonnes. You may tow a larger trailer, providing the MAM of the trailer does not exceed the unladen weight of the vehicle, and the combined MAM does not exceed 3.5 tonnes. Almost all horse trailers fall outside these limits because they usually have a MAM of over 2 tonnes. You should note, too, that it is the trailer's MAM that matters and not its actual weight at the time.

Drivers who passed their test after 1 January 1997 need to sit a separate test in order to tow a trailer that exceeds these weight limitations. This is a B + E test. To drive a vehicle with a MAM of over 3.5 tonnes, additional tests must be taken, both theory and practical. This can be one of two tests, depending on your age:

■ If you are under 21 years of age, you can take the sub-Category C1, which is for medium-sized goods. The minimum age for this category is 18.
■ If you are over 21 years of age, you can take category C for large goods vehicles over 7.5 tonnes; this will give you entitlement to sub category C1.

If you wanted to tow a trailer with a vehicle in either of these categories, you would need to take an additional test C1+E or C+E. Taking C+E would automatically entitle you to drive vehicles in C1+E and B+E. The minimum age for C1+E or C+E is 21. There is no theory test for C1+E or C+E.

You may be considering buying, or using, a vehicle with automatic transmission, the pros and cons of which are covered elsewhere in this chapter (see page 214). However, be aware that if you take your B+E test in an automatic car, you will be restricted to B+E Automatic – hence you may only tow with an automatic. If you take your B+E test in a manual, you may drive either.

Before applying for provisional entitlement for either test, you will be required to have a D4 form which has been filled out by your doctor.

At the time of writing, you can drive a vehicle for which you hold provisional entitlement for as long as you are insured on the vehicle, are accompanied by someone who has held that class of licence for more than three years and is over 21 years of age, and you display L-plates to the front and rear of the vehicle. Before taking the C1 or C test, an LGV theory test needs to be passed.

The towing and minibus tests are based on the large goods vehicle test, and so they include reversing and braking exercises at a lorry driving test centre followed by an on-the-road driving test. For the B + E test, you will not be expected to carry out an emergency stop, reverse around a corner or reverse

Minibus tests

Vehicles with nine to sixteen seats are legally minibuses, and include the Land Rover Defender 110 Station Wagon, a capable and popular towing vehicle. To drive a minibus, the post–1997 driver needs to be at least 21 years old and will need to take the minibus driving test (category D1), followed by a D1+E if you want to tow a trailer over 750 kg. Even then, you will be restricted to trailers with a MAM less than the vehicle's unladen weight and a combined MAM not exceeding 12 tonnes. The trailer must not be used to carry passengers. This does not apply to any other Defender version or pre–1997 drivers.

park or turn in the road. You can find out more from your local Driving Standards Agency office or their website (see page 284). If you have to take a test, then seek professional tuition because lorry

ABOVE: *Make sure that you always close the top door before setting off.*

driving schools, many of which offer trailer courses, can teach you what you need to know for the test.

Warning

Finally, you should be aware that if you tow a trailer or drive a horsebox when your licence does not include these vehicle classes, you will face serious charges with heavy fines.

9.2 Horsebox or trailer?

If you are touring the country three-day eventing, then a lorry makes sense, but if you only go to the occasional local show it would not be an economical investment. A decent lorry costs more to buy than a trailer, needs much more expensive servicing, costs more to insure and must be taxed and given the equivalent of an annual MOT, which is generally called a plate. You also have to run a car for other journeys.

If you have to buy a suitable towcar to pull a trailer, it could work out as expensive as a lorry, but you will not have to run a second car. A trailer is cheaper both to insure and maintain, with DIY maintenance a practical proposition, and there is no trailer MOT, although regular servicing is essential. We shall focus on trailers because most amateur horse owners have them.

Horses' weights

Whatever transport you use, you must know how much your horse weighs in kilogrammes (the motor industry is metric). A vet's surgery can accurately weigh your horse for you, but weigh tapes, available from most saddlers and feed manufacturers, will give a good indication.

Alternatively, you can use the following simple calculation: (girth in cm, squared x length in cm) ÷ 8717 = weight in kilogrammes.

The horse's length is measured from the withers to the point where the tail joins the body. The average 16 hand riding horse weighs about 550 kg, but a shorter cob may weigh the same, so it is important that you have a good idea of what your horse weighs.

Breakdown cover

Ordinary car breakdown cover does not cover vehicles over 3.5 tonnes. The RAC, along with a number of other companies, will recover a trailer with horses aboard if the towing vehicle cannot be fixed. It is important to shop around and find a deal that suits your needs and budget, as a large number of different types of cover are available.

If you run a lorry it is highly advisable to join a specialist horsebox breakdown organization because even changing a wheel needs special equipment. If you travel long distances with a trailer, it may be worth joining these organizations because they give backup like getting the horses home or to overnight livery and providing vet services. The RAC allow towing vehicle drivers to add these services from ESS to their standard breakdown cover.

Horseboxes

If you are planning on having a lorry built from scratch, then a horsebox body may be put onto a new or used chassis, depending on your budget. If you go for a used chassis, check that the builder will renovate it. Some horseboxes are converted from lorries that already have box bodies but the bodywork is often not well insulated or thick enough to withstand horses

kicking. You must also ensure that the floor is strengthened because horses put their weight down through a small area, unlike most lorry cargos.

Only buy a lorry with living accommodation if you really need it because it adds to the original cost of the lorry and reduces its payload. Payload is the maximum weight that you can put in the lorry and is the difference between the lorry's kerb (empty) weight and MAM, so the more you add to the kerb weight the lower the payload. With smaller lorries, you should check that the payload is enough for the horses you want to carry plus people and everything you need to take with you.

BELOW: *If you have only one horse, a trailer is the best option and is more economical than a lorry.*

Choosing a trailer

Weight is important when choosing trailers and towing vehicles because you want the car to have the best chance of staying in charge. With this in mind you need to know the towing capacity of the towing vehicle and the MAM weight of the trailer that you wish to buy. Not only should the towing vehicle be capable of towing the MAM weight of the trailer but

Insurance and security

Car insurance normally provides third party cover only for a trailer while it is hitched to the insured car, but that means that the trailer is not covered for theft or damage to itself – you need to check this with your insurance company. To comprehensively cover the trailer you must either add an extension to the car policy or take out a separate trailer policy. The advantage of the latter is that it covers the trailer with other towing vehicles and is usually provided by equestrian insurers who better understand horsy problems.

Insurers normally demand that a security device is fitted when the trailer is parked. Most require a wheel clamp because there have been cases where thieves have pulled trailers with hitchlocks away from the owner's yard. Fit the clamp to a rear wheel because thieves can pull the trailer with the front wheels off the ground. Also think of making your trailer look different with your own artwork, roof-top postcodes or reflective stripes.

the laden weight of the trailer should ideally not exceed 85 per cent of the unladen weight of the towing vehicle.

All car manufacturers quote a maximum towing weight for their cars, but this is purely a maximum. It is based on the car's ability to pull away on a slope and is usually more than the car weighs – considerably more with off-roaders. However, when the trailer weighs more than the car, the tail can wag the dog.

The ideal trailer weight is no more than 85 per cent of the car's unladen weight, as long as it is less than the maximum towing weight. That is difficult to achieve with a trailer and two horses, which will weigh around 1850 kg in a lightweight trailer, meaning that only the heaviest off-roaders could maintain the 85 per cent rule, so give yourself as much leeway as possible and drive very carefully. With a single horse trailer, you can tow safely with some large cars, like the big Volvo estates, or a leisure off-roader like a Land

BELOW: *You must ensure that your towing vehicle is suitable for pulling the trailer, so be sure to check the maximum towing weight.*

one. Lift the mats to check the floor and prod any suspect areas with a screwdriver: if it is rotten, then the screwdriver will easily sink in. Check that the floor supports are also sound. If the trailer's floor has been replaced, seek evidence that it was done by a horse trailer specialist who should understand the stresses horses put on a floor.

Finally, you must check that everything works, that the tyres are in good condition, and ask what servicing has been done.

Choosing a towing vehicle

This means finding a suitable vehicle that is able to cope with the trailer's weight, as explained above. It also needs a maximum noseweight of at least 75 kg, which is the maximum downwards pressure that a trailer can put on the towball. If the noseweight is too high, it pushes the car's tail down and affects stability and handling.

Consider the torque

A good towing engine will have good flexibility at low engine speeds for pulling away and getting the outfit moving, so do make sure that you look at the torque figures that are featured in the brochures.

Torque is twisting or pulling power and for a towcar you will need lots at fairly low engine speeds. Thus for an engine that will develop, say, 130 bhp (brake horsepower) but 200 lb per ft of torque at 2500 rpm should tow better than a 200 bhp engine that will develop 150 lb per ft at 4500 rpm.

Rover Freelander or Honda CR-V, but always check the weights ratios.

Before you buy, ask others about their trailers and from whom they bought them. Look at how well finished trailers are: there should be no rough edges or projecting screw heads, and the materials and fittings should look substantial. Check also that the partitions and ramps are not too heavy for you.

When you have decided which trailer you like, see if you can hire or borrow one to test drive it, but make sure that you are insured.

If you buy a used one, check that it is not stolen or you risk losing the trailer and all you paid for it. Demand proof of ownership and be suspicious of vendors who have no paperwork. Note the trailer's chassis number on the chassis plate – you should not buy a trailer on which the plate is missing – and check it out on the Trailerwatch website (see page 284).

Some manufacturers register trailers with The Equipment Register and they display a 'TER' sticker with a phone number so you can ring them or visit their website (see page 284) to check the chassis number for a fee.

Floors, ramps and tyres

Horses suffer horrific injuries if they go through trailer floors and ramps, so do not buy a trailer with a suspect

ABOVE: *A side ramp will make unloading your horse much easier.*

Manual or automatic?

Which type of gearbox is best for you? Whichever you prefer, a manual gearbox should always have sensibly spaced ratios so that you do not find that, say, third gear is too busy but fourth gear is too high.

Whether you choose a towing vehicle which is fitted with a manual or an automatic gearbox is entirely up to you. Manuals are usually much cheaper and they will give the driver more control, although the modern automatics with their adaptive electronic control and manual touch changes have closed that gap.

As a general rule, it is much easier to tow smoothly with an automatic although some hunt between gear ratios in certain circumstances when towing. Automatics should change down readily on gentle throttle but they should not be too over-eager, and should kick down smoothly and instantly when you floor the throttle.

You should note that if you passed your test after 1 January 1997 in an automatic, your licence entitlement will be restricted if you take your B+E test in an automatic (see page 208).

Towing equipment

Towing vehicles that were registered after 1 August 1998 must only be fitted with towbars bearing an EU type approval label to prove it meets safety standards. Towbars may be fixed or detachable, with the latter often invisible once the towball has been removed. The standard height for a towball is 46 cm (18 in) from the ground to the top of the ball.

Electrical sockets

The towing vehicle may have one or two electrical sockets. The British system has a black-capped socket that connects the lights and also a white-capped socket to run a caravan's electrics, which you do not need for trailers.

Many European car makers supply a single multi-pin socket that does the job of both UK sockets and with which you can either fit a

matching plug to the trailer or you can use an adapter instead.

Stabilizers

It is worth using a stabilizer when towing horse trailers. Friction stabilizers replace the trailer hitch with one that has friction plates which grip the towball to reduce side-to-side movement in the trailer. Bar or blade stabilizers have either a bar or a single-blade leaf spring between the towbar and a bracket on the trailer's A-frame and stabilize the outfit by widening the point of contact between the car and trailer. A few types that are made specially for large trailers have blades on both sides of the A-frame.

Stabilizers make the outfit feel more like one vehicle, reducing the effect of passing trucks and side winds as well as making it more stable. Bar and blade stabilizers have the additional benefit of greatly reducing pitching, which makes the ride more comfortable for people and horses. However, stabilizers must be properly set up and maintained, and cannot turn a badly matched outfit into a good one.

Towing mirrors

When you are driving, you must have a good view past the trailer, so with a narrow car you may need to fit some towing mirrors which attach to the door mirrors or are on outriggers strapped to the wings.

Hitching up is made much easier with a Trailer Coupling Mirror (see page 284), which is fitted to the trailer nose and allows you to see the hitch and ball coming together.

BELOW: *This horse is kitted out ready for travelling and loading into his trailer with his legs protected by padded travelling boots, his tail bandaged, and wearing a cooler rug.*

Horse wear

Horses will always need protection when travelling to avoid abrasion and knocks and to keep them warm in cool weather. Rugs should be suitable for the weather. Leather headcollars are safest because they will break if they get caught up instead of strangling the horse. Although you should always take a bridle for control if you have to unload your horse in difficult circumstances, never transport a horse in one because of the damage the bit will do if it gets hooked up.

Legs should be protected with travelling boots or bandages over some padding. Boots are much quicker and easier to put on than bandages but must fit well or they can slip down.

A tail guard or bandage is also essential because it stops the tail being rubbed against the trailer ramp, especially with large horses. Again, a guard is easier to put on but it must be designed so that it does not slide down. Very tall horses will also benefit from a poll guard to protect their head. When buying a trailer, you must take into consideration the height of your horse and its natural head carriage as these factors may well affect what height of trailer is suitable.

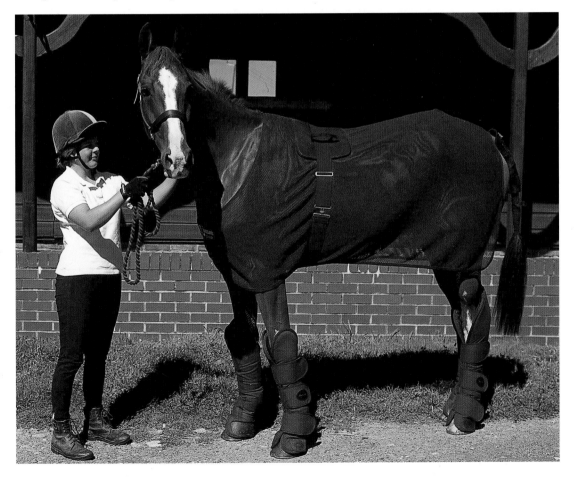

9.3 Pre-travel checks

Before you embark on any journey with your horse, however short, there are certain fundamental checks that you must carry out as well as some basic maintenance.

Check the tyres

The tyres are vital to the outfit's stability so they must be checked on every trip. You will need a pressure gauge that is capable of measuring the high pressures trailers require, so digital and dial ones are best. A pump that plugs into the car's cigarette lighter saves effort.

The correct tyre pressures are given in the trailer and car handbooks and sometimes on labels on the vehicles. If the car's handbook does not give a towing pressure, then use the one for the fully laden car. If it has only one pressure, some cars tow better with an extra 3 psi in the rear tyres.

While you are checking pressures, also check tyre condition. If a tyre has cuts deep enough to show the reinforcing or has bulges, which mean that the tyre is breaking up, it must be replaced. A blow-out while towing can be disastrous.

Other basic checks

Before setting out, you should also check the towcar's oil, water and washer bottle levels and that the towball has some clean grease applied. Check that the lights and

mirrors are clean and in good condition. Make sure also that the trailer's ramps and floor are sound.

Maintenance

Your trailer handbook should explain the maintenance that it requires. All moving parts will need lubrication, including the hitch, hinges and catches. The hitch is attached to a sliding drawbar which applies the brakes as the car slows down and has at least one grease nipple on the housing into which grease must be injected every 2000 to 3000 miles. Dirty grease should be washed out of the hitch cup with white spirit and then some clean grease applied. Brakes will also need adjusting for wear at about the same mileages.

Older trailers need their wheel bearings regreasing every two years, although since the mid-1990s trailers have increasingly had sealed-for-life bearings. If you have the former, the nut under the hub cap is shaped like battlements with a pin through the slots. If you do not have the ability to carry out these tasks yourself, they must be done professionally once a year for your safety.

RIGHT: *Before setting out on any journey, do check the tyres of the towing vehicle and the trailer for any damage as well as the tyre pressures.*

9.4 Hitching up and reversing

It is an excellent idea to establish a routine for hitching up so that you do not forget anything. If you follow the simple guidelines for hitching and reversing that are outlined here, you will find that they will get easier with practice.

Hitching up procedure

1 Start by applying the trailer handbrake and removing any security devices, then wind the hitch up with the jockey wheel to clear the towball. Reverse up to the trailer. It helps to have a marker on the rear window directly above the towball.

2 If a helper is guiding you back, agree some hand signals in advance and have them stand where they can be seen through the rear window but cannot be squashed against the trailer. When you stop, apply the car's handbrake and turn off the engine.

3 Lower the hitch onto the towball with the jockey wheel. On some hitches you have to hold the locking handle up; others are self locking and on some you only hold back a safety catch. When it clicks on, raise the hitch again to make sure it has locked, then fully raise the jockey wheel and lock it in position.

4 Attach the breakaway cable to the purpose-made ring on the towbar or to a substantial part of the car. If the trailer becomes unhitched, this cable applies the brakes before snapping. Therefore it must not be attached to something that might break first, such as a plastic bumper.

5 If you use a stabilizer, fit it now. Plug in the electrics, then check that the car's handbrake is on before releasing the trailer's handbrake.

6 Check that everything is stowed properly, and then, finally, check that the trailer's lights are working properly. This is best done with a helper shouting out what they can see coming on. Remember the brake lights and check the indicators separately, not with the hazard switch which is on a separate circuit.

Reversing

Reversing often frightens many new trailer owners but it will become second nature to you with plenty of practice. If you find that you have difficulty with it, or are taking the towing test, you should seek some professional tuition. Here are a few basic rules to help you succeed:

■ Always check behind the trailer before reversing because it creates a huge blind spot.

■ To reverse a trailer you have to turn the wheel the opposite way to the way you want the trailer to go because if the back of the trailer is going left, its front must go right and as that is attached to the back of the car, that must go the same way. But that only starts the trailer turning and there comes a point at which you must steer the other way to bring the car round.

■ Recognizing that point can come only with practice, and even experts get it wrong sometimes.

Reverse to the right

To practise your reversing, you should start by learning to reverse to the right because that is easiest. Set up a 'gate' to reverse into using objects that will not cause damage if hit. Start with the outfit in a straight line and about half its length in front of the gate. Practise with this until you can do it from various positions. On tight turns, you have to pull forwards to straighten the outfit after getting the tail through the gate, and it is always easier to pull forwards than it is to correct its line in reverse.

Reverse in a straight line

To reverse in a straight line, you should use the door mirrors alone, and when you can see more of the trailer in one mirror than the other, you should steer a little towards that mirror in order to straighten the outfit.

Reverse to the left

Finally, you should try reversing left into a 'gate'. This is the hardest manouevre of all to master because you have such a limited view of the trailer, especially in a van. But, again, with practice and patience, it can be mastered and you will soon become proficient at this skill.

9.5 On the road

Before you take your new horse trailer out with horses, try it on a good mix of roads to get accustomed to it, especially if you have never towed before. Pay particularly attention to pulling away smoothly, changing gear correctly and allowing for the extra width and turning space of the trailer. However, when you take the horses out for the first time, remember that the trailer will feel and handle differently and will take longer to stop because of the extra weight.

Drive considerately

Always drive with consideration for the horse which cannot anticipate the trailer's movement and does not have comfortable seats and a car's long travel suspension to absorb any bumps in the road.

Anticipate hazards

Look well ahead so you can better anticipate hazards, junctions and bends and thus avoid harsh braking or sudden manoeuvres. Trailers also exaggerate poor gear changing, so slow down early to complete gear changes smoothly and before you reach the bend or junction. When you change down, the throttle foot should come down slightly before the clutch foot comes up and vice versa when changing up.

By slowing and changing down early, you can take corners under gentle power because if you drift round with your foot off the throttle the trailer's weight tries to push you straight on. A cornering trailer will follow a tighter line than the car, so allow extra space on the inside and look out for any other road users, especially cyclists, getting into that

space. Use mirrors to check how far the trailer's wheels are from the kerb.

Roundabouts need special care because horses do not like the sudden direction changes, especially if they come at the end of a long straight stretch. Read the Highway Code to make sure that you get the signalling right because it is essential that other motorists know where you are going. Take it steady: remember

that others may not have noticed the trailer behind you or correctly judge the difference between your speed and theirs. Allow extra room on the left as you enter and leave and on the right around the island, keeping a constant mirror check. Mirrors also need frequent checking on straight roads to make sure that you are not taken by surprise by passing trucks, whose slipstream always gives the trailer a sideways push.

Above all, remember that most other road users have no idea what it is like to drive a large trailer outfit, so be prepared for them to do stupid things, such as not allowing you the time and the space to get round obstacles or driving straight at the trailer on roundabouts.

RIGHT: *Always take care when pulling a trailer – try to anticipate potential hazards and road conditions which might have an effect on your vehicle.*

Snaking

It is normal to feel some side-to-side movement in the trailer when you are towing, but when this becomes a rhythmic swing that starts to affect the towing vehicle it is called snaking and can result in your total loss of control if not remedied. Snaking has many triggers, ranging from uneven tyre pressures to side winds, but the underlying factor is always speed. The fault that had little effect at 40 mph (64 km/h) might become more significant at 50 mph (80 km/h), and often the driver has ignored the early gentle movements that predicted a problem so if the trailer starts to feel unstable, slow down.

When a trailer snakes, it is important to lose speed without further destabilizing it. Ease off the power and hold the steering steady without trying to counter the movement. It may help to ease your left hand's grip so that your hands are not fighting each other. It is best not to brake but if you are running out of road you may have to and must do it gently, backing off if it makes things worse. Stop to check the trailer has no faults, like a soft tyre, overheated wheel bearing or seized brake.

9.6 Loading

Teaching a young horse to load calmly into a trailer or a horsebox should be part of his general education, and most experienced animals which have been trained correctly will take this in their stride. However, inconsiderate handling or simple lack of thought can turn what should be an easy task into a problem, so always follow a common sense checklist.

Checklist

Before loading your horse into the trailer or horsebox, you should take the following into consideration:

1 The horse should be properly equipped for travelling (see page 215), and it is best to load him with a bridle over his headcollar for more control. The bridle should be removed once he is inside the horsebox or trailer. The handler and, if available, a helper should both wear gloves, a hard hat and suitable footwear.

2 The vehicle must be parked so that the ramp is level, to give secure footing and so that the horse can see where he is going. If necessary, you should let down a trailer's front ramp so the horse can see all the way through.

3 Move the partition over so that the entrance is as wide as possible, and then you can load the heavier of two horses, or a single horse, on the driver's side to help counter the road's camber. Note that single horse trailers are a rarity in the UK because they are less stable than two-horse ones.

Loading a horse

1 Calmly lead the horse straight up to the ramp of the trailer, not at an angle, walking alongside his head or slightly in front. Do not look round at him if he halts on the ramp – keep looking ahead. Horses often pause as they put their first foot on the ramp to check its stability. Never scold a horse for doing this; let him reassure himself and then encourage him to go straight forwards by looking ahead and stepping forwards yourself.

2 Once he is in place in the trailer, tie your horse up via a piece of strong string or some twine, which should be attached to the tying-up ring, as before. If you are travelling with a single horse in a trailer without a centre partition – which gives him more room to position himself where he finds it easiest to balance – you should use a rope on each side. This procedure is known as cross-tying.

3 A helper, if available, should adjust the partitions and put the trailer breeching bar in place, then raise the ramp whilst the handler reassures the horse. Whoever raises the ramp should talk quietly and reassuringly to the horse whilst this is being done so that the horse's attention is drawn to the movement without him being startled.

Safety tip

You should *always* stand to one side when you are raising or lowering the ramp so if the horse kicks out, there is minimal risk of you being hit by it.

Unloading a horse

Take as much care when unloading a horse. It is often best to put on the horse's bridle before unloading him, as this gives you more control. Do not stand directly in front of a horse as unloading preparations are being made, or you risk being knocked down if he is eager to come off.

Take care

You should also be aware that even the quietest horse or pony will become more alert or even excited when he goes somewhere different, such as a show. No matter how well you know him, you must keep your wits about you – it may be that as soon as he comes off the ramp of the trailer, he will see other horses cantering and jumping nearby and will become very animated. Make sure that you are holding firmly and he is under your control at all times.

Reluctant horses

If you are faced with a horse or pony that is reluctant to load, get expert help from someone who can be relied upon not to become angry or try and punish the horse. Punishing a horse who is reluctant to load acts as negative reinforcement, and this will only make him even more convinced that this is an experience to avoid in future.

Loading a horse

1 Prepare your horse by kitting him out in his travelling boots or leg bandages, tail bandage and rug. Lead him towards the trailer or horsebox talking reassuringly to him.

2 Lead the horse straight up to the ramp of the trailer, looking ahead and walking slightly in front of him. By walking calmly, you will encourage him to follow you.

3 When the horse is safely inside the trailer, go under the bar and tie him up securely, via some strong string or twine, to the tying-up ring.

4 Close the front door of the trailer. The horse will enjoy looking out and watching what is going on outside, but it is safer to close the top door when on the move.

5 Go round to the back of the trailer and secure the breeching bar behind the horse. If you have an assistant with you, probably they will have done this already.

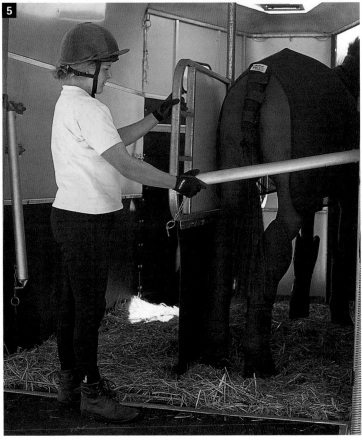

6 Lift the ramp of the trailer, taking care to stand to the side of it. If the breeching strap should break and the horse backs out, the ramp would drop down and trap you.

7 If the ramp is heavy, you may require an assistant to help you lift it. If your horse is nervous, get someone to do this for you while you talk to your horse at the front.

Chapter 10
Showing and competitions

• •

Competing with your horse or pony is a great way to measure the progress you are making, both as a rider and in training your horse. It should not be the be-all and end-all of why you ride, but it can give you goals to aim for in your partnership, and it is also a good incentive to improve your standards of equitation and horsecare. More importantly, it's fun — for you and your horse. All horses will enjoy going to a 'party', as long as you are well prepared for the event and are realistic about what you expect them to do.

10.1 Shows

'Showing' is a very broad term that covers everything from the Hack Championship at the Horse Of The Year Show to a best Pony Club pony class at your local show. It is always best to start your showing career at local level, where you will have the opportunity to try out different sorts of classes and learn what is required of you both.

Local shows

To find out when shows in your area are taking place, you can check out the tackshops and riding schools for schedules, contact your local riding clubs and Pony Clubs, and read the local and national equestrian press for advertisements.

Some shows require you to fill out entry forms and enter in advance, but many allow you to enter on the day. Just make sure that you check which system is operating — it is not much fun spending hours polishing yourself and your horse to turn up and find you are not allowed to compete!

At the show

Allow enough time for your journey, and arrive in plenty of time. There is nothing worse than being hurried and getting you and your horse into a fluster. Find the secretary's tent or caravan and then collect your number, which you will have to wear in each class. Traditionally, at local shows you wear your number round your waist with the number in the middle of your back.

Find out which ring each class you have entered is due to take place in, and also whether the show is running approximately to time.

You should take time to relax your horse or pony and work them in. Try to stay calm — we all get nervous, but make an effort not to communicate these nerves to your horse.

Turn-out for horses

For most showing classes, except those for natives, traditional Cobs and Palominos, horses and ponies should have plaited manes, and tails should be either pulled or plaited. Show Cobs should have hogged manes. Heels and chins should be trimmed. Tack should be made of plain leather, and only show ponies and riding horses should wear coloured browbands. If you have to wear a numnah, make sure that it follows the line of the saddle and is a discreet colour — brown, black or white. Girths should be dark — unless your horse is grey, in which case, white is acceptable. Horses and ponies should not wear boots in showing classes — the only exception to this is the jumping phase of a working Hunter class.

Turn-out for riders

It is correct to wear a tweed jacket in most classes, except to show riding ponies, hacks and riding horses. Children under 16 years should wear pale-coloured jodhpurs and jodhpur boots with jodhpur clips that pass under the foot to stop them riding up, as should adults showing small native breeds. Adults should wear breeches and long boots. A discreetly coloured shirt and tie should be worn, not a stock. Gloves should be

RIGHT: *A well turned-out rider and horse at a local show. Looking smart is essential and you will be required to wear breeches, long boots, gloves, a smart jacket and a suitable hard hat when you are competing.*

Preparation

The better prepared you are for any equestrian activity, then the more successful it will be and the more fun you will have. Remember that you ride your horse for fun — if jumping a round of hefty show jumps scares the living daylights out of you or dressage bores you senseless, then don't do it! Nowadays there are so many different types of competitive and non-competitive events from which to choose that there will definitely be one to suit you and your horse – TREC (see page 238) is rapidly becoming very popular. The more you have practised at home — your show, your dressage test or your jumping skills — the better the day will go and the more successful you will be. Learn from your mistakes, and make sure that you practise the things that did not go quite to plan before you have another go. Practice really does make perfect.

plain brown or black. Be careful of wearing leather gloves if you have plain leather reins — if it rains or you sweat a lot, it all gets rather slippery!

However, at local level it is more important that you and your horse are clean and tidy, and the tack fits correctly and is clean, rather than having all the most fashionable kit.

Whatever you wear, do make an effort — be proud of the way you and

Showing tip

Always keep it short and sweet when you perfom your indivdual show. The judge may have hundreds of horses to watch that day, and will appreciate you keeping it brief. Trotting 20 circles or walking for five minutes before you trot won't do you any favours.

your horse look, and do the judge the courtesy of being well turned-out. It will be an enjoyable occasion for you both — and a good excuse to spend extra time with your beloved equine!

The class

Obviously all shows are different and will run different classes, but what you will be expected to do does not change much. In the ridden classes, everyone will ride round the ring together in walk, trot and canter before being asked to line up in the centre and, one by one, perform an individual show. Usually the judge will then expect you to walk, trot and canter on each rein with perhaps a short gallop to finish, but they may ask you to do something specific, so make sure that you listen carefully to anything they say.

ABOVE: *Going to a show can be an enjoyable day out for all the family. Many people take a picnic and some folding seats so that they can settle down in comfort to watch the horses being put through their paces.*

The steward may then ask you on behalf of the judge to 'strip'. This is nothing to do with the 'Full Monty' so keep those breeches on. What they want you to do is to take your horse's saddle off and run him up in hand, so that the judge can assess his conformation and movement better.

If you have someone at the show who is helping you, ask them to come into the ring at this point with a body brush, so that you can remove any sweat marks under the saddle, and perhaps bring a stable rubber too for last-minute polishing.

LEFT: *At local shows, the jumps are not usually very high. Your aim is to get round the course without any faults and complete a clear round.*

and will help to present the horse to his best advantage.

Remember that showing is very subjective, and different judges will be looking for different things in their winner. Just because you don't come first every time does not mean your horse is any less lovely! Never be afraid to ask judges for their comments and tips on improving your performance, but don't badger them for lengthy lectures and never be rude, no matter what you may think of their decision.

It's a cliché, but at the end of the day it is the way that your horse performs and behaves that matters, not the colour of your rosette.

BELOW: *These horses are patiently waiting in line for the judge to watch each one perform in turn. The rider with the judge is about to give her own individual show.*

You should walk your horse out of the line-up and stand him up square sideways-on to the judge, who will look at him from all sides. When the judge tells you to, walk your horse away in a straight line, and then trot him back briskly on a fairly loose rein, continuing on past the judge so that he can watch the horse move from all angles. Then return to the line and tack up again and remount. You will then usually be asked to walk round again as a class before being called in to your final positions.

It is always a good idea to practise getting your horse to stand up square at home, both in-hand and while he is being ridden. It looks professional

10.2 Types of show class

There are myriad classes that are open to competitors, but here are a few examples of some of the ones that you may commonly encounter at smaller local shows.

Riding Club horse/ Pony Club pony

This class is suitable for most types of horse. Manners should be considered more important than conformation. The judge will be looking for harmony between the horse and rider as well as the horse's suitability for the job: a general all-rounder that provides his rider with a safe, happy ride. You may be asked to jump a small jump, and will usually be expected to perform a short show. It is unlikely that the judge will ride the horses himself.

Working Hunter/ working Hunter pony

You will be expected to jump a round of rustic fences at a height that is appropriate to the height of your horse or pony. Competitors who jump a clear round or, in some cases, only incur a few faults will then be asked to come back in to the ring in order to perform their individual shows, which should include a gallop.

At some local shows and at bigger shows, the judge will ride each horse (or those in the top line) instead of the rider performing their show for them. The marks will then be divided between jumping performance, conformation and ride/show.

Riding horse classes

These may include ridden Hunter, Cob, hack and show pony classes. Horses are judged on conformation and performance, and you will be asked either to perform an individual show or the judge will ride your horse.

In-hand classes

There are all sorts of classes in which you may show your horse in-hand, including assorted young stock and breeding classes, heavy horses, natives and Arabs in particular.

Leading properly

It is important to ensure that your horse or pony leads properly – you should always walk at his shoulder and the horse must walk forward well, keeping his head straight. Do not ever get in front of the animal's shoulder and pull him along behind you — this will not make him move any more freely and will look very unprofessional.

Horses and ponies in-hand are usually shown in a bridle, with a coupling and leather or webbed lead rein. Some native breeds and heavy horses are shown in halters.

Handlers usually wear trousers, rather than jodhpurs or breeches, and a tweed jacket, shirt and tie. A hairnet (if necessary), hat and gloves should be worn.

LEFT: *This combination is competing in a show jumping class. Note the number round the rider's waist.*

Mountain and Moorland

These classes are for our native breeds, and at a small show, these may only be divided into:

• The 'Large breeds', i.e. Fell, Dales, Highland, New Forest, Connemara, Welsh Pony (Cob type) Section C and Welsh Cob Section D.

• The 'Small breeds', i.e. Dartmoor, Exmoor, Shetland, Welsh Mountain Section A and Welsh Pony Section B.

However, at bigger shows there are usually classes for each specific breed, often in-hand and under saddle. Adults are allowed to compete in the same classes as children.

Novelty classes

There is a huge variety of 'novelty' classes at small shows, ranging from the likes of 'pony with the best tail' and 'horse most like its owner' to fancy dress classes. These classes are often a good way for less experienced competitors to get some practice in the ring without a lot of pressure.

Best conditioned

These classes can be held in-hand or ridden – or mixed. The judge is looking for a very high standard of turn-out from both horse and rider and will inspect both carefully, but usually there is no performance element. Make sure your horse or pony is looking his absolute best. Except for native breeds, manes should be carefully plaited, the coat should be clean and shining, and hooves should be well picked out and oiled. Tack should be immaculate, and even more attention than usual should be paid to your own clothing.

Do not get disheartened if you try your best and still do not win anything. Because conformation and performance are not involved, the judging is even more subjective than usual, and the five-year-old on the snowy white pony which is scrubbed to within an inch of its life by the child's mother and a team of international grooms will always win!

Handy pony/handy horse

If your pony is immune to flapping washing lines and walking over plastic bags, this is the class for you. All shows vary, of course, but you will be expected to complete a course of obstacles within a certain amount of time, or against the clock. If there is a jump, it will be relatively small, and the rest of the round depends on the imagination of the organizers.

Common tasks will include posting letters, bending, reversing out of a box made from poles on the ground, and loading in and out of a trailer.

Veteran

As our care of horses and ponies gets more sophisticated, there are more elderly animals still in work. Veteran classes have become very popular, and the Veteran Horse Society now runs affiliated classes split into different age groups of horses. These culminate in a final at the Horse Of The Year show in Birmingham. Almost every local show runs a veteran class of some sort, but the age at which a horse is judged to have become a veteran may differ, so remember to check the schedule. The requirements are much the same as for any ridden show class, although you may not be asked to gallop in your individual show. Some classes will cater for ridden and in-hand veterans together.

RIGHT: *This line of ponies are being led in-hand ready to be judged. Most children enjoy going to shows and competing against their peers.*

10.3 Other events

In addition to the more familiar show jumping and dressage events, there is now a wide range of exciting competitions and riding activities that you and your horse can try. These include cross-country events, hunter trials, long-distance endurance riding, fun rides and the increasingly popular TREC.

Hunter trials

These are cross-country competitions run by hunts, riding clubs and Pony Clubs, usually in the spring and the autumn, and they are an excellent introduction to cross-country riding. Many of them run qualifiers for the BHS cross-country series and final.

There is usually a wide range of classes, with special sections for novice horses/ponies, novice riders, age ranges and opens. Do check the schedule for the heights of the fences, although these are not always printed – if you are in doubt, ring the person organizing the competition. The fence heights will range from under 0.6 m (2 ft) to around 1.05 m (3 ft 6 in) for the 'Open' class.

The judging can be arbitrary: some classes are judged on style, some carry an optimum time (usually not revealed) that you have to try to achieve, and others have a timed specific section of the course. Aim for a 'hunting pace', i.e. a strong canter that covers the ground but is not a flat-out charge, and you will not be far off the mark.

The jumps are rustic and varied, and are designed to replicate, to a certain extent, those that you may encounter if you are out hunting.

A good way to start is to do a pairs class with a more experienced combination. You are not usually expected to jump upsides each other as a pair all the way round – there will be certain 'dressing' fences (ones that must be jumped as a pair) listed on the course plan.

Dress

A few hunter trials still specify that hunting kit must be worn – jacket and tie/stock. A back protector is compulsory at all cross-country competitions, such as one-day events, hunter trials and team chases. Some

BELOW: *In this ultimate Endurance Ride in Dubai, the competitors are tested by riding across the desert sand under the scorching sun.*

trials will accept cross-country dress: breeches and boots or jodhpurs and jodhpur boots, sweat shirt or rugby shirt, back protector and approved hard hat. Check the schedule to see which standard of hat is permitted: you will not be allowed to compete if yours is not up to standard.

You may want to put brushing boots and/or overreach boots (see page 111) on your horse to protect him from knocks and scrapes, and possibly put some studs in his shoes to prevent him from slipping. Ask your farrier about this.

One-day events

Eventing is perhaps the most exciting and demanding horse sport open to the average horse and rider. The three elements – dressage, show jumping and cross-country – require a horse to be obedient and supple on the flat, accurate and careful in the show –

ABOVE: *Here Matt Ryan is competing on Balmoral Mr Slinky at Gatcombe in 2002. Horse trials and one-day eventing have become increasingly popular in recent years.*

jumping, and bold and forward-going across country, and all on one day! However, a small one-day event is within the grasp of every horse, and provides great goals towards which to work for both of you.

Events run by and affiliated to the sport's governing body, British Eventing, are at levels ranging from Intro, where the jumps are about 0.9 m (3 ft), to Advanced, where the jumps are 1.18 m–1.2 m (3 ft 11 in–4 ft) high. However, nearly every Pony Club and riding club runs more basic competitions, with classes for both the novice and the more experienced competitor, in which you are less likely to have to gaze in awe at the Olympic gold medallist competing in the arena next to you.

For dressage and show jumping, you should wear cream or white breeches or jodhpurs, a tweed or black/navy jacket with a tie or stock and an approved hat.

Across country, body protectors and cross-country colours should be worn. At Pony Club, Riding Club and British Eventing (BE) events, you must also wear an armband containing personal and medical information in case of an accident – you can obtain them from British Eventing, your local riding club or Pony Club, or the BHS Bookshop. Your cross-country sweatshirt should also have long sleeves – Pony Clubs will not let you compete in short-sleeved shirts for safety reasons.

Fun rides

Local hunts and riding clubs often run fun rides, which basically involve having an enjoyable and informal ride in pleasant countryside. There are usually optional jumps, and the length of the ride will vary from approximately three to fifteen miles. Try to get a group of like-minded friends and their horses together; it's no fun if you want to go fast while others stay in a steady trot, and equally you may wish to mooch along enjoying the view while others take off. This is a cheap and fun way to get used to riding in open spaces in public. Start times are staggered so that it does not turn into the Charge of the Light Brigade.

Endurance

Endurance riding is long-distance riding across various types of terrain. A discipline that is well known for its friendliness and approachability at the lower levels, it can be a really rewarding competitive sport for those who don't want to jump – although many of its participants do, of course. And you do not need any special equipment nor a particular breed or type of horse to get started – all that is required is just you, your horse and your normal riding tack.

Types of ride

There are four main types of rides, and these are as follows:

■ Pleasure rides, sometimes called training rides, which are of distances up to 34 km (21 miles). The only sort of rides open to people who are not members of endurance's governing body, Endurance GB, they are the place to dip your toe in the endurance waters. The speed required is quite low: minimum 8 km/h (5 mph), maximum 13 km/h (8 mph).

■ Set speed rides, of between 30 and 80 km (19 and 50 miles), form the next level. Riders do not have to be members of Endurance GB, but their horses must be registered and have a logbook from the society. There are compulsory vet inspections before and also half an hour after the ride is

Fitness

To compete in one-day events and hunter trials, your horse will have to be fairly fit. It is unfair to expect him to carry you round a long course of jumps at a fast pace if he is not, and you risk putting excess strain on his heart and legs. Your horse or pony does not need to be as fit as a racehorse, but he does need all-round strength and stamina. To get a horse fit enough from complete rest to run safely and competitively in a small one-day event will take 10–12 weeks.

Obviously, the more lofty your ambitions, the fitter and better trained you and your horse need to be, but to start your competitive career, you must ensure that you can both complete a round of show jumps and a short cross-country course without getting too out of breath. The speed of the horse's recovery after exertion is the measure of his fitness: if he is still puffing 20 minutes later, he's not fit enough.

Rider fitness is equally important, and an area that is much-neglected by many. There is nothing worse than the sight of a rider finishing a course blowing harder than his or her horse – and the fitter you are, the better you will ride and the better your horse will go.

RIGHT: *Even youngsters can enjoy their first taste of competition in the wide range of Pony Club events that are now on offer for young riders.*

completed, with a trot-up and heart-rate check for the horse.

■ Graded rides are usually between 30 and 80 km (19 and 50 miles). Speeds vary between 8 and 20 km/h (5 and 12 mph), but there are restrictions on higher speeds for novice horses and lower speeds for more advanced combinations. Vet inspections are more rigorous, with penalties given for certain speeds, heart-rates and other parameters. The total number of penalties will denote the grade that is awarded.

■ Endurance Rides (ERs) are the most advanced of all the rides. All FEI and international competitions are ERs. They vary from 65–160 km (40–100 miles) in a single day, or longer over several days.

Rides begin with a mass start, and the competitors aim to cover the distance as fast as they can, taking into account the terrain and welfare of their horse.

There are vet inspections at set intervals, and very high levels of fitness and recovery are required. Following this are rest periods, which are called 'holds', where the horse and rider can eat and take a breather before continuing.

TREC

TREC is a relatively new competitive discipline, which is designed to test a horse/rider combination through a whole range of activities rather than focusing on a single one.

The competition combines the requirements of trail riding with some jumping and flatwork. It tests the partnership's ability to find their way across country – using basic map-reading skills – and to deal with

all types of terrain; to show a safe degree of control and riding ability; and to deal with the sort of obstacles and common problems that can be encountered by a rider on their own in the countryside.

The competition is conducted in three phases, and at Championship level it takes place over two days. Even at the lower levels, competition is usually conducted over two days, as great emphasis is placed on the social side of the event.

Phase One

POR is orienteering on horses. Riders must follow a route on a map, at specific speeds. The POR is not a race and the majority of the course is conducted in walk and trot. Although the course can be up to 45 km (28 miles) long at Championship level, generally the higher levels of equine fitness associated with endurance or eventing are not necessary.

Phase Two

This is the control of paces phase. Normally conducted as the first part of the second day, this phase is designed specifically to demonstrate that the rider can control their horse first in canter, then in walk, following a straight-line course 150 m (450 ft) long and a couple of metres wide. The slower the horse travels in canter, and the faster it moves in walk, the greater the marks awarded.

Phase Three

In PTV, the final phase, which can be up to 5 km (3 miles) long, is the cross-country element. Although this phase does include some jumping, it also features dismounted exercises.

Scoring

The scoring is based on accumulating the most points, and one of the major parts of the appeal of this discipline is that if a horse or rider is unable to perform any part of the competition, they are not eliminated – they merely lose points.

Hunting

Although it is not strictly a show or a competition, hunting (or drag hunting) is one of the best ways to educate you and your horse. You will learn to ride cross-country in the most natural and exhilarating atmosphere possible, to conserve your horse's energy across country, and to ride as part of a large group safely. Those riders who wish to jump will get ample opportunity to do so, depending on the hunt, and those who don't want to, don't have to.

To find out which is your local hunt, consult the equine magazines or contact the Masters of Foxhounds Association (see page 284). You must telephone the master to ask for permission to come out hunting. Explain if you or your horse are novices – there will not be a problem, but the master likes to know and will be able to advise you if the day you have chosen is suitable.

The best time to start is during autumn hunting – literally early-morning hunting during September and October. The pace is slower and the day is less formal.

You will be asked to pay a sum of money for your day out hunting, which is called a 'cap'. If you get really hooked, you can pay for a whole season at once, and this is called a subscription.

Checklist for competitions

If you go to a competition with your horse, you will need some of the following clothing and equipment items, depending on the type of event in which you are taking part.

Horse

- Saddle and numnah
- Stirrups and stirrup leathers
- Girth
- Bridle
- Martingale/breastplate if worn
- Basic first-aid box
- Plaiting bands/needle and thread
- Grooming kit: dandy brush, body brush, curry comb, hoof pick, stable rubber, hoof oil and brush, mane comb, etc.
- Two buckets – one to wash your horse, one to offer drink
- Sponges and sweat scraper
- Sweat rug and surcingle
- Travelling boots
- Tail bandage
- Headcollar and rope
- Water carrier and lots of water

For jumping:

- Brushing boots/bandages and gamgee
- Overreach boots

For cross-country:

- Studs and kit
- Cross-country surcingle
- Tape for boots

Rider

- Approved standard hat
- Jacket
- Shirt and tie or stock and stock pins
- Some light-coloured breeches or jodhpurs
- Boots or jodhpur boots and chaps as necessary
- Hair net
- Basic human first-aid kit
- Whip/spurs if required
- Gloves

For cross-country:

- Back protector
- Cross-country colours/sweatshirt
- Armband
- Spare pair of breeches (and underpants) in case you fall off into the water...

Chapter 11

Keeping your horse healthy

••••••••••••••••••••••••••••

For some people, keeping horses is a new experience and there is a lot to learn, whereas others will feel confident about equine health care, having looked after a horse for years. It is wise to keep up to date: procedures change as new research provides useful information. You need to recognize when your horse is well and realize when he is ill. This includes understanding how some signs of ill health may be more serious than others and when or if you need to contact your vet. Practising preventive medicine – good general management, parasite control, regular foot trimming and shoeing, dentistry, a good diet and routine vaccinations – will help to keep your horse healthy.

11.1 Observing a horse

Routine, regular observation of all horses under your care is crucial. It is obvious when a horse is seriously sick, but are you really sure that you know whether your horse is feeling 100 per cent? The more you know what a horse is usually like, the easier it is to spot a problem.

Think ABC

The simplest way of remembering what to look for in your horse is to think of ABC: Appearance, Behaviour and Condition. Make sure that you check each one in turn. A responsible horse owner should also know their horse's normal vital signs, namely its temperature, pulse and respiratory rate, which are known as TPR.

■ T: the normal temperature for a horse is 37.5–38.5°C (99–101.5°F).
■ P: the normal pulse for a horse is 36–42 beats per minute.
■ R: the normal respiratory rate at rest is 8–14 breaths per minute.

Taking the temperature

An easy-to-read digital thermometer is ideal for this. If you use a glass thermometer, make sure the mercury is shaken down to the end of the thermometer first or it will not record accurately. A horse's temperature is measured in the rectum. Grease the measuring end of the thermometer with some lubricating petroleum jelly or even saliva. It is safest to have

RIGHT: *To take a horse's temperature, move the tail aside and gently insert a lubricated thermometer into the anus at an angle so that it presses against the rectal wall.*

someone steadying the horse's head and reassuring it. Stand to one side of the rear of the horse, run your hand over the quarters and grasp the base of the tail firmly. Gently lift it and carefully insert the thermometer through the anus. Keep hold of the tail so the horse does not clamp it down, and hang onto the thermometer, so you do not lose it. Stay standing to the side and be careful to avoid being kicked. Insert the thermometer for about a minute, making sure you

tilt it against the wall of the rectum, rather than in the centre of a ball of droppings. Remove gently, wipe clean and read it. Afterwards, clean it with cold water and disinfectant.

Increased temperature

A slightly increased temperature is not usually serious and is quite normal after exercise. However, a high temperature – much more than 39.5°C (102.5°F) – is potentially serious. It suggests that the horse is unwell: you should contact your veterinary surgeon for advice.

Low temperature

A very low temperature also indicates that the horse could be unwell and may be shocked. Check with your vet.

RIGHT: *Healthy horses should have access to a field or paddock for grazing and exercised regularly.*

Measuring the pulse

The best place to feel a horse's pulse is where the facial artery passes under the jaw. Make sure that the head is still and that the horse is not eating when you do this. The horse's resting pulse is slow, so it can be difficult to detect. You can practise finding your horse's pulse after exercise, when it is more obvious.

Finding the pulse

To find the pulse, run your fingers along the inside of the bony lower edge of the jaw. The pulsing artery will be felt as a tubular structure. If you lightly press this against the jaw with the flat of your first three fingers, you will feel the pulse. Count the number of beats in 15 seconds and then multiply by four to get the pulse rate per minute. Do be sure to bear in mind that the pulse rate will increase with exercise, excitement, a high temperature or pain.

If you cannot feel the pulse, feel for the heartbeat between the ribs on the left side of the lower chest, just behind the elbow in the girth area.

Respiratory rate

To check this, you can either hold a hand close to the horse's nostrils to feel each breath or count the flank movements. On a cold day, you will be able to see when the horse exhales.

Other observations

As well as checking your horse's behaviour, taking his temperature and measuring his pulse, you can observe his general appearance to assess his level of health.

Eyes and gums

The mucous membranes around the eyes and on the gums should be a healthy pink colour, apart from the occasional horse that has dark pigmented gums. With serious illness, the membranes change colour. It is possible to check the circulation by measuring the 'capillary refill time'. Firmly press a pink area of the horse's gums with your fingertip. Initially this

ABOVE: *To take a horse's pulse, which is normally 36 to 42 per minute, place your first three fingers under the back of the lower jawbone. You will feel the artery pulsating beneath the skin just on the inside of the jaw, but it requires practice.*

RIGHT: *To measure your horse's respiratory rate, hold your hand close to his nostrils and feel each breath. On a very cold day, you will be able to see easily when he exhales.*

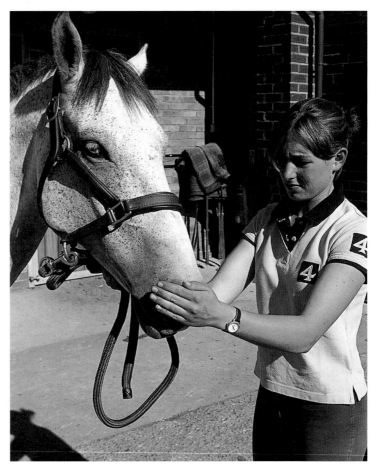

should be pale (blanched), but normal colour should return within three seconds. A delay may suggest a circulatory problem, such as shock. Sweating for no obvious reason implies that something is wrong and is sometimes a sign of pain.

Mental state

A horse's mental state is yet another relatively reliable indicator of how healthy he is. If your horse appears to be unusually dull or excited, then something may be wrong.

Lameness

Although it will be obvious when a horse is very lame, milder lameness can be difficult to assess. If you are unsure, you should ask someone to trot the horse away from you in a straight line and then back towards you, with the horse's head held loosely, so you can watch it move.

A horse that is lame in the front legs will lift its head up as the lame leg hits the ground. Its head nods down as the sound leg hits the ground.

Hind-limb lameness is easiest to observe as the horse is trotted away from you. The hip on the painful lame side will appear to rise and fall more obviously as the horse tries to avoid taking any weight on that leg.

However, if the horse is severely lame it is unwise to trot it up. If it is lying down more than normal it may be due to severe lameness, usually in more than one foot, e.g. laminitis.

What goes in

Ponies are almost always hungry, so if they stop eating it usually means that something is wrong. Horses are fussier and will stop eating if they are

excited or disturbed. Very fit animals can be surprisingly 'picky' eaters.

You should know what your individual horse's appetite is like. For many, being off their food is the most obvious clue that they are unwell. Horses drink about 20–45 litres (4–9 gallons) of water a day, but this will vary with the individual, the weather, their work load and also the moisture content of their diet. Dehydration has to be severe before it is obvious; if your horse is not drinking, then it is important to double-check everything else.

What comes out

Loose droppings or diarrhoea should always be a cause for concern. You should also be concerned if a horse passes fewer droppings than normal

ABOVE: *To detect signs of lameness ask someone to trot up your horse and study its movement closely for any changes in its natural gait.*

as this may signal constipation or even impending colic.

Urine should also be checked. It is normal for a horse's urine to be a cloudy yellow colour, but it varies from a pale yellow to brown. If you notice that there is a change in its colour, and particularly if it appears red, be concerned. Similarly, if a horse is repeatedly straining to pass urine, it suggests there is pain somewhere.

In all these instances, you should consult your vet without delay and get some expert advice. Do not adopt a wait and see policy; it is better to be safe than sorry.

Digital pulses

If a foot problem is present, a stronger than normal digital pulse may be felt where the digital artery runs over the sides of the fetlock. Compare the different feet. If there is a foot abscess developing, the pulse will be stronger and easier to find. If you find a pounding digital pulse in more than one foot, the most likely cause is laminitis.

11.2 Healthcare check

The more you get to know your horse or pony, the easier it will be to spot any warning signs of ill health and nip them in the bud before they worsen. Inspect your horse regularly, especially when grooming him, to detect any abnormalities.

Whether your horse is kept at grass or in a stable, you should visit him and check him over at least twice a day as a matter of course. Make this an enjoyable part of your daily routine. Look closely at him and watch him moving. Run your hands over his body and legs. Listen to his breathing. You will soon learn to recognize any telltale warning signs and can take steps to prevent ill health. As we have already seen in earlier chapters, feeding your horse a good diet and exercising him regularly will help to keep him fit and healthy.

Daily checklist

■ Stand back and take a good look at your horse or pony. Is he alert and pleased to see you? Are his general behaviour and posture normal?
■ Is your horse walking and standing normally without any signs of lameness or favouring one leg rather than another? Are his legs puffy when you run your hands over them? Can you feel any lumps or bumps?
■ Is he eating and drinking as he normally does?
■ Is his breathing normal? Are there any signs of wheezing or a cough?
■ Is his coat smooth and shiny? It should not be dull or sweaty.
■ Is his skin supple? If you pick up a fold over the neck and then release it, does it flatten out again?

■ Are the horse's ears alert and do they follow you around?
■ Are the eyes bright with no signs of discharge? The membranes should be moist and a pale salmon pink.
■ Are the droppings normal?
■ Is the urine clear and pale yellow without straining?

Skin

The coat should never be dull and staring. However, a thick winter coat, of course, will not shine like a summer one.

Anus

The area around the dock should always be clean. If in doubt about your horse's health, take its temperature before ringing the vet.

Legs

Look and run your hands over the legs to check for swellings, puffiness and injuries. Watch the horse moving for any signs of lameness.

Withers and back

Check for swellings or saddle sores. The back should not be arched ('roached'), which may signify pain. Nor should it be hollow or dipped, which can also indicate discomfort.

Demeanour

The horse or pony should stand normally, alert and full of interest in his surroundings and in you.

Head

The horse should not be unusually nervous and excitable.

Eyes

The eyes should be bright and the membranes moist and pale salmon pink in colour.

Lungs

Listen for coughs and wheezes. The breathing should be normal.

Feet

A horse should take his weight on all four feet without limping. There should be no vertical cracks or horizontal grooves in the hooves. Look for stones and signs of injury or disease on the sole or frog as well as signs that he needs re-shoeing.

11.3 Body condition

This is an important reflection of a horse's diet, exercise and general state of health. By monitoring the body condition of your horse, you can discover a lot about his physical state.

Underweight

Common reasons for a horse to be in poor condition and underweight are:

■ Insufficient feed or grazing
■ Inadequate care, which is possibly associated with parasite infestation, dental disease, inadequate shelter in cold wet weather, or even bullying by other horses which can prevent the horse from eating enough.

Overweight

Many horses, and particularly ponies, are 'good doers', gaining weight all too easily, particularly as many are given too much feed and too little exercise. Obesity is an issue with horses as well as with people, and it is wrong for any animal to be overweight. There is a much higher risk of laminitis and other serious lameness in overweight animals. Native ponies are most at risk, since naturally they inhabit the mountains and moorlands, yet are often kept on lush lowland grazing. Spring and autumn are the critical times of year for fatties, because the new grass is too rich for them. Any overweight animal should not be turned out at grass, as they will only get fatter. Laminitis is most common in ponies out on lush spring grass, but it is also seen in horses that have had too much feed. However, some laminitis cases are not related to feeding.

Condition scoring

This system is used to assess a horse's physical state. There are a variety of scoring systems that can be used, but they all work on the principle of assessing fat deposits. With horses, it is important to rely on feeling areas such as over the ribs, as a shaggy winter coat or rugs may disguise thinness. The simplest advice for condition is that you should be able to feel but not see a horse's ribs, although there are better systems (see the table below).

Condition scoring

To obtain the condition score for any horse or pony, first score the pelvis, then adjust the pelvis score up or down by 0.5 if it differs by one or more points from the back or neck score.

Score	Condition	Pelvis	Back and ribs	Neck
0	Very poor	Angular, skin tight; very sunken rump; deep cavity under tail	Skin tight over ribs; very prominent and sharp backbone	Marked ewe neck; narrow and slack at base
1	Poor	Prominent pelvis and croup; sunken rump but skin supple; deep cavity under tail	Ribs easily visible; prominent backbone with skin sunken on either side	Ewe neck; narrow and slack at base
2	Moderate	Rump flat either side of backbone; croup well defined, some fat; slight cavity under tail	Ribs just visible; backbone covered but spine can be felt	Narrow but firm
3	Good	Covered by fat and rounded; no gutter; pelvis easily felt	Ribs just covered and easily felt; no gutter along back; backbone well covered but spine can be felt	No crest (except for stallions), firm neck
4	Fat	Gutter to root of tail; pelvis covered by soft fat; need firm pressure to feel	Ribs well covered; need pressure to feel	Slight crest; wide and firm
5	Very fat	Deep gutter to root of tail; skin distended; pelvis buried and cannot be felt	Ribs buried; cannot be felt; deep gutter along back; back broad and flat	Marked crest; very wide and firm; fold of fat

Weight loss tips

An instant diet is never the best approach if your horse is overweight and needs to lose some weight. Instead, you should implement any weight loss plan slowly and gradually. Always seek professional advice from your vet to ensure that you are correct in your assumption that your horse needs to lose weight and to devise a suitable programme of diet and exercise. Here are some general guidelines to help you.

Always be patient

Weight reduction should always be a slow, steady process so as not to stress the horse or to create any metabolic disturbance. Hyperlipaemia, a serious disorder of fat metabolism, can be triggered by cutting the feed too drastically or by a period of starvation. It is particularly common in fat ponies and Shetlands. So if your horse is overweight, don't rush it – aim for a gradual weight loss.

Change the diet

You should make any changes in both the type and amount of feed given to the horse gradually. Unless recommended otherwise by your vet, reduce the rations by no more than 10 per cent over a seven-to-ten-day period. On rare occasions, your vet may need to use total starvation, as when treating certain colic cases.

Monitor progress

You can easily monitor your horse's progress by using a weigh tape or even just a long piece of string to measure the reduction in your horse's girth. Remember that a weigh tape will only provide an approximation.

It can be out by a significant margin, especially in fit, lean or odd-shaped animals, such as a pregnant mare or a donkey. A calibrated weighbridge is far more accurate. When the horse's weight plateaus, you can gradually cut back its ration again.

Increase the horse's workload

Gradually up the time and intensity of exercise as your horse's fitness improves. Never feed him more in anticipation of increased work.

Provide plenty of fresh water

It is important that you continue to provide plenty of fresh water for your horse or pony, even though the food intake is reduced. This can help the horse's digestive and other systems to function efficiently.

Forage feeds

You should use forage feeds with plenty of high-quality fibre which are low in total energy; for example, you could switch from alfalfa to meadow hay. Hay that is made from older plants, i.e. late cut, has an increased fibre content, a lower percentage of leaves and is less digestible and likely to be less fattening.

Weigh the rations

Always measure your horse's feed by weight, not by volume (as in the case of scoops or buckets) to determine the appropriate rations.

Time and amounts

A horse is naturally a grazing animal which spends a lot of time nibbling. Try to maximize the time taken to eat a given amount by using double or treble haynets to reduce the amount

pulled out with each bite. When you are seriously restricting feed intake, e.g. with a laminitic, your veterinary surgeon may suggest scattering the hay in among non-edible bedding, so that the horse has to hunt for it and will take longer to eat it. You should always feed the overweight horse separately from others, so that it cannot steal any other horse's feed.

Balance the diet

Balance the diet against the horse's age and activity level. Never feed more than is needed for the horse's level of work. An overweight animal can have a forage-based diet, i.e. grass and/or hay. For many horses doing a small amount of work per day, this is enough except in winter. Any extra hard food required should be 'non-heating', i.e. it does not give your horse too much energy. There are many different types of nuts and mixes on the market. Your vet or a specialist nutritionist will advise you on which one is best for your horse.

Soaking the hay

You could consider soaking the hay for fat ponies, especially those that are affected with laminitis, in order to leach out soluble carbohydrates.

Maintaining condition

If you do manage to slim your horse down to its ideal body condition, it is important to maintain it, and this means carefully readjusting its rations to stabilize its weight. Exercise will continue to be important for weight maintenance, and you should never forget the fattening effect of grass; just think of it as being like chocolate for the human weight watcher.

11.4 Preventing problems

You can prevent a wide range of common health problems in horses by putting some simple measures into practice. These include worm control, foot and dental care, and vaccination.

Worm control

This is important because internal parasitic infestation with different equine worms produces many health problems, ranging from loss of appetite, reduced performance, loss of weight and poor coat condition to potentially fatal conditions, such as colic or diarrhoea. The main factors leading to infection are as follows:

- High stocking density
- Over-grazed pasture, so that horses are forced to graze close to piles of droppings and eat grass close to the ground where larvae live.
- Use of the same fields by mixed age groups of horses, especially young horses, which are more likely to be heavily infected with worms.
- The presence of horses with high worm egg counts: they are significantly infected and will infect other horses.
- Warm damp weather, such as is common in the UK.

Designing a programme

A variety of effective parasite control measures are available to protect your horse, even if there are no apparent signs of worms. General guidelines are available, often from wormer manufacturers. However, such information is no substitute for an individually designed worm control programme to fit your horse's particular circumstances available from your veterinary surgeon, who will advise you on the following issues.

Pasture hygiene

The daily removal of droppings is a highly effective means of controlling the spread of worms between horses. It is tedious, but effective.

Keeping your horses off the fields allows infective eggs and larvae on 'resting' paddocks to die before they can infect another horse. Depending on the weather conditions, this can take a long time – a minimum rest period of six months. However, in warm weather a year or more may be needed – so it is rarely practical.

Mixed species grazing is helpful. Cattle and sheep act as 'biological vacuum cleaners', eating the eggs and larvae, which cannot survive in species other than the horse. Do not over-stock pasture, otherwise horses will graze closer to dung piles and any worm-infected grass. Harrowing of the pastures is not ideal as it merely spreads parasites around the paddocks.

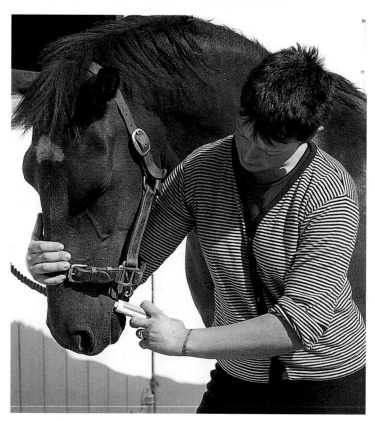

LEFT: *A common way of worming a horse is to use a special worming syringe. Hold the horse's head with one hand and squirt the contents into the animal's mouth.*

Using worming medication

Different worming treatments will eliminate different parasites. Your vet will advise what is most appropriate. Read medication instructions carefully and ensure you know what compound you are giving: there are various brand named products, which have the same key ingredients. Follow the instructions, so they are not used more frequently than recommended and the correct dose is given for the size of horse.

Diagnostic testing

This is a very cost-effective way of determining whether your horses actually require treating for worms. Diagnostic testing can also be used once or twice a year to check worm control programmes are working.

A faecal worm egg count simply requires you to submit a small (teaspoon-sized), labelled sample of fresh droppings to your vet or lab for analysis. This will assess the number of worm eggs present, which is useful for checking the parasite

Failure of worm control

Owners are often shocked when told that their horse has worms and complain that they have already been treated. There are several reasons for failure of worm control which are as follows:

■ Drug resistance is developing, so some wormers may no longer be effective. Check with your veterinary surgeon.

■ Lack of synchronization of dosing within an entire group. This is a common problem in big livery yards, where there is no co-ordinated control programme and the untreated horses may re-infect the treated animals. Check the yard's policy if your horse is at livery.

■ Underdosing due to underestimating the horse's body weight.

■ Introducing new animals into the grazing without treating them.

■ Extending the interval between doses beyond the period of activity of the various wormers.

■ Using the wrong treatment; for instance, only certain wormers (containing pyrantel or praziquantel) are effective against tapeworms.

■ Drug treatment will not destroy all the immature or larval worms. A particular problem is some forms of cyathostomes (small red worms) encyst or bury themselves inside the equine gut wall, where they are relatively inaccessible to treatment. They will then hatch out at a later date and will cause problems, particularly severe diarrhoea, if many such worms emerge at once.

status of a particular horse and deciding whether or not it needs treatment. A result of less than 200 eggs per gram is acceptable and usually indicates that treatment for

worms is not required. A blood sample can be taken and sent for a specific antibody test for tapeworms. Routine worm egg counts do not detect tapeworms, so blood tests are useful to screen healthy horses as well as those with recurrent colic.

LEFT: *Effective pasture management will help to control worms. Tests on blood and droppings are useful to see if treatment is needed.*

Warning

If you are administering a wormer treatment, ensure your horse eats it immediately. There have been instances of dogs being poisoned by eating leftover wormer powders or paste. The treatment itself is less effective if left in the feed.

11.5 Foot care

Hooves should be checked, trimmed and, if they are shod, the shoes should be regularly renewed by a registered farrier. To avoid lameness, it is essential to pay regular, careful attention to your horse's feet. Good foot shape or conformation is a critical part of lameness prevention because of its relationship to biomechanical function, i.e. the way in which the foot is a working part of the horse's body as it moves.

You need to be certain that you and your farrier are doing everything to maintain your horse's feet in the best possible condition. The Farriers Registration Council maintains a register of farriers (see page 284), but personal recommendation is best.

Being well shod

Farriers frequently say correctly that they are not consulted often enough. Mostly, a horse's feet need attention every four to six weeks. Regular trimming and shoeing are essential to keep the feet in good shape. After six weeks, the shoe may not be falling off but the toe will be getting long, so the horse is more likely to stumble.

Signs of foot problems

■ A low heel/long toe shape, especially in the Thoroughbred type of horse. This results in collapsed heels and extra pressure on the back of the foot, especially the navicular bone and surrounding soft tissue structures. It will increase the chance of heel pain developing, so avoid this. Frequently the heels will gradually collapse as the balance of the foot deteriorates. Once a horse has collapsed heels, it is a difficult and lengthy procedure to correct. It can take nearly a year for the hoof to grow down from the coronary band to the ground.

■ Sheared heels, which is when there is a disparity between the medial and lateral heel heights of more than half a centimetre, i.e. the side to side balance is wrong.

■ Small feet and narrow heels in relation to the size of the horse, so that there will be too much weight on too small a surface area.

Take advice

It can be hard to spot the gradual changes in a horse's feet that you pick out every day. For this reason, it is best to consult both your vet and farrier. To successfully trim and shoe a horse is a skilled task. Remember to look after your farrier and appreciate what he does – so that he can look after your horse's feet.

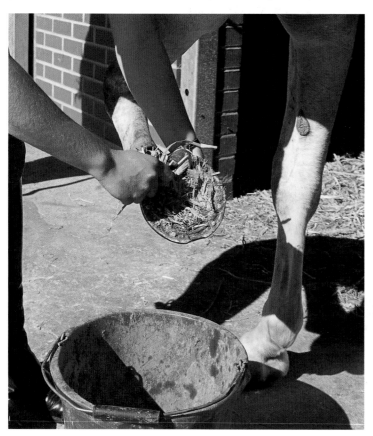

LEFT: *You should pick out your horse's feet twice every day to prevent thrush and other problems.*

Structure of the hoof

The horse's hoof forms an insensitive covering for the internal parts of the foot. It consists of the wall, the sole and the frog. The wall is the external visible part of the hoof when the foot is on the ground. It is thicker at the toe than at the heels, and it grows from the coronary band, taking nine to twelve months before coming into wear at the toe; six months at the heel.

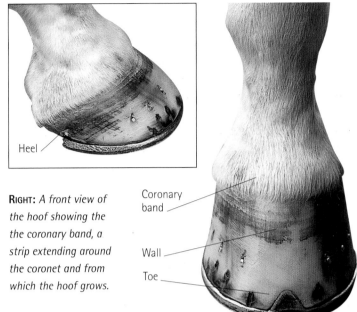

Heel

Coronary band

Wall

Toe

RIGHT: *A front view of the hoof showing the the coronary band, a strip extending around the coronet and from which the hoof grows.*

LEFT: *An unshod hoof, clearly showing the internal structure with the sole and sensitive frog (plantar cushion) visible.*

Parts of the shoe

You need some knowledge of the different parts of the shoe so that you can understand the terminology and how it works.

■ The web is the width of the material from which the shoe is made.

■ The branch is the parts of the shoe from the toe to the heel.

■ The quarter is the part of the hoof between the toe and heel.

■ The bearing surface is the part of the shoe in contact with the foot.

■ The clips assist in keeping the shoe in place.

■ Studs or nails can be fitted on both heels but only if some additional grip is considered essential.

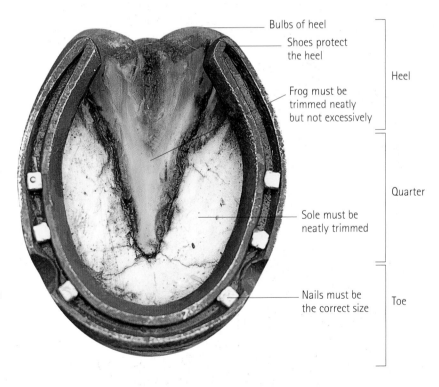

Bulbs of heel

Shoes protect the heel

Frog must be trimmed neatly but not excessively

Heel

Sole must be neatly trimmed

Quarter

Nails must be the correct size

Toe

11.6 Dental care

Your horse's teeth should be examined at least once every six to twelve months. This will assist with comfortable riding for the competition horse and it will also aid early detection of any dental problems, particularly in older horses.

Dental checks

It is very important to use veterinary surgeons and qualified equine dental technicians (EDTs) to care for your horse's teeth. You must always ensure that a competent qualified individual performs any dentistry.

Unlike humans, horses' teeth continually erupt or grow. In addition, the standard practice of feeding hay in a net or feed from a raised manger means that that they eat with their head up – an unnatural position for a horse designed to graze at ground level. Consequently, their different jaw movements result in uneven tooth wear and the development of sharp hooks and points, which require removal, usually by rasping.

Signs of discomfort

By checking your horse on a daily basis, you will learn to look for and recognize any early warning signs of future dental problems and an uncomfortable mouth. Look for:
■ Quidding – messy eating with partially chewed food being spilt as the horse eats.
■ Slower eating or reluctance to eat.
■ Tossing the head more than usual.
■ Chewing or playing with the bit.
■ Stiff-backed action, bucking or disobedience when schooling.

If you are in doubt, you should have your horse's mouth properly checked by the vet, which may require the use of a gag to fully open the mouth. Occasionally, sedation may even be necessary to allow a thorough dental examination.

LEFT: *Always ensure that your vet or a qualified dental technician cares for your horse's teeth.*

Types of teeth

Your horse or pony has three types of teeth, which are as follows:
■ Molars, or grinding teeth. These are used for chewing the food.
■ Incisors, or biting teeth. These are used for cutting through grass and collecting food.
■ Tushes are found in the mouths of adult male horses and some mares, yet have no real purpose. They are between the incisors and molars.

11.7 Contagious diseases

Currently in the United Kingdom there are a limited number of contagious equine diseases. However, with the increasing international travel of horses, there is an ever-present threat of the emergence of new or 'exotic' diseases.

Major diseases

Respiratory infections are the most important contagious diseases that can infect the horse population. These include the influenza virus, equine herpes viruses and strangles. Different preventive strategies are used for combating them.

Many measures can be taken to reduce the risk of infection of horses by infectious and contagious diseases. Precise precautions vary with the individual diseases and depend on factors such as the natural history of the disease, its means of spread and the horse's immunity.

Vaccination

For some infectious diseases, such as influenza virus, the widespread use of vaccination has an important role to play in prevention. A large percentage of the horse population needs to be vaccinated to prevent major outbreaks.

Vaccination may not eliminate the risk of infection in a horse completely but it reduces the spread and is a major component in the overall preventive strategy for the horse population. Suitable vaccines, correctly administered at the correct times, are vital. A small number of horses may demonstrate reactions to vaccines, but only rarely, and this is not a logical reason why vaccination should not be undertaken.

Vaccinations currently available

There are five diseases of horses for which vaccinations are currently available in the UK. These are as follows:

Tetanus

Otherwise known as lockjaw, this is a serious (often fatal) disease of horses caused by toxins produced when spores of the bacteria Clostridium tetani multiply within a wound. The toxins produce paralyzing muscle spasms and death by respiratory arrest. Humans and horses are especially susceptible to tetanus and should be vaccinated. Vaccination regimes for horses vary but all involve a primary course of two injections four to six weeks apart, followed by boosters at intervals of two to three years. In situations where an unvaccinated horse sustains a wound, tetanus antitoxin can be given to provide emergency protection. Your horse must be vaccinated against tetanus.

Equine influenza

Vaccination is compulsory for horses competing under the rules of the Jockey Club and most other sporting organizations. For many horses it is essential that their equine influenza vaccination record is properly up to date, otherwise they will not be allowed to compete.

More frequent booster vaccinations may be indicated for high-risk horses, such as young racehorses, or in the face of a big influenza outbreak.

Equine viral arteritis (EVA)

This can cause fever, infertility and illness. It is called 'pink eye' because of inflammation in and around the eyes. It is a problem in breeding horses, where stallions can become carriers of the infection. Currently any case involving a stallion or breeding mare in the UK is notifiable, i.e. your vet will inform DEFRA if it is suspected.

Equine herpes virus

Vaccination is available. It has been shown to provide some immunity against infection by the respiratory and abortion forms of the infection. It is uncertain whether it protects against the neurological form.

Strangles

A new vaccine has been developed against strangles and may be very beneficial in areas where the disease is a problem. It is recommended that the whole yard is immunized; frequent boosters are needed. The vaccine is administered as a tiny pinprick into the upper lip.

11.8 Preventing ill health

You can take a wide range of practical measures to keep your horse or pony fit and healthy and to help prevent ill health. These are all relatively easy to put into practice, need not cost you a lot of money, and they will benefit your horse and may help to prolong his life.

Dust-free environment

All horses will benefit from being kept in a dust-free environment, as will the people who care for them. Foot associated lameness, coughs and respiratory disease are the commonest problems for many horses and a concern for their owners. The respiratory ideal is to turn your horse out to pasture and, with decent rugs, many horses can happily live out all year round, grazing permitting.

However, for many performance horses this is not practical. Instead, it is important to keep the stable environment as dust free as possible by selecting dust-free bedding (see page 53) and using good-quality hay.

Most respiratory disease in the horse is either caused or made worse by inhaling a combination of dust, bacterial endotoxins (toxic substances produced by bacterial cell walls) and moulds or fungal spores. The most common source is mouldy hay or straw.

Good ventilation is vital, so keep the top stable door open at all times and install a vent with a baffle in the opposite wall to ensure a constant flow of fresh air. Keeping dust levels low in a stable environment is important for human health, as it will reduce the chances of people developing dust-induced coughs and asthma.

Stereotypic behaviour

In the past, certain types of abnormal behaviour were known as vices. These are now called stereotypies, which are repetitive behaviour patterns with no function, and may be an equine response to a stressful environment. Their significance to equine health is controversial, as shown by the fact that many experts link crib-biting with colic, whilst others refute this.

LEFT: *Some horses that are confined in stables may develop abnormal forms of behaviour, such as weaving. Fitting a special V-shaped grille to the stable door will help prevent this but turn-out is a better step to take.*

Horses are naturally free-ranging, social-grazing animals. In stables, they are provided with food, water and shelter, but their choice of food, social interaction and movement are all limited. Undesirable stereotypical behaviours may sometimes develop in horses that are kept confined.

■ Locomotor stereotypies, such as weaving and box walking, may be related to lack of exercise.

■ Oral stereotypies, such as wind-sucking and cribbing, have been associated with feeds, which are highly digestible but contain little dietary fibre. Giving horses more turn out in a field or paddock with plenty of forage and social contact may help to reduce this behaviour.

Foals and young horses

Oral stereotypies will often arise after weaning when foals still want to suckle but they cannot do so. At this stage, concentrate feeds are often increased; this can cause problems because foals' digestive tracts are adapted essentially to cope with a diet of milk and grass. Many foals are fed concentrates, which are high in starch and sugar, from early in life in preparation for weaning. Such rations cause increased acidity in the gastro-intestinal tract, which may lead to inflammation and the ulceration of the gut lining in the young horse. Research shows that foals that received high-concentrate rations early on had a greater risk of developing crib-biting, so this may be a response to a disturbance of the normal digestive process.

Essentially, the more turn out that young horses have, the lower the risk of them developing these problems. Recent studies have shown that foals weaned by confinement in a stable or barn were more than twice as likely to develop abnormal behaviour than paddock-weaned foals. Foals kept in after weaning were also more likely to develop abnormal behaviour than foals that were kept at grass.

Bad behaviour

Certain abnormal behaviours, such as pawing or door kicking, may be reinforced by attention. Many horses carry out this 'bad behaviour' prior to feeding, and are subsequently 'rewarded' for it by their owner. However, horses in the wild never show stereotypic behaviour, and this is a good reason for trying to manage your horse in the most natural way that is practical for you.

Avoiding injury

Horses are especially prone to injury. All possible precautions should be taken by a responsible owner including the following:

■ Turn your horse out in a safe environment, e.g. avoid barbed wire.

■ Care with companions: a high-stocking density, limited grazing and the introduction of new horses will increase the risk of injury.

■ Maintain a safe, healthy environment in and around any stable yard.

Preventing contagious diseases

■ Be familiar with the clinical signs associated with the main infectious diseases.

■ Seek veterinary attention immediately if you suspect a contagious disease in your horse. Confirmation of infection is vital so that appropriate control measures can be implemented.

■ If there is a known outbreak of a contagious disease in the area, seek veterinary advice about the risks and measures that can be taken to minimize the chance of infection in your own horse.

■ It is important to maintain an adequate vaccination programme for your horse. Influenza vaccination is recommended in most horses, and is essential if your horse attends shows. You should consider increased frequency of vaccination, e.g. six monthly, for 'high-risk' horses. Strangles vaccination is another consideration.

■ Establish a quarantine procedure for new arrivals. Isolation for three weeks is usually adequate. Get veterinary advice concerning any testing of new arrivals that may be indicated. Some horses carry strangles but show no signs.

■ Maintain adequate ventilation for all stabled horses, especially in barns.

■ Maintain high levels of hygiene in the stable, yard, trailers and lorries. Seek veterinary advice concerning the routine use of disinfectants and 'cleaning-up' following an outbreak of disease.

■ You should attempt to minimize stress at all times for your horse.

Chapter 12
Health disorders and injuries

· ·

As we have seen, the way in which you keep your horse and how you care for him will affect his general health and wellbeing. If your horse appears to be unwell, you must identify the cause and ensure that he receives the necessary care and treatment to restore him to good health. If a horse is ill or in pain, you should contact your vet without delay. Early veterinary advice is essential for all but the most minor problems. Delaying may prolong a health problem or even, in some cases, make the condition worse.

12.1 Special features

Horses possess some special features which are unique to them and it is worth examining these so that you can better understand your horse's anatomy and how his body works. This will help you to understand equine illnesses and diseases.

Limbs

As horses have evolved, their limbs have lengthened. This allows them to run faster by covering more ground per stride. Unfortunately, because they go fast and have such long legs, they are prone to injury in many ways.

The modern horse stands virtually on permanent tiptoe and uses the equivalent of our middle fingers and toes, in a permanent ready-to-run stance. Humans only stand up on tiptoe to run or if they are standing on high heels (which is uncomfortable for any length of time). This stance means that the horse has long tendons stretching towards the feet from below the knee and the hock.

Particularly crucial are the flexor tendons, which act to bend the lower limb. These are susceptible to injury, particularly in the horse at speed.

If a horse injures a flexor tendon it is termed 'broken down', which indicates the potential severity of such damage. A horse with such an injury will require a lengthy period of rest and often will not return to the same level of work as before.

To permit this tiptoe position, a specialized foot covered with a hoof has evolved, protecting the extremity of each limb like the human nail. The hoof and other soft tissues deeper within the foot serve to protect the underlying bones from damage and

act as shock absorbers for the limb. Unfortunately, this design is not perfect, especially for fast work on hard ground. Foot lameness is common in the horse, and regular farriery is important to help protect it, otherwise the old saying 'no foot, no horse' may become all too true.

The legs are long and streamlined, with powerful muscle masses which are confined to the upper limbs. The skin is relatively thin, and there is very little protection over many of the numerous synovial structures (vital joints, tendon sheaths and bursae) that are present in the legs. In many places on the lower limbs, and to a lesser extent in the upper limbs, important synovial structures lie immediately beneath the skin. As a result, these structures are prone to damage from penetrating wounds and external trauma. Such injuries are potentially serious as they can lead to

BELOW: *A racehorse has been bred to run fast, using its long legs and powerful muscular strength.*

ABOVE: *A heavy horse such as this Shire Horse has the same basic body systems as a Shetland pony or a Thoroughbred, although they all look very different.*

LEFT: *Ponies are frequently more robust than larger horses. There are nine mountain and moorland breeds that are indigenous to the British Isles. These are Exmoor ponies.*

the development of an infection, which can be difficult to treat and can result in permanent disability.

The equine abdomen

As herbivores, horses have a large abdomen, which is designed to digest their natural high-fibre diet. This, plus the way in which they have been domesticated, makes them prone to abdominal pain, which is properly called colic. There are several reasons for this, which are listed below.

Worm infestation

Horses suffer from parasitic worms that damage the gut, and can block the blood supply so that the gut no longer functions properly. Red worm infestation, in particular, is notorious for causing an area of bowel to die from lack of blood. It is now known that tapeworm can cause colic, too.

However, as the danger from worms has become better understood and general parasite control has improved, worm-related disease has diminished. If you need more information on worm control by strategic worming and pasture management, see page 252.

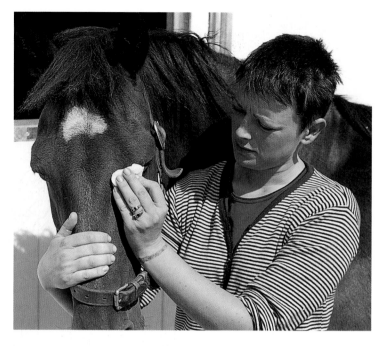

Design faults

The equine digestive tract has some definite design faults. Horses have a small stomach for their size. If they over-eat, which most will do given half a chance, the stomach all too easily becomes distended and painful. In severe cases of colic, a ruptured stomach may be the cause of death.

Horses also have long loops of intestine, which are poorly anchored to the body wall. A Thoroughbred will

ABOVE: *To bathe a horse's eye, use boiled, clear lukewarm water. Apply gently with a wad of cotton wool.*

have more than 20 m (60 ft) of small intestine floating fairly freely inside it and 4–8 m (12–24 ft) of large intestine folded into several U-bends. Both the large and small intestines have a high potential to twist, telescope or otherwise become entangled, causing severe pain. This makes the horse roll to try to get relief from the agony.

Contrary to popular belief, it is not normally the repeated rolling with colic that causes the horse's gut to twist, but nature's attempt to relieve the condition. When such a catastrophe occurs, major surgery is often the only answer.

Another design fault is that as food passes through the gut, it has to move round several U-bends and areas where the width of the intestine changes suddenly. And just like the

Accident prone

Almost the worst equine fault is the horse's extremely accident-prone nature. Not only do they have an amazing tendency to catch themselves on the only protruding nail on a fence, but also as herd animals they have a 'pecking order' which means they sustain all sorts of kicks and cuts as they sort out their rank in the herd hierarchy. Finally, we ask our horses to perform athletically and as they gallop, jump and generally work hard for us, they run the risk of injury.

In general, the majority of horses are relatively healthy and with good management can live long and healthy lives. The responsible owner must know what to watch out for, have a basic understanding of first aid procedures and know when they need veterinary help.

worst road works on our motorways, traffic jams result, and in the horse this means an intestinal blockage.

Stabling and concentrates

We also disrupt our horses' digestive systems by stabling and feeding concentrates. In the wild, horses and ponies graze continuously. By eating little and often, they can control the supply of food to their stomachs. Most horses are greedy and will eat everything that is put in front of them. Certainly there is a higher incidence of colic in stabled animals, although when a horse at grass gets colic, it is frequently more serious.

Good stable management with a regular routine, especially for feeding, will help to reduce the risk of colic in your horse. Unfortunately, abdominal catastrophes as the result of a twisted gut can occur even in a well-managed yard.

Avoiding hazards

The horse's instinct is to flee from danger – the 'fight or flight reaction' – often disregarding any obstacles, such as fences, people or vehicles in the way. If they stopped and looked, they could avoid many accidents, but they do not have the brainpower to think logically and, for this reason, humans need to do the thinking for them. We must ensure they avoid potential hazards such as barbed wire.

Senses

Horses have very sophisticated senses of sight, hearing and smell, which, together with rapid reflexes, enable them to respond rapidly to what they perceive as danger, whether this is a

plastic bag rustling in the hedge or a vet approaching. Sadly, however, horses sometimes react too rapidly and end up damaging themselves.

Eyesight

The horse's eye sticks out on the side of the head, which is attached to a long, flexible neck. This gives good all-round vision, with a slight turn of the head and neck allowing the horse to see right behind it. The advantage of this is that horses see movement easily, but may respond

ABOVE: *The horse's eyes, unlike those of a human, are positioned on the sides of the head, making them more easily prone to injuries.*

by moving rapidly or kicking out, resulting in harm to themselves or another horse (or human) nearby.

Equally, because the eyes are so prominent, they are also at risk of injury. Horses commonly sustain wounds to the eyelids when they blink to protect the eyeball. Such injuries may require surgical repair.

12.2 When to call the vet

If a horse suffers a major injury, or is clearly in pain, it will be obvious that you need a vet straightaway. Yet there are some apparently minor injuries, which would also benefit from urgent veterinary attention, such as some small puncture wounds which can be more serious than larger lacerations.

A major responsibility of all vets in practice in the UK is to provide 24-hour emergency care for all animals under their care. However, do not abuse this by disturbing your vet unnecessarily. It is unreasonable to ring your vet at midnight for a horse that has been ill for three days, but it is also unfair to leave a sick horse if it requires urgent attention. Hopefully, you will establish a friendly working relationship with a vet who is experienced in dealing with a wide range of equine emergencies.

With all potential emergencies, experience helps in recognizing what is a true crisis. The vet may resolve an apparent crisis with some simple first aid advice and reassurance. Vets are trained to ask the right questions but rely on the horse's owner to provide accurate answers. The person who contacts the vet should be the one who knows most about the horse. There is nothing worse than discussing a potentially serious problem third hand. If you have not actually seen the horse yourself, you will find it hard to explain accurately what is wrong. It helps if you make a basic assessment before consulting the vet.

BELOW: *If your horse is lying down and is unable to get up but is trying to do so, consult the vet immediately.*

Key points to consider

Pain
How much pain is the horse in? What are the frequency and duration of the signs of pain? Common indications of significant pain, such as sweating, refusal to eat, agitation or depression, mean that the horse may need to be seen by your vet.

Vital signs
Check the horse's vital signs. Can you take the horse's temperature? Can you measure the pulse and breathing rate? Have they altered from normal?

Signs of injury
What does any wound look like and whereabouts on the body is it? Any significant wound in association with obvious lameness will warrant a discussion with your vet as, although wounds themselves are not very painful at first, any associated lameness may mean damage to deeper structures or maybe the presence of infection.

Change from normal

Has there been any change from the horse's normal routine that may be significant? Abdominal pain, namely colic, may affect a horse suddenly changed to a different diet. Grass sickness notoriously affects young animals that have just been turned out on different grazing.

Special circumstances

There may be a whole range of special circumstances, such as when a mare is pregnant. Foaling difficulties are a number one emergency. If something goes wrong, minutes are vital if you are to end up with a live mare and foal.

How many are affected?

Multiple animals getting sick at once should raise a red flag. Signs of illness in several animals could indicate such dangers as infectious diseases or, rarely, a toxin in the pasture, water, or feed.

Lameness

If your horse is lame, then you should consider the following points:

How lame is the horse?

Is it lame and unable to stand on the affected limb? If you suspect that the bone might be involved, because it is exposed, or the leg is misshapen or abnormally floppy, urgent attention is essential as the horse could have a broken limb. If a horse is only mildly lame, it may be safe to wait and see.

Lame horses should never be worked until the cause has been determined. Certainly, if the lameness does not respond to a few days' rest or cannot be resolved by your farrier checking the foot, then it is time for you to call your vet.

Catch the problem early

Most conditions are more likely to have a successful outcome if they are caught early and treated before any disease process has really taken hold. When calling your vet, try to give as much notice as possible. If you notice a problem in the morning and are unsure of its significance, ring and talk to your vet so that a visit can be planned for the same day if needed. Your vet may be slightly less sympathetic if a problem has been ongoing for several days before you decide to ring, and valuable time has been lost!

Sometimes, it is necessary to transport a horse to an equine hospital where the facilities exist for more in-depth examination and treatment. Bear in mind that it is much better for the horse to travel before its condition deteriorates any further, and also that horse transporters are easier to arrange during working hours as opposed to late at night!

Degrees of urgency

It is impossible to describe every conceivable situation or to provide set rules for when you should call your vet, but the following conditions all constitute various degrees of emergency. Perhaps the best rule of all is when in doubt, call!

Urgent attention required:
- Possible fractured limb
- Abdominal pain (colic) that is violent and/or continuous
- Uncontrollable major bleeding
- Difficulties at foaling

Veterinary attention needed without delay:
- A horse lying down and unable to stand
- Non-weight-bearing lameness coupled with distress
- Non-weight-bearing lameness coupled with a wound
- Diarrhoea that is continuous and/or painful
- Foreign objects protruding from the horse's body – you should never be tempted to remove them yourself
- Injury to the eye or eyelids
- Sudden onset of disorientation and lack of co-ordination
- Difficulty in breathing

Prompt veterinary attention required:
- Choke coupled with obvious distress that does not clear within 30 minutes
- Wounds that may require stitching
- Any ill donkey as they are so stoical that by the time they look off colour they may be seriously unwell
- Sick foals

12.3 First aid

Horse owners need to know how to use appropriate first aid for any minor injuries as well as recognizing real emergencies.

It is always best to be prepared and to consider things in advance in order to avoid panic in a crisis. This means that you must: know how to contact your vet in an emergency; know where or how you can obtain horse transport in a hurry; and keep a well-stocked first-aid kit available.

Bandages

There are now many new bandaging materials available, so ask your vet to advise on the best options for your requirements. There will be occasions when you will need to bandage your horse's legs. Bandaging can provide both protection and support for the horse whilst working, travelling, resting or recovering from an injury.

Regardless of the purpose, it is essential that proper leg bandaging techniques are used (see page 122). If they are applied incorrectly, bandages will not only fail to help but they will also cause discomfort, by restricting the blood flow and potentially damaging tendons and other tissue. It is better to leave a horse's legs unbandaged than to bandage them incorrectly. If you have never bandaged a horse's legs, ask a vet or an equine nurse to show you.

Three layers

A bandage should have three layers which are as follows:
■ The inside, which is a non-stick clean dressing, such as melonin® (or rondopad®), which is attached next to a wound. If there is no wound but you are just applying a protective or support bandage, this is unnecessary.
■ The middle, which is the crucial padding that protects injuries, absorbs discharges, controls swelling and prevents bandage rubs. If this is skimped, the horse will suffer.
■ The outer wrapping is important as this holds the bandage in place and provides extra support.

Bandaging knees/hocks

With a knee bandage, it is important to avoid any pressure on the two prominent points at the back and inside of the knee. Similarly, the point at the back of the hock is vulnerable to pressure sores. It is best to apply a figure-of-eight bandage, avoiding pressure on these vulnerable areas.

Bandaging feet

Disposable babies' nappies make an effective dressing for a horse's foot. Their absorptive capacity and also

Key bandaging rules

■ Always start with clean, dry legs and bandages.
■ Use a thickness of at least 2 cm (3/4 in) of soft, clean padding to protect the leg beneath the bandage. Apply padding, so it lies flat and wrinkle-free against the skin. Cotton wool fits well around the limb and is not expensive.
■ Bandage front to back, outside to inside (counter clockwise on left legs, clockwise on right legs) using a spiral pattern and smooth uniform pressure, working down the leg and up again, overlapping the preceding layer by 50 per cent.
■ Avoid applying bandages too tightly or too loosely. Tight bandages cause injury, and loose bandages slip and will not provide proper support. Equally, ensure they are attached firmly, so they cannot come undone; use sticky tape over adherent bandages.
■ If there is a potential problem with bedding or debris getting into the bandage, seal the openings with a loose layer of flexible adhesive bandage.
■ Bandage limbs in pairs. A horse will favour the injured limb, putting more weight on the sound leg. By bandaging limbs in pairs, the undamaged leg is supported, hopefully minimizing further injury.
■ Most bandages mean the horse will need to be stabled, as a loose bandage on a loose horse is potentially disastrous.
■ Always watch for swelling above the bandage, increased lameness, or if the horse begins to chew at the bandage. If worried, contact your vet.

their waterproofing powers are really phenomenal. A size 3 or 4 will fit the average riding horse's foot instead of a baby's bottom.

A poultice or other dressing can be inserted as an inside layer within the nappy. If extra padding is needed for a tender foot, then an additional nappy can be used to provide it.

Duct tape

Duct tape is extremely useful as an outside layer to hold everything in place and provide a seal. If a horse does not like bandaging, a star-shape of sticky tape can be made up easily and then stuck on.

Changing bandages

In summary, you should not overdo this. A support bandage should be changed at least once a day. Wound dressings should be changed in accordance with veterinary advice, but most can be left on for longer than a day. If it is clean and dry, a leg bandage may stay for a few days, but most foot dressings get wet and need daily replacement.

If you are in doubt, ask your vet. Every time that you put on a clean dressing, it is expensive, and your vet will be able to advise you how often it really needs doing.

Tetanus vaccinations

In addition to a well-stocked first aid kit, it is important that both you and your horse or pony are up to date with vaccinations for tetanus. Many puncture wounds that are a potential source of infection go unnoticed, so proper protection against this dangerous disease is very important. Check with your vet and your doctor

First aid kit

The contents of your equine first aid kit can be simple or elaborate, but at least some of the following are worth having:

- A list of key phone numbers, e.g. vet and insurance company
- Some paper and a pen
- A torch, ideally a small pen torch and a larger torch (with some spare batteries)
- A thermometer
- A pair of curved stainless steel scissors
- A small pair of tweezers or forceps
- A clean bucket or big bowl
- Some antiseptic wound cleaner, e.g. povidone-iodine (pevidine®) or chlorhexidine (Hibiscrub®)
- An antiseptic spray
- Surgical spirit
- Petroleum jelly e.g. Vaseline®
- Wound gel e.g. Derma-gel®, Intrasite gel®, Nugel ®
- A range of dressings and bandages including those listed below
- Cotton wool
- Gamgee
- Ready-to-use poultice e.g. Animalintex®
- Non-stick sterile dressing squares to go over wounds e.g. melonin®
- Cotton stretch bandages e.g. K band®
- Adhesive bandages e.g. Elastoplast®
- Self-adhesive bandages e.g. Vetrap®
- Zinc oxide tape or strong sticky tape
- Exercise bandages
- Stable bandages

Extras:
- Shoe removing kit
- Pliers and wire cutters
- Spare hoof pick
- Epsom salts
- Sterile saline bag to flush wounds
- Moist baby wipes to clean wounds
- Some sterile antiseptic impregnated nail brushes to clean wounds, e.g. E-Zscrub®
- Proprietary ice wrap or cooling bandage
- Clean old towels
- Bailer twine and some rope

Medications:
These should be discussed with your own vet and prescribed as necessary. It is dangerous to keep things on a 'just-in-case' basis.

12.4 Dealing with wounds

Wounds are the most common first-aid condition which everyone encounters with horses. Your immediate first aid aims should be to: prevent further injury, control blood loss, minimize contamination, and, finally, maintain cleanliness and thereby reduce the risk of infection.

Controlling bleeding

Remember that even a small amount of bleeding will look colossal when it is your favourite horse (or yourself). Just think of a spilt cup of coffee: it looks like a flood on the floor.

All but the most severe bleeding can be controlled by applying a clean, dry bandage pad with moderate pressure. If you are out in the middle of nowhere, sacrifice your T-shirt or whatever else is to hand to hold over the wound. If you can tape it in place or hold it there for at least five minutes, then it should allow blood clotting to occur.

Contact your vet if:

■ Any wound is bleeding profusely.
■ The horse is very lame, even if the wound itself is small.
■ Any wound is more than about 5 cm (2 in) long and has gone right through the skin, so that it is gaping open and may need to be stitched by your vet.
■ There is any suspicion of a foreign body in the wound.
■ There is any suspicion that a vital structure, such as a joint, may be involved.
■ The horse has NOT had an anti-tetanus vaccination.

The ideal is to use a sterile or, at least, clean bandage to reduce any contamination by dirt and dust. However, you may not have one to hand, and you will have to utilize what is available to you.

The three rules

The three rules to remember when treating every wound are as follows:

1 Encourage clotting

First, you must stop the bleeding.

2 Check and clean the wound

Contamination and infection will both prevent wound healing. If an infection penetrates vital structures, such as joints or tendon sheaths, a horse may be permanently crippled. It is vital to establish the position, depth and severity of any wound. You will need to clean the wound, so you can see what is involved, provided that this can be done without making it bleed further.

3 Cover the wound

Cover the wound where possible to protect it. People often apply all sorts of potions and powders. Remember that raw tissues are exposed, so never put anything on a wound which you would not put in your eye.

Covering wounds

A useful development in covering wounds is the water-soluble wound gels. Originally designed for human burns patients, they are also great for horses. When applied to the area of damage, they help to keep a wound clean and moist. They will reduce the number of bacteria in the wound, bind bacterial toxins and speed up healing. They are essential in any first-aid kit and a safe way of covering wounds.

Surgical skin staples are often used instead of stitching for certain skin wounds. They can be inserted quickly and are ideal when a horse does not want to stand still.

Staples do not work well for jagged lacerations, or when the wound edges are under a lot of tension. However, they are often a way to repair clean cuts, such as head injuries.

Suturing a wound

A wound may need to be sutured (stitched or stapled) if:
■ The edges are gaping apart.
■ It is very large or deep.
■ It is in an awkward place where it will scar.

If you think a wound may need to be sutured, consult your vet as soon as possible, since it will heal more effectively if it is sutured whilst fresh. There is a six to eight hour optimum period for wound repair.

Deep punctures, very swollen or crushed wound edges, and severely contaminated or infected wounds will not be suitable for suturing, nor will most wounds that are more than eight hours old. Your vet will advise on the best course of action for any particular injury. Many wounds heal amazingly well without stitching.

12.5 Lameness

The horse's foot is the most common area of forelimb lameness, and hence the old adage 'No foot, no horse'. It helps to understand the basic design of the equine foot in order to avoid and treat the more common foot problems.

Anatomy of the foot

A horse's foot is primarily composed of two-and-a-half bones:

■ The third phalanx or coffin bone or the pedal bone.
■ Half the second phalanx or the short pastern bone.
■ The distal sesamoid or navicular bone.

The short pastern and coffin bones support the horse's weight while the navicular bone serves as a pivot for the deep digital flexor tendon. The joint between the first and second phalanges is the proximal interphalangeal or pastern joint, and the joint between the second and the third phalanges is the distal interphalangeal or coffin joint.

Soft tissue structures

As well as bones, there are numerous soft tissue structures including:

■ The deep digital flexor tendon which runs down the back of the limb and angles around the navicular bone to attach to the back of the coffin bone.
■ The navicular bursa is a fluid-filled pouch which sits between the navicular bone and the deep digital flexor tendon and helps cushion and protect the bone and tendon.
■ The navicular bone also has three ligaments attaching it to the second and third phalanges.

■ There are two large collateral ligaments attaching the second and third phalanges.
■ Underneath the pedal bone is the digital cushion, a fibrous pad, which functions as a shock absorber.

External structures

There are also numerous key external structures of the foot, which are important for its overall health.

■ The coronary band is where the skin and the hair intersect with the hoof wall.
■ The hoof wall grows from the coronary band at a rate of 5–10 mm ($1/4$–$1/2$ in) per month.
■ On the bottom of the foot are the sole, frog, white line and bars.

Wounds and infections

The foot is vulnerable to penetrating wounds and infections, particularly as a horse is so heavy, with a relatively large weight on a small surface area. Also the hoof treads in dirty areas. Stones, mud and dirty bedding do not help foot health.

Preventing lameness

You can help prevent the possibility of lameness occurring in your horse by checking the feet regularly for any injuries, cracks in the wall of the hooves, bruising or thrush (infection of the frog). It is also very important to make sure that the horse is shod correctly with well-fitting shoes and that they are not left on for too long. A good diet and a well-drained, clean stable are also essential in preventing problems with the feet.

Warning signs

You may spot your horse is lame when it is standing still in its stable or field, or when it is moving. It may shift its weight from foot to foot, rather than spread it evenly across all four feet. It may hold a front foot up in the air or rest one of its feet when standing.

A way of identifying the lame leg is to get someone to trot the horse up in-hand for you on some level, hard ground. They should allow the horse a little loose rein to enable it to move its head. Whereas a sound horse will hold its head level, a horse with a lame foreleg will nod its head. To identify lameness in a hindleg, watch the horse's hindquarters as they move. When the sound hindleg touches the ground, the hindquarter on that side will dip, taking the weight.

Lameness examination

If a horse remains lame, consult the vet or farrier. Most lameness is in the foot, and in many cases the farrier can solve it. If it persists, the vet will need to investigate with a comprehensive clinical examination including:

■ Palpation of the limbs.
■ Checking the foot, including using a hoof-tester examination.
■ Joint manipulation.
■ Examining the horse when it is moving to determine the severity of the lameness and which limb or limbs are affected.

Diagnosing lameness

If it is not immediately obvious, the site of pain may be pinpointed by use of a local anaesthetic injected around the nerves and/or within the joints (nerve blocks). Modern technology can be used to diagnose lameness, e.g. nuclear scintigraphy (bone scans), and MRI (magnetic resonance imaging). More frequently, X-rays and ultrasound are used to provide answers.

All technology can be costly and, frustratingly and sadly, the treatment available is not always as sophisticated or successful. Unfortunately, in order to perform well, our horses need to be 100 per cent sound, and this is sometimes unachievable.

Laminitis (founder)

Laminitis is quite common in horses. Basically, there are two types:

■ Acute laminitis is always treated as an emergency even if the horse or pony is in the early stages of the condition, as it may be reversible if it is treated promptly by the vet.

■ Chronic laminitis is when the pedal bone has rotated or sunk. Such cases are not always such an immediate emergency, but you should always contact your vet as soon as possible if your horse or pony is in pain.

The laminae are the lining tissues in the equine foot that connect the coffin bone to the inside of the hoof. There are sensitive laminae that cover the coffin bone and interlock with the insensitive laminae on the inside of the hoof wall.

Generally, the laminae between the front edge of the coffin bone and the front hoof wall are the worst affected. As that area weakens, the deep digital flexor tendon continues to pull on the back of the pedal bone causing rotation of the bone.

If the entire foot is affected, then the support for the pedal bone is compromised everywhere and the

BELOW: *This horse is displaying the characteristic stance of a horse with laminitis. It shifts its weight from foot to foot and leans back.*

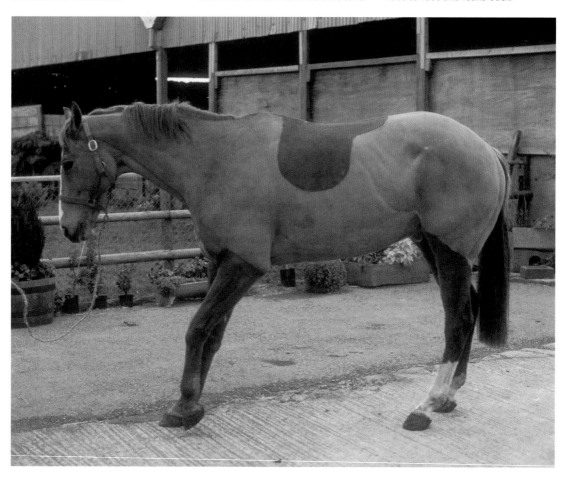

coffin bone sinks within the foot without rotation. This is the so-called 'sinker', which is unusual but serious.

If you suspect laminitis in your horse or pony, you should contact your vet without delay as severe cases will need urgent treatment, and prompt action may help to reduce the severity. Chronic cases can benefit enormously from good farriery.

Signs of acute laminitis

The tell-tale signs of laminitis to look out for include the following:
■ Lameness, especially when a horse is turning in circles, or shifting lameness when it is standing, or sometimes so much pain that the horse may not want to move at all.
■ Hooves that feel hot and feet that are painful when pressure is applied to the sole.
■ The horse may have a raised pulse and respiratory rate, especially an increased digital pulse over the fetlock in all four of its feet.
■ A stiff 'sawhorse stance', with the front feet stretched out in front to alleviate pressure on the toes, and the hind feet 'camped out'.
■ The horse will move better on a soft surface.
■ Occasionally, the hind feet are worse, so look carefully. Watch for horses shifting their weight from one foot to the other.

Signs of chronic laminitis

These may be milder and less obvious than the symptoms that are described above and include the following:
■ Recurrent lameness or feeling footsore, especially after trimming or on hard ground.
■ Odd-looking feet with rings in the

hoof wall that become wider as they are followed from toe to heel and a wider white line on the sole, which is often flatter than normal.
■ Foot problems associated with bruised soles or recurrent abscesses.
■ A thick, 'cresty' neck in a fat pony indicates a high risk of laminitis.

Preventing laminitis

You can help to prevent this painful health problem by making sure that you feed a good diet to your horse or pony. You must avoid over-feeding, especially in the spring and autumn when animals are susceptible to laminitis. If you need to slim your horse down, reduce the amount of concentrates in its diet and allow it only limited grazing when grass is lush. Make sure also that you exercise it regularly. Look after its feet carefully and inspect them daily for the tell-tale signs (see left). If you are in doubt, it is important to consult your vet immediately – don't delay until it is too late. Laminitis should always be treated as an emergency.

Treating laminitis

Your vet will have to identify the underlying cause before the laminitis can be treated successfully. The horse or pony will need total box rest and must not be ridden; in severe cases, it should not be walked out. Keep it warm indoors in a clean stable with plenty of thick, soft bedding. You may also need to adjust its diet.

Your vet will probably prescribe painkillers, anti-inflammatory drugs or even a mild sedative, depending on the severity of the laminitis, and the feet should be trimmed and have regular attention from the farrier.

Common problems

Other causes of lameness in the horse may include the following:

Pus in the foot

This is the commonest cause of severe lameness in horses and is summarized by the saying that 'the best treatment for shoulder lameness in the horse is to drain the pus from the foot'. Always consider this if a horse goes lame. Horses can be so uncomfortable that they can barely put their affected foot to the ground. If you suspect this, you should arrange for your vet or farrier to visit as soon as possible in order to investigate the problem.

Bruising and other foot pain

Other common causes of foot pain in horses include bruising or, less frequently, lameness after shoeing, where a nail has pinched the sensitive tissues. Again, your vet or farrier should check this out for you.

Navicular Disease/syndrome

Poor foot conformation can lead to increased stress in the foot, especially the heel region and predisposes the development of degenerative changes of the navicular bone and surrounding structures. This condition causes much anxiety, but work with MRI has shown that many such cases actually have soft tissue damage rather than bone disease. Your vet and farrier will be able to advise you on the most effective treatments that are available.

12.6 Colic

Colic is any abdominal pain and it can affect horses of all ages and types. It can vary from a mild bout of discomfort that sorts itself out, to something more serious that requires medical treatment. Most dramatically, it can be a serious abdominal crisis requiring rapid skilled surgery.

The majority of cases can be cured medically, but 5–10 per cent will need emergency surgery to survive. It is not possible to diagnose the cause purely on the basis of the horse's behaviour.

Colic is always best controlled if the treatment is started early on. Regular checks on your horse will allow early detection of any problems.

What to look for

The signs of colic vary, but studies have shown that in horses with colic, 44 per cent roll; 43 per cent paw continuously or intermittently; 29 per cent lie down for long periods; 21 per cent get up and down; 14 per cent repeatedly look at their flank; 13 per cent curl their upper lip; 10 per cent back into a corner; 7 per cent kick at their abdomen; 4 per cent stand in a stretched position as if trying to pass urine; and 1 per cent fail to pass droppings for longer than 24 hours.

Often, the first clue you have that something is wrong with your horse is an unfinished feed, an untouched haynet or a churned-up bed. With severe colic, a horse can thrash around alarmingly and obviously will need urgent veterinary assistance. You should contact your vet if even mild colic signs persist for more than half an hour.

How often does it happen?

Colic is relatively common: studies have shown a background incidence of 0.1 to 0.2 episodes per horse per year. This means that if you have, say, 10 horses, you should expect one to two cases of colic per annum. Any more than this would be well worth discussing with your vet.

What to do

If colic is violent, the first essential thing that you must do is protect yourself against getting injured.

Try to calm the horse

Many horses will panic with the pain. Getting them up and walking on hard ground, e.g. concrete, where they are less likely to want to roll may help in the short term. If they are determined to go down, make sure that they have a big enough box with a deep bed, where they will not get cast.

Preventing injury

You must ensure also that the horse cannot get injured on stable fittings, such as mangers or buckets. You could remove them if they are not fixed or turn the horse out into a field or an arena, where it cannot damage itself. Although it is not ideal, rolling is unlikely to make the colic worse. By the time that the horse rolls, the guts may already be twisted and it is only nature's way of attempting to relieve the problem.

Warning

- It is wrong to walk a horse around for hours as this will only cause exhaustion. It should only be a stopgap whilst waiting for the vet.
- You must remove all feed from within the horse's reach.
- Do not give any treatment, such as colic drenches, without consulting your vet first.
- Have some clean water, soap and a towel ready for the vet's arrival.
- Make sure you have transport available if the option of further treatment for the horse at an equine hospital is considered.

Surgery

If surgery has to be carried out, the chances of success are far greater than they were 10 or 20 years ago. Essentially, you can assume that, at present, a horse with surgical colic will have about a 75 per cent chance of survival, provided that you can get it to an equine hospital quickly and that the surgery and aftercare are undertaken by an experienced team.

Obviously, a horse that has been sick for a day before it reaches a clinic has a much poorer chance of survival than one that is presented for surgery immediately.

Many horses have undergone colic surgery and successfully returned to full work. You should think now about whether it would be right to submit your horse to expensive surgery. It is well worth having insurance to cover the costs of any operation.

12.7 Caring for a sick horse

If your horse is unwell, he will need your extra attention, especially if he is kept in a stable. Be vigilant and watch carefully for any changes in his demeanour or behaviour, and pay attention to his comfort, diet and stable hygiene.

Box rest

Just as humans get tucked into bed, sick horses may be confined to their stable. Box rest is useful for many conditions, especially lameness, but also following surgery.

Key care points

Many lame horses need to be kept in, although they may not feel ill and will become bored. Regular grooming may help to keep them happy. You should choose their stable carefully: some horses like to watch activity around them while others are better somewhere quiet. Stabled horses that do not have access to grazing are more likely to develop stereotypical or abnormal behaviour, such as crib-biting, wind-sucking or weaving. Stable toys may help prevent this.

Feeding

It is necessary to cut the hard feed if a horse is kept in and is not being exercised. Change to a high-forage diet, so that he has plenty to munch, as eating keeps the horse occupied. Hay or short-chop forages that take longer to eat are better than haylage.

If a horse has no exercise and is fed high-energy feeds, it can develop

muscle problems, which are known commonly as azoturia or 'tying-up'. Colic is a risk for horses stuck inside because of the change in their eating patterns, e.g. reduced grass intake will predispose them to constipation.

When a horse is kept in, count the droppings and if they reduce, you can feed a bran mash as a laxative. A one-off mash is a useful transition from a normal diet to convalescence rations. Frequent short walks to graze in-hand will help, if permitted as part of their treatment. Your vet will advise you.

Take care leading out

Always ensure your horse is adequately restrained. Horses that are normally relaxed may become difficult after being 'confined to barracks'. If you are in doubt, use a bridle or a Chifney anti-rearing bit.

Watch for complications

A horse that is being box rested for severe lameness is at risk of damage to its legs as a result of their increased weight-bearing. Check all the feet daily for warning signs of laminitis, including increased warmth, digital pulses or soreness. A deep bed that encourages the horse to lie down will help. The other legs should be support bandaged (see page 112). These bandages should include plenty of padding, and they should be checked regularly for bandage rubs. The legs should be massaged each time that the bandages are changed.

RIGHT: *Some sick horses are kept inside their stable on box rest.*

12.8 Complementary therapy

Although your vet will always be the first person whom you ring in an emergency, for chronic problems many owners may consider complementary therapies, particularly when conventional medicine has not provided a cure.

Qualified practitioners

Any alternative or complementary treatment should only ever be undertaken using a practitioner who works on vet referral. It is important to follow the maxim 'above all, do no harm', so ensure that anyone who treats your horse is competent and is approved by your vet.

The commonest therapies are the manipulative techniques which are similar to those used on people. Chartered physiotherapists, who hold recognized qualifications, and those belonging to the Association of Chartered Physiotherapists in Animal Therapy (ACPAT), will treat animals only with veterinary authorization. The same applies to osteopaths and chiropractors, who use manipulation, and they should also be registered with their governing body.

The law permits treatment of animals by 'physiotherapy', which is interpreted as including all manipulative therapies, following vet referral or permission and states that a vet should administer all other forms of complementary therapy, including homeopathy and acupuncture.

If you decide to call in an unregistered therapist, you could regret it. Chartered physiotherapists, osteopaths and chiropractors are all required by their regulatory bodies to have indemnity insurance whereas unregistered 'therapists' may not have proper insurance cover. Most equine insurance companies may include complementary therapies as part of your veterinary fee cover, but any policy will state that they must be carried out under the direction of or on referral from your vet.

BELOW: *It is important to know what is wrong with your horse before you embark on complementary treatment.*

12.9 Humane destruction

Unfortunately, if you have horses, you will become involved with the issue of humane destruction. This provokes strong emotions, and it helps to plan ahead as to what you want for your horse. Rather like leaving a will, it makes it less stressful when it happens. If others know your intentions, it makes decision-making possible if something serious happens in your absence. You will need to consider the following.

Is the horse insured?

Do the insurers need to be notified before proceeding? In general, the best advice is to contact insurers before doing anything irreversible. In a crisis, if a horse has sustained a major injury, it may be necessary to put the horse down immediately to prevent further suffering.

If you proceed to have your horse put down without seeking permission from the insurer, you may be unable to make a claim later on. Your vet will be able to advise you.

Before making a decision, find out whether the insurers need a second opinion from another vet before your horse is put down and/or a post mortem afterwards. Clarify this as it may help to resolve practicalities, such as where and how the humane destruction is performed.

Procedure

There are two methods of humane destruction – by free-bullet pistol or intravenous injection. The advantages of using a free-bullet pistol are that, if performed correctly, death is instant and painless and the animal's carcass can be easily disposed of. It is also a relatively cheap and efficient form of humane destruction. However, there may be some bleeding and the noise may be distressing for owners to witness. Occasionally, there may be involuntary movements of the limbs after death.

Alternatively, humane destruction may be performed by an intravenous lethal injection. Prior placement of an intravenous catheter and sedation makes the procedure less stressful. However, as with a pistol, there are both advantages and disadvantages. Quiet and painless, it can only be administered by a vet. Although the horse collapses slowly, death may not be instantaneous. The horse may try to counter the effects of the injection, and it is likely to twitch for a few moments after death, making it upsetting to witness. If you are unsure about which method to choose, your vet can offer further practical advice and guidance. There are limited options for carcass disposal (see below). Whatever you decide, the welfare of the horse must always come first.

Carcass disposal

This must be carefully considered, particularly following lethal injection. The various options are usually cremation/incineration or burial with appropriate permission. In 2003, the legislation was changed in the UK, preventing the burial of farm animals, although it is still possible to bury pets, but permission must be sought. In general, burial may be allowed and confirmation can be obtained from your local authority (the trading standards department). For up-to-date information, check with DEFRA.

Location

This is your choice. Most vets and knackermen will come to the yard, so the horse can be put down at home. Some owners prefer the horse to be taken elsewhere, which may be more practical, especially if a post mortem is required. Removal of the carcass can also be distressing for observers and quite difficult in a muddy field. Another option is going to a licensed slaughterhouse or to use your local hunt kennelsmen. It is rarely essential for you to be present so it is your decision as to whether you want to be there or not. It may be better remembering the good times you enjoyed with your horse and leaving him in the hands of professionals when he is put down and removed.

Other horses?

People always ask about what should be done with the other horses. If a horse is being put down because it is injured and the other healthy horses are moved, the horse that is left may become distressed, which is not the ideal situation – its welfare should always take priority. The other horses are rarely disturbed for more than a moment, as they do not comprehend what has happened.

Glossary

• •

Action The movement of the horse's legs.

Backing The process of getting a horse accustomed to having a rider's weight on its back.

Bars The ends of the hoof wall, extending towards the centre of the sole from the heels.

Bars of the mouth Another term for the diastema, the space where the bit fits.

Bay Brown colour of the body with black mane, tail and lower legs.

Blaze A broad white stripe running down the face.

Brushing The knocking of one inside leg by its opposite number when the horse is moving.

Cantle The back of the saddle.

Cast When a horse is unable to get up and stand because it is stuck against a wall or a fixture in a loosebox.

Cast a shoe When a shoe comes off by accident.

Cavesson A piece of equipment used for lungeing a horse with rings to which the lunge line is attached.

Chaff Chopped straw or a straw/hay mix.

Chestnut Ginger-red colour of the body with similar or lighter mane and tail.

Clench The hook formed by the end of each horse shoe nail when it is bent over to hold it in place.

Cob A sturdy carrying-weight type of small horse, not exceeding 15.3 hh (155 cm).

Coldblood Applies to heavy workhorses, such as Shires, Percherons and Clydesdales.

Colic A painful stomach/bowel condition.

Colt An uncastrated male horse under four years of age.

Concentrates Types of food that are not roughage, e.g. cereals, legumes, lucerne hay or compound feeds, that are offered to provide high levels of nutrition – the additional energy part of the horse's ration.

Conformation The way a horse is put together. Conformation affects the horse's soundness, ability to perform and comfort to ride.

Crib-biting A stable 'vice' whereby a bored horse grabs hold of something and takes in air.

Croup The highest point on the horse's hindquarter.

Curb A type of bit with a strong effect on the horse.

Dam A horse's mother.

Dishing The front foot is thrown outwards, particularly in trot.

Dock The top of the tail that contains the bony vertebrae.

Dorsal stripe A dark stripe along the back of a horse.

Dun Gold or cream body colour with black mane, tail and lower legs.

Entire A male horse that has not been castrated.

Fetlock The joint between the cannon bone and the long pastern bone.

Filly A female horse under four years of age.

Forging Hitting the underneath of the forefoot with the toe of the hind foot. You can hear a sound as it happens.

Frog The V-shaped pad on the sole of the hoof.

Gait The leg movement of a horse.

Gamgee A form of padding to go under bandages.

Gelding A castrated male horse of any age.

Grey A coat colour produced by a mixture of white and dark hairs.

Groove This may refer to the chin groove where the curb chain from a curd bit sits.

Gullet The channel underneath the seat of a saddle.

Half-bred A horse of whom one parent is a Thoroughbred.

Hand A unit of measurement for horses and ponies, equivalent to 10 cm (4 in).

Hock The joint in the middle of the back leg.

Hogged mane A mane that has been shorn down to the horse's neck.

Hotblood A horse bred from Thoroughbred or Arab stock.

Hunter A type and usually a half- or threequarter-bred animal, ranging from 15.3 hh (155 cm) upwards. Bred for stamina and jumping ability.

Knee rolls Front of the saddle flap that the knees rest behind.

Laminitis A painful disease caused by the inflammation of tissues within the hoof. It can be recurrent.

Livery Rent-paid accommodation for horses, sometimes with daily care included.

Lungeing A method of exercising a horse from on the ground whereby the horse moves around the handler on a long rein.

Manger A feed trough.

Mare A female horse of any age.

Near side The horse's left side.

New Zealand rug A tough waterproof rug for continuous use outdoors.

Numnah A wool or cotton pad used under the saddle to relieve pressure and absorb sweat, shaped to fit the saddle.

Off side The horse's right side.

Over-reaching The hind limb over-extends and the toe of the hind shoe strikes the forelimb.

Palomino A bright chestnut or gold body colour with a white mane and tail.

Pastern The part of the foot between the fetlock and the hoof.

Piebald Black and white patches on the coat.

Plaiting Also called lacing; at walk and trot the horse places one foot in front of the other.

Points of horse The names of each part of the horse.

Poll The point at the top of the head immediately behind the ears.

Polo pony A thoroughbred type under 16 hh (162 cm) with weight-carrying ability and suitable for adult riders.

Pommel The raised front of the saddle.

Pony A horse that is smaller than 14.2 hh (148 cm) when fully grown.

Rig A male horse that has one testicle retained in the abdomen.

Roan A mixture of white and other coloured hairs evenly distributed over the body.

Roller A broad strap around the belly to keep a rug in position. It must always be used with a wither pad.

Sire The father of a horse.

Skewbald Any other two-colour coat other than black and white.

Snaffle The commonest type of bit, usually with one ring on each side.

Sock White pastern and fetlock.

Sound horse A horse that is not lame.

Stallion An uncastrated male horse of any age.

Star A white patch on the forehead.

Staring coat A dull coat, often with the hairs standing up.

Stifle The joint where the hind leg appears to join the barrel.

Strawberry roan A pink-looking colour composed of a mix of chestnut and white hairs.

Stripe A narrow white marking down the face.

Surcingle A strap going round the belly to fix a rug in place. It should be used with a wither pad.

Tendon A gristly band of tissue that attaches a muscle to a bone.

Thoroughbred A horse that is registered in the General Stud Book and can trace its ancestry in the male line to three Arab stallions imported into Britain in the seventeenth and eighteenth centuries.

Toes turned out Horses that stand with either the forefeet or hind feet pointing outwards which usually brush their legs.

Tushes Teeth found in the mouths of male adult horses between the molars and incisors.

Type Includes hunters, hacks, polo ponies and cobs. They are usually cross-breds and are distinguished from breeds as they are not registered in a stud book.

Vice A bad and undesirable habit.

Wall-eyed One or two blue eyes.

Warmblood A horse whose ancestry includes coldbloods and hotbloods. Used for riding or driving.

Weaving A stable 'vice' in which a bored, stabled horse rocks its head and neck from side to side stereotypically.

White line The junction between the insensitive and sensitive parts of the foot.

Whorls Changes in the direction of hair growth.

Wind The horse's breathing.

Withers The high point of the back, located at the base of the neck between the horse's shoulder blades.

Useful addresses

● ●

British Association of Homeopathic Veterinary Surgeons (The)
Chinham House
Standford in the Vale
Nr Faringdon
Oxon SN7 8NQ

British Connemara Pony Society
Glen Fern
Waddicombe
Dulverton
Somerset TA22 9RY
Tel: 01398 341490
Email:
secretary@britishconnemaras.co.uk
Website:
www.britishconnemaras.co.uk

British Dressage Ltd
National Agricultural Centre
Stoneleigh Park
Kenilworth
Warks CV8 2RJ
Tel: 024 7669 8830
Fax: 024 7669 0390
Email:
office@britishdressage.co.uk
Website: www.britishdressage.co.uk

British Driving Society
27 Dugard Place
Barford
Nr Warwick
Warks CV35 8DX
Tel: 01926 624420
Fax: 01926 624633
Email:
email@britishdrivingsociety.co.uk
Website:
www.britishdriving society.co.uk

British Equestrian Federation
National Agricultural Centre
Stoneleigh Park
Kenilworth
Warks CV8 2RH
Tel: 024 7669 8871
Fax: 024 7669 6484
Email: info@bef.co.uk
Website: www.bef.org.uk

British Equestrian Trade Association
East-Wing
Stockeld Park
Wetherby
West Yorks LS22 4AW
Research and enquiry: 01937 587062
Directory and trade: 01937 582111
Email: info@beta.org.uk
Website: www.beta-uk.org

British Equine Veterinary Association
Wakefield House
46 High Street
Sawston
Cambs CB2 4BG
Tel: 01223 836970
Fax: 01223 835287
Email: info@beva.org.uk
Website: www.beva.org.uk

British Eventing
National Agricultural Centre
Stoneleigh Park
Kenilworth
Warks CV8 2RN
Tel: 024 7669 8856
Fax: 024 7669 7235
Email: info@britisheventing.com
Website: www.britisheventing.com

British Horse Society (The)
Stoneleigh Deer Park
Kenilworth
Warks CV8 2XZ
Tel: 01926 707700
Fax: 01926 707800
Email: enquiry@bhs.org.uk
Website: www.bhs.org.uk

British Show Jumping Association
National Agricultural Centre
Stoneleigh Park
Kenilworth
Warks
CV8 2RJ
Tel: 024 7669 8800
Fax: 024 7669 6685
Email: bsja@bsja.co.uk
Website: www.bsja.co.uk

British Percheron Horse Society
Three Bears Cottage
Burston Road
Diss
Norfolk
IP22 5UF
Tel: 01379 740554
Email: secretary@percheron.org.uk
Website: www.percheron.org.uk

British Veterinary Association
7 Mansfield Street
London W1G 9NQ
Tel: 020 7636 6541
Fax: 020 7436 2970
Email: bvahq@bva.co.uk
Website: www.bva.co.uk

Driving Standards Agency
Website: www.dsa.gov.uk

Department for Environment, Food & Rural Affairs (DEFRA)
Nobel House
17 Smith Square
London SW1P 3JR
Helpline: 08459 335577
Fax: 020 7238 6609
Email: helpline@defra.gsi.gov.uk
Website: www.defra.gov.uk

Endurance GB
National Agricultural Centre
Stoneleigh Park
Kenilworth
Warks CV8 2RP
Tel: 024 7669 8863
Fax: 024 7641 8429
Email: enquiries@endurancegb.co.uk
Website: www.endurancegb.co.uk

Equestrian Support Services (ESS)
Tel: 01300 348997
Website: www.equestriansupport.co.uk

Equipment Register (The)
Website: www.ter-uk.com

Farriers Registration Council
Sefton House, Adams Court
Newark Road
Peterborough
Cambs PE1 5PP
Tel: 01733 319911
Fax: 01733 319910
Email: frc@farrier-reg.gov.uk
Website: www.farrier-reg.gov.uk

Ifor Williams Trailers Ltd
The Old Station
Bridge Street, Corwen
Denbighshire LL21 0AD
Tel: 01490 412527
Fax: 01490 413216
Email: info@iwt.co.uk
Website: www.iwt.co.uk

Master of Foxhounds Association
The Old School
Bagendon, Cirencester
Glos GL7 7DU
Tel: 01285 831470
Fax: 01285 831737
Email: office@mfha.co.uk
Website: www.mfha.co.uk

National Association Farriers & Blacksmiths
Avenue B, 10th Street
National Agricultural Centre
Stoneleigh Park
Kenilworth
Warks CV8 2LG
Tel: 024 7669 6595
Fax: 024 7669 6708
Email: nafbae@nafbae.org.uk
Website: www.nafbae.org.uk

National Trailer & Towing Association
1 Alveston Place
Leamington Spa
Warks CV32 4SN
Tel: 01926 353445
Fax: 01926 335445
Email: info@ntta.co.uk
Website: www.ntta.co.uk

Organization of Horsebox and Trailer Owners
Tel: 01408 657651
Website: www.horsebox-rescue.co.uk

Pony Club (The)
National Agricultural Centre
Stoneleigh Park
Kenilworth
Warks CV8 2RW
Tel: 024 7669 8300
Fax: 024 7669 6836
Email: enquiries@pcuk.org
Website: www.pcuk.org

Royal College of Veterinary Surgeons
Belgravia House
62-64 Horseferry Road
London SW1P 2AF
Tel: 020 7222 2001
Fax: 020 7222 2004
Email: admin@rcvs.org.uk
Website: www.rcvs.org.uk

Society of Master Saddlers (UK) Ltd
Green Lane Farm
Green Lane
Stonham, Stowmarket
Suffolk IP14 5DS
Tel: 01449 711642
Email: enquiries@mastersaddlers.co.uk
Website: www.mastersaddlers.co.uk

Trailer Coupling Mirror
Equibrand
Tel: 01327 262444

Trailerwatch
Website: www.trailerwatch.com

Worshipful Company of Farriers
19 Queen Street
Chipperfield
Kings Langley
Herts WD4 9BT
Tel: 01923 260747
Fax: 01923 261677
Email: theclerk@wcf.org.uk
Website: www.wcf.org.uk

Worshipful Company of Saddlers
Saddlers' Hall
40 Gutter Lane
Cheapside
London EC2V 6BR
Tel: 020 7726 8663
Email: clerk@saddlersco.co.uk

Bibliography

The BHS Directory of Where to Ride, Train and Stable Your Horse (The British Horse Society)

The BHS Instructors' Manual for Teaching Riding, Islay Auty FBHS (The British Horse Society)

The BHS Manual of Equitation, Consultant Editor Islay Auty FBHS (The British Horse Society)

The BHS Manual of Stable Management, Consultant Editor Islay Auty FBHS (The British Horse Society)

The BHS Riding and Road Safety Manual: Riding and Roadcraft (The British Horse Society)

The BHS Training Manual for Progressive Riding Tests 1–6, Islay Auty FBHS (The British Horse Society)

The BHS Training Manual for Stage 1, Islay Auty FBHS (The British Horse Society)

The BHS Training Manual for Stage 3 and PTT, Islay Auty FBHS (The British Horse Society)

The BHS Training Manual for Stage 2, Islay Auty FBHS (The British Horse Society)

The BHS Veterinary Manual, P. Stewart Hastie MRCVS (The British Horse Society)

Driver Licensing Information pamphlet (The Stationery Office)

Driving, The Official Driving Test and The Highway Code (available from bookshops)

The Glovebox Guide to Transporting Horses, John Henderson (J A Allen)

Learn to Ride, Islay Auty (The British Horse Society)

Pony Handbook, David Taylor BVMS, FRCVS, FZS (HarperCollins)

Riding and Roadcraft (The British Horse Society)

The SMMT Guide to Towing and the Law (Society of Motor Manufacturers and Traders' publications department – 020 7235 7000)

Towing Trailers, Preparing for the Towing Test and Trailer Maintenance, John Henderson (J A Allen Photographic Guides)

Index

• • • • • • • • • • • •

Numerals in italics refer to illustrations